THE BIG BEAN
COOKBOOK

THE BIG BEAN COOKBOOK

185 healthy, wholesome and delicious low-fat recipes for every day, from breakfast or lunch to special occasion dishes – all shown step by step in more than 800 photographs

Everything you need to know about beans, grains, pulses and legumes, including rice, split peas, chickpeas, couscous, bulgur wheat, lentils, quinoa and much more

Nicola Graimes

HERMES
HOUSE

This edition is published by Hermes House
an imprint of Anness Publishing Ltd
info@anness.com
www.annesspublishing.com

If you like the images in this book and would like to investigate using
them for publishing, promotions or advertising, please visit our
website www.practicalpictures.com for more information.

A CIP catalogue record for this book is available from
the British Library.

Publisher: Joanna Lorenz
Editorial Director: Helen Sudell
Editor: Simona Hill
Designer: Ian Sandom
Production Controller: Ben Worley

PUBLISHER'S NOTE
Although the advice and information in this book are believed to be
accurate and true at the time of going to press, neither the author nor
the publisher can accept any legal responsibility or liability for any
errors or omissions that may have been made nor for any
inaccuracies nor for any loss, harm or injury that comes about from
following instructions or advice in this book.

COOK'S NOTES

Bracketed terms are intended for American readers.
For all recipes, quantities are given in both metric and imperial
measures and, where appropriate, in standard cups and spoons.
Follow one set of measures, but not a mixture, because they
are not interchangeable.
Standard spoon and cup measures are level.
1 tsp = 5ml, 1 tbsp = 15ml, 1 cup = 250ml/8fl oz.
Australian standard tablespoons are 20ml. Australian readers
should use 3 tsp in place of 1 tbsp for measuring small quantities.
American pints are 16fl oz/2 cups. American readers should use
20fl oz/2.5 cups in place of 1 pint when measuring liquids.
Electric oven temperatures in this book are for conventional ovens.
When using a fan oven, the temperature will probably need to be
reduced by about 10–20°C/20–40°F. Since ovens vary, you should
check with your manufacturer's instruction book for guidance.
The nutritional analysis given for each recipe is calculated per portion
(i.e. serving or item), unless otherwise stated. If the recipe gives a
range, such as Serves 4–6, then the nutritional analysis will be for the
smaller portion size, i.e. 6 servings. The analysis does not include
optional ingredients, such as salt added to taste.
Medium (US large) eggs are used unless otherwise stated.

CONTENTS

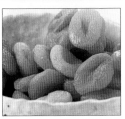

INTRODUCTION

For thousands of years, grains and pulses (encompassing peas, beans and lentils) have been staple foods for many civilizations. They are both culturally and historically significant. The lentil, for example, is believed to be one of the first plants ever "farmed" by humanity. In fact, within some cultures the humble lentil almost reached mythical status – the Egyptians praised the lentil for its ability to enlighten the mind. In China, sprouted beans and grains were used to treat a wide range of illnesses, from constipation to dropsy. In India, remains of green peas, red lentils and kesari beans have been found dating from 1800–2000BC.

Mung beans and urd beans have also been consumed on the subcontinent since ancient times. Written records from different periods of history confirm that pulses have been a major component of our diets. Early texts mention a number of pulses that are still farmed today, including chickpeas, cowpeas and pigeon peas. More recent introductions include jackbeans, lima, broad (fava) and kidney beans, which were introduced from South America.

When it comes to grains, climate and growing conditions have influenced the popularity of certain types throughout the world: wheat, barley, oats and rye in Europe; maize in America; buckwheat in Russia and central Asia; quinoa in South America; rice in the Far East; and sorghum and millet in Africa. Although the consumption of grains in the form of bread is more prevalent in the West, in the East noodles and rice are the supplement to a main meal.

VERSATILITY
What is truly remarkable about these staple ingredients is their versatility and how they have been transformed by

Above: Different varieties of lentils are available. Red lentils need no soaking and less cooking time than other types.

civilizations throughout the world into a staggering range of foods. In India, which produces more pulses than any other country, there are at least 60 different kinds of dhal made from peas, beans and lentils. Pulses are also finely ground to make pancakes, flatbreads, poppadums and dosa.

Pulses and grains are experiencing a resurgence in popularity. They've become "upwardly mobile" – no longer seen as a poor man's food or that of the puritanical wholefood fanatic. With this renewed interest, we've seen new, or more accurately previously unseen, varieties on many restaurant menus and in food shops. Spelt, quinoa, polenta, soba and freekah are becoming increasingly fashionable.

HEALTH ATTRIBUTES
Both pulses and grains contain a high concentration of nutrients, considering their size. Wholegrains contain a balance of carbohydrates, protein, fat and vitamins and minerals, which is higher when unrefined. When processed or refined, however, as in white flour, much of the fibre, B vitamins, vitamin E, iron and other trace minerals are lost.

Left: Burritos are a popular Mexican fast food. These wheat-flour tortillas are often filled with spicy bean mixtures.

Above: Chickpeas are one of the oldest crops farmed by man. Dried chickpeas need soaking before cooking but canned chickpeas are ready to use.

Pulses contain proportionately less carbohydrates yet more protein than grains. Additionally, they are very low in fat, mostly the unsaturated kind, and are a good source of B vitamins, iron, magnesium and fibre. While dried beans lose most of their vitamin C content in the drying process, canned beans manage to retain half of their vitamin C and contain a higher percentage of calcium and vitamin E than dried. Soya beans are nutritionally superior to other pulses being richer in protein, iron and calcium.

Below: Polenta is available in different forms and is a versatile grain.

Both grains and pulses can be sprouted, which greatly enhances their nutritional value.

Recently, scientists at University College, London discovered that a diet rich in beans, nuts and cereals could be a way to help prevent cancer. They found that these foods contain a potent anti-cancer compound, which, researchers say, in the future may be possible to mimic in an anti-cancer drug.

STORAGE
One of the biggest advantages of many grains and dried beans is that they have a long shelf life if kept in dry, cool airtight containers away from sunlight. However, it's best to eat dried beans as fresh as possible as they toughen with age and consequently take longer to cook.

Some wholegrains can be kept for up to 2 years, although flaked and cracked grains and flour should be used within 2–3 months of purchase.

Modern canning methods mean that canned pulses are not only often more nutritious than fresh but are also more convenient. No pre-soaking or long cooking times are necessary, and since canned beans are softer in texture they only need heating through. Some argue, however, canned beans can't compete on flavour.

Below: Noodles are a staple food for many cultures. Many varieties are available, such as rice, cellophane, wheat and egg noodles.

PULSES
A pulse is the collective term for the edible dried seeds of plants belonging to the Leguminosae, including beans, peas and lentils. There are around 13,000 species and the Leguminosae family is the second largest in the plant kingdom. Pulses sustain a large number of people in the world and are important economically. Surprisingly, the groundnut or peanut is also part of this family.

GRAINS
The word cereal has its origin in the name of the Roman goddess of grain, Ceres. Grains, otherwise known as cereals, are the edible seeds of plants, usually members of the grass family, although there are exceptions. They are grown in greater quantities worldwide than any other crop and provide more food energy to the human race than any other crop. They are annuals that have to be planted every year. Like all seeds they are very nutritious.

LEGUMES

LENTILS, PEAS AND PULSES PROVIDE THE COOK WITH A DIVERSE RANGE OF FLAVOURS AND TEXTURES.
THEY HAVE LONG BEEN A STAPLE FOOD IN THE MIDDLE EAST, SOUTH AMERICA, INDIA AND THE
MEDITERRANEAN, BUT THERE IS HARDLY A COUNTRY THAT DOES NOT HAVE ITS OWN FAVOURITE
LEGUME-BASED DISH, FROM BOSTON BAKED BEANS IN THE USA TO LENTIL DHAL IN INDIA. IN
MEXICO, THEY ARE SPICED AND USED TO MAKE REFRIED BEANS, WHILE IN CHINA THEY ARE
FERMENTED FOR BLACK BEAN AND YELLOW BEAN SAUCES.

LENTILS AND PEAS

The humble lentil is one of our oldest foods. It originated in Asia and north Africa and continues to be cultivated in those regions, as well as in France and Italy. Lentils are hard even when fresh, so they are always sold dried. Unlike most other pulses, they do not need soaking.

Red Lentils

Orange-coloured red split lentils, sometimes known as Egyptian lentils or masoor dal, are the most familiar variety. They cook in just 20 minutes, eventually disintegrating into a thick purée. They are ideal for thickening soups and casseroles and, when cooked with spices, make a delicious dhal. In the Middle East, red or yellow lentils are cooked and mixed with spices and vegetables to form balls known as *kofte*.

Yellow Lentils

Less well-known yellow lentils taste very similar to the red variety and are used in much the same way.

Green and Brown Lentils

Also referred to as continental lentils, these disc-shaped pulses retain their shape when cooked. They take longer to cook than split lentils – about 40–45 minutes – and are ideal for adding to warm salads, casseroles and stuffings. Alternatively, green and brown lentils can be cooked and blended with herbs or spices to make a nutritious pâté.

Puy Lentils

These tiny, dark, blue-green, marbled lentils grow in the Auvergne region in central France. They are considered to be far superior in taste and texture than other varieties, and they retain their bead-like shape during cooking, which takes around 20–30 minutes. Puy lentils are a delicious addition to simple dishes, such as warm salads, and are good braised in wine and flavoured with herbs.

Umbrian Lentils

These golden-brown Italian lentils are often cooked with onion, garlic and herbs, and served with pasta or rice.

Peas

Dried peas come from the field pea not the garden pea, which is eaten fresh. Unlike lentils, peas are soft when young and require drying. They are available whole or split; the latter have a sweeter flavour and cook more quickly. Like split lentils, split peas do not hold their shape when cooked, making them perfect for dhals, purées, casseroles and soups. They take about 45 minutes to cook.

Below: Puy lentils.

Right: Green and brown lentils.

Left: Red lentils.

COOKING LENTILS

Lentils are easy to cook and don't need to be soaked. Split red and green lentils have a soft consistency when cooked, while whole lentils hold their shape when cooked.

Green, Brown and Puy Lentils

1 Place 250g/9oz/generous 1 cup whole green, brown or puy lentils in a sieve and rinse well under cold running water. Drain, then tip the lentils into a pan.

2 Cover with water and bring to the boil. Simmer for 25–30 minutes until tender, replenishing the water if necessary. Drain and season with salt and freshly ground black pepper.

Split Red and Yellow Lentils

1 Place 250g/9oz/generous 1 cup split lentils in a sieve and rinse thoroughly under cold running water. Drain, then tip the lentils into a pan.

2 Cover with 600ml/1 pint/2½ cups water and bring to the boil. Simmer for 20–25 minutes, stirring occasionally, until the water is absorbed and the lentils are tender. Season to taste.

PEANUTS

Not strictly a nut but a member of the pulse family, peanuts bury themselves just below the earth after flowering – hence their alternative name, groundnuts. They are a staple food in many countries, and are widely used in South-east Asia, notably for satay sauce, and in African cuisines, where they are used as an ingredient in stews. In the West, peanuts are a popular snack food; the shelled nuts are frequently sold roasted and salted, and they are used to make peanut butter. Peanuts are particularly high in fat and are best eaten in moderation.

Buying and Storing Legumes: Lentils and peas toughen with time. Buy from shops with a fast turnover of stock and store in airtight containers in a cool, dark place. Look for bright, unwrinkled pulses. Rinse before use.

Health Benefits of Legumes: Lentils and peas have an impressive range of nutrients including iron, selenium, folate, manganese, zinc, phosphorus and some B vitamins. Extremely low in fat and richer in protein than most pulses, they are reputed to be important in fighting heart disease by reducing harmful low density lipoprotein (LDL) cholesterol in the body. They are high in fibre, which aids the functioning of the bowels and colon, and provide the body with a steady supply of energy.

Above and right: Yellow and green split peas.

Left: Marrow fat peas.

PULSES

THE EDIBLE SEEDS FROM PLANTS BELONGING TO THE LEGUME FAMILY, PULSES, WHICH INCLUDE CHICKPEAS AND A VAST RANGE OF BEANS, ARE PACKED WITH PROTEIN, VITAMINS, MINERALS AND FIBRE, AND ARE EXTREMELY LOW IN FAT. FOR THE COOK, THEIR ABILITY TO ABSORB THE FLAVOURS OF OTHER FOODS MEANS THAT PULSES CAN BE USED AS THE BASE FOR AN INFINITE NUMBER OF DISHES. MOST PULSES REQUIRE SOAKING OVERNIGHT IN COLD WATER BEFORE USE, SO IT IS WISE TO PLAN AHEAD IF USING THE DRIED TYPE; ALTERNATIVELY, CANNED ARE VERY CONVENIENT.

Aduki Beans

Also known as adzuki beans, these tiny, deep-red beans have a sweet, nutty flavour and are popular in Oriental dishes. In Chinese cooking, they form the base of a red bean paste. Known as the "king of beans" in Japan, the aduki bean is reputed to be good for the liver and kidneys. They cook quickly and can be used in casseroles and bakes. They are also ground into flour for use in cakes, breads and pastries.

Above: Aduki beans.

Black Beans

These shiny, black, kidney-shaped beans are often used in Caribbean cooking. They have a sweetish flavour, and their distinctive colour adds a dramatic touch to soups, mixed bean salads or casseroles.

Black-eyed Beans

Known as black-eye peas or cow peas in the USA, black-eyed beans are an essential ingredient in Creole cooking and some spicy Indian curries. The small, creamy-coloured bean is characterized by the black spot on its

Black beans (left), black-eyed beans (above right) and borlotti beans.

CANNELLINI BEAN PURÉE

Cooked cannellini beans make a delicious herb- and garlic-flavoured purée. Serve spread on toasted pitta bread or to use as a dip with chunky raw vegetable crudités.

SERVES FOUR

INGREDIENTS
400g/14oz/2½ cups canned or
200g/7oz/1¼ cups dried
   cannellini beans
30ml/2 tbsp olive oil
2 large garlic cloves, finely chopped
2 shallots, finely chopped
75ml/5 tbsp vegetable stock
30ml/2 tbsp chopped fresh flat
   leaf parsley
15ml/1 tbsp chopped fresh chives
salt and freshly ground black
   pepper

1 If using dried beans, soak them overnight in cold water, then drain and rinse. Place in a pan and cover with cold water, then bring to the boil and boil rapidly for 10 minutes. Reduce the heat and simmer for about 1 hour, or until tender. If using canned beans, rinse and drain well.

2 Heat the oil in a pan and sauté the garlic and shallots for about 5 minutes, stirring occasionally, until soft. Add the beans, stock, parsley and seasoning, then cook for a few minutes until heated through.

3 To make a coarse purée, mash the beans with a potato masher. Alternatively, place in a food processor and blend until thick and smooth. Serve sprinkled with chopped chives.

Right: Butter beans.

side where it was once attached to the pod. Good in soups and salads, they can also be added to savoury bakes and casseroles, and can be used in place of haricot (navy) or cannellini beans in a wide variety of dishes.

Borlotti Beans

These oval beans have a red-streaked, pinkish-brown skin and a bitter-sweet flavour. When cooked, they have a tender, moist texture, which is good in Italian bean and pasta soups, as well as hearty vegetable stews. In most recipes, they are interchangeable with red kidney beans.

Broad (Fava) Beans

These large beans were first cultivated by the ancient Egyptians. Usually eaten in

their fresh form, broad beans change in colour from green to brown when dried, making them difficult to recognize in their dried state. The outer skin can be very tough and chewy, and some people prefer to remove it after cooking. They can also be bought ready-skinned.

Butter Beans and Lima Beans

Similar in flavour and appearance, both butter beans and lima beans are characterized by their flattish, kidney shape and soft, floury texture. Cream-coloured butter beans are familiar in Britain and Greece, while lima beans are popular in the USA.

In Greek cooking, large butter beans, called gigantes, are oven-baked with

tomato, garlic and olive oil until tender and creamy. The pale-green lima bean is used in succotash, an American dish that also includes corn kernels. Butter and lima beans are also good with creamy herb sauces. Care should be taken not to overcook both butter and lima beans as they become pulpy and mushy in texture.

Right: Broad beans.

Left: Cannellini beans.

Cannellini Beans

These small, white, kidney-shaped beans have a soft, creamy texture when cooked and are popular in Italian cooking. They can be used in place of haricot (navy) beans and, when dressed with olive oil, lemon juice, crushed garlic and fresh chopped parsley, make an excellent warm salad.

Chickpeas

Also known as garbanzo beans, robust and hearty chickpeas resemble shelled hazelnuts and have a delicious nutty flavour and creamy texture. They need lengthy cooking and are much used in Mediterranean and Middle Eastern cooking – falafel and hummus being two of the most popular dishes made from chickpeas. In India, they are known as gram and are ground into flour to make fritters and flat breads. Gram flour, also called besan, can be found in health food shops and Asian grocery stores.

Flageolet Beans

These young haricot beans are removed from the pod before they are fully ripe, hence their fresh delicate flavour. A pretty, mint-green colour, they are the most expensive bean to buy and are best treated simply. Cook them until they are tender, then season and drizzle with a little olive oil and lemon juice.

Right:
Chickpeas.

Haricot (Navy) Beans

Most commonly used for canned baked beans, these versatile, ivory-coloured beans are small and oval in shape. Called navy or Boston beans in the USA, they suit slow-cooked dishes, such as casseroles and bakes.

Pinto Beans

A smaller, paler version of the borlotti bean, the savoury-tasting pinto has an attractive speckled skin – it is aptly called the painted bean. One of the many relatives of the kidney bean, pinto beans feature extensively in Mexican cooking, most familiarly in refried beans, when they are cooked until tender and fried with garlic, chilli and tomatoes. The beans are then mashed, resulting in a wonderful, spicy, rough purée that is usually served with warm tortillas. Soured cream and garlic-flavoured guacamole are good accompaniments.

Red Kidney Beans

Glossy, mahogany-red kidney beans retain their colour and shape when cooked. They have a soft, "mealy" texture and are much used in South American cooking. An essential ingredient in spicy chillies, they can also be used to make refried beans (although this dish is traditionally made from pinto beans). Cooked kidney beans can be used to make a variety of salads, but they are especially good combined

Above: Clockwise from left: Haricot beans, red kidney beans, flageolet beans and pinto beans.

with red onion and chopped flat leaf parsley and mint, then tossed in an olive oil dressing.

It is essential to follow the cooking instructions when preparing kidney beans as they contain a substance that causes severe food poisoning if they are not boiled vigorously for 10–15 minutes.

COOKING KIDNEY BEANS

Most types of beans, with the exception of aduki beans and mung beans, require soaking for 5–6 hours or overnight and then boiling rapidly for 10–15 minutes to remove any harmful toxins. This is important for kidney beans, which can cause serious food poisoning if not treated in this way.

1 Wash the beans well, then place in a bowl that allows plenty of room for expansion. Cover with cold water and leave to soak overnight or for 8–12 hours, then drain and rinse.

2 Place the beans in a large pan and cover with fresh cold water. Bring to the boil and boil rapidly for 10–15 minutes, then reduce the heat and simmer for 30 minutes to 2 hours, until tender, depending on the type of bean. Drain and serve.

Ful Medames

A member of the broad (fava) bean family, these small Egyptian beans form the base of the national dish of the same name, in which they are flavoured with ground cumin and then baked with olive oil, garlic and lemon, and served topped with hard-boiled egg. They have a strong, nutty flavour and tough, light brown outer skin. Ful medames need to be soaked overnight in cold water, then cooked slowly for about 1½ hours until soft.

Below: Ful medames.

Soya Beans

These small, oval beans vary in colour from creamy-yellow through brown to black. In China, they are known as "meat of the earth" and were once considered sacred. Soya beans contain all the nutritional properties of animal products but without the disadvantages. They are extremely dense and need to be soaked for 12 hours before cooking. They combine well with robust ingredients, such as garlic, herbs and spices, and they make a healthy addition to soups, casseroles, bakes and salads.

Soya beans are also used to make tofu, tempeh, textured vegetable protein (TVP), flour and soy sauce.

Above: White and black soya beans.

HOW TO PREPARE AND COOK PULSES

There is much debate as to whether soaking pulses before cooking is necessary, but it certainly reduces cooking times, and can enhance flavour by starting the germination process. First, wash pulses under cold running water, then place in a bowl of fresh cold water and leave to soak overnight. Discard any pulses that float to the surface, drain and rinse again. Put in a large pan and cover with fresh cold water. Boil rapidly for 10–15 minutes, then reduce the heat, cover and simmer until tender.

COOKING TIMES FOR PULSES

As cooking times can vary depending on the age of the pulses, this table should be used as a general guide.

Aduki beans	30–45 minutes
Black beans	1 hour
Black-eyed beans	1–1¼ hours
Borlotti beans	1–1½ hours
Broad beans	1–½ hours
Butter/lima beans	1–1¼ hours
Cannellini beans	1 hour
Chickpeas	1½ –2½ hours
Flageolet beans	1½ hours
Ful medames	1½ hours
Haricot beans	1–1½ hours
Kidney beans	1–1½ hours
Mung beans	25–40 minutes
Pinto beans	1–1¼ hours
Soya beans	2 hours or more

Mung Beans

Instantly recognizable in their sprouted form as beansprouts, mung or moong beans are small, olive-coloured beans native to India. They are soft and sweet when cooked, and are used in the spicy curry, moong dhal. In several Asian countries mung bean ice cream or ice lollies are popular, as is a "porridge-like" dish in Indonesia. Mung beans are also used to make transparent cellophane noodles, also called glass noodles. Soaking is not essential, but if they are soaked overnight this will reduce the usual 40 minutes cooking time by about half.

Left: Mung beans.

USING CANNED BEANS

Canned beans are convenient store-cupboard stand-bys, because they require no soaking or lengthy cooking. Choose canned beans that do not have added sugar or salt, and rinse well and drain before use. The canning process, according to recent research can help to retain certain nutrients such as calcium and vitamin E.

Canned beans tend to be softer than cooked dried beans so they are easy to mash, which makes them good for pâtés, stuffings, croquettes and rissoles, and they can also be used to make quick salads. They can, in fact, be used for any dish that calls for cooked, dried beans: a drained 425g/15oz can is roughly the equivalent of 150g/5oz/¾ cup dried beans. Firmer canned beans, such as kidney beans can be added to stews and re-cooked, but softer beans, such as flageolet, should be just heated through.

Tepary Beans

Native to Southwest America and Mexico, the name tepary derives from the Papago phrase *t'pawi* or "it's a bean". Cooked teparies are light and mealy, while in their uncooked state they can be toasted then ground into a meal and mixed with water.

Urd Beans

Also known as black gram, the urd is thought to be native to India where it is used to make different purées or dhal. The blackish seeds are similar in size and shape to the mung bean and similarly are sold whole, split and skinned.

Pigeon Peas

The cultivation of the pigeon pea goes back 3,000 years, probably to Asia. Today, they are widely cultivated in India, Africa and Central America. In India it is one of the most important pulses, next to chickpeas, where they are used to make dhal or they are combined with grains.

Buying and Storing Pulses: Look for plump, shiny beans with an unbroken skin. Beans toughen with age so, although they will keep for up to a year in a cool, dry place, it is best to buy them in small quantities from shops with a regular turnover of stock. Avoid beans that look dusty or dirty and store them in an airtight container.

Health Benefits of Pulses: Beans are packed with protein, soluble and insoluble fibre, iron, potassium, phosphorous, manganese, magnesium, folate and most B vitamins. Soya beans are the most nutritious of all beans. Rich in high-quality protein, this wonder-pulse contains all eight essential amino acids that cannot be synthesized by the body but are vital for the renewal of cells and tissues. Insoluble fibre ensures regular bowel movements, while soluble fibre has been found to lower blood cholesterol, thereby reducing the risk of heart disease and stroke. Studies show that eating pulses on a regular basis can lower cholesterol levels by almost 20 per cent. Beans contain a concentration of lignins, known as phytoestrogens, which protect against cancer of the breast, prostate and colon. Lignins may help to balance hormone levels in the body.

QUICK COOKING AND SERVING IDEAS FOR PULSES

• To flavour beans, add an onion, garlic, herbs or spices before cooking. Remove whole items before serving.

• Spoon spicy, red lentil dhal and some crisp, fried onions on top of a warm tortilla, then roll up and eat.

• Dress cooked beans with extra virgin olive oil, lemon juice, crushed garlic, diced tomato and fresh basil.

• Mix cooked chickpeas with spring onions (scallions), olives and chopped parsley, then drizzle over olive oil and add lemon juice.

• Mash cooked beans with olive oil, garlic and coriander. Pile on to toasted bread. Top with a poached egg.

• Fry cooked red kidney beans in olive oil with chopped onion, chilli, garlic and fresh coriander (cilantro) leaves.

• Sauté some chopped garlic in olive oil, add canned flageolet beans, canned tomatoes and chopped fresh chilli, then cook for a few minutes until the sauce has thickened slightly and the beans are heated through.

• Roast cooked chickpeas, which have been drizzled with olive oil and garlic, for 20 minutes at 200°C/400°F/Gas 6, then toss in a little ground cumin and sprinkle with chilli flakes. Serve with chunks of feta cheese and naan bread.

SPROUTED BEANS, LENTILS AND GRAINS

SPROUTS ARE QUITE REMARKABLE IN TERMS OF THEIR NUTRITIONAL CONTENT. ONCE THE BEAN OR GRAIN HAS GERMINATED OR SPROUTED, THE NUTRITIONAL VALUE RISES DRAMATICALLY. THERE ARE ALMOST 30 PER CENT MORE B VITAMINS AND 60 PER CENT MORE VITAMIN C IN THE SPROUT THAN IN THE ORIGINAL BEAN, LENTIL OR GRAIN. SUPERMARKETS AND HEALTH FOOD SHOPS SELL A VARIETY OF SPROUTS, BUT IT IS EASY TO GROW THEM AT HOME — ALL YOU NEED IS A JAR, A PIECE OF MUSLIN AND AN ELASTIC BAND.

Beansprouts or Mung Beansprouts

The most commonly available beansprouts, these have long, translucent white shoots and are popular in Chinese and Asian cooking, where they are used in soups, salads and stir-fries. They have a crunchy texture and a delicate flavour. Bought varieties tend to be larger than home sprouted.

Below: Mung beansprouts.

Wheat Berry Sprouts

Sprouts grown from wheat berries have a crunchy texture and sweet flavour and are excellent in breads. If they are left to grow, the sprouts will become wheat-grass, a powerful detoxifier that it is often made into a juice.

Chickpea Sprouts

Sprouts grown from chickpeas have a nutty flavour and are substantial in size. Use in salads and stews.

Lentil Sprouts

These sprouts have a slightly spicy, peppery flavour and thin, white shoots. Use only whole lentils: split ones won't sprout.

Aduki Bean Sprouts

These fine wispy sprouts have a sweet nutty taste. Use in salads, stir-fries, bakes and stews.

Buying and Storing Sprouts: If you can, choose fresh, crisp sprouts with the bean, lentil or grain still attached. Avoid any that are slimy or musty-looking. Sprouts are best eaten on the day they are bought but, if fresh, they will keep, wrapped in a plastic container or clean, dry jar, in the refrigerator for 2–6 days. Rinse and pat dry before use.

Health Benefits of Sprouts: Sprouted beans, lentils and grains supply rich amounts of protein, B vitamins and vitamins C and E, calcium, iron, potassium and phosphorus, which, due to the sprouting process, are in an easily digestible form. Sprouting also boosts the enzyme content. Plant enzymes are said to boost the metabolism and are good for the skin, stress and fatigue. In Chinese medicine, sprouts are highly valued for their ability to cleanse and rejuvenate the system.

SPROUTING BEANS, LENTILS AND GRAINS

Larger pulses, such as chickpeas and whole grains, take longer to sprout than small beans, but they are all simple to grow and are usually ready to eat in 2–4 days. Store sprouts in a covered container in the refrigerator for 2–6 days.

2 The next day, pour off the water through the muslin and fill the jar again with water. Shake gently, then turn the jar upside down and drain thoroughly. Leave the jar on its side in a warm place, away from direct sunlight. The ideal temperature is 17–24°C.

1 Wash 45ml/3 tbsp beans, lentils or grains thoroughly in water, then place in a large jar. Fill the jar with lukewarm water, cover with a piece of muslin (cheesecloth) and fasten securely with an elastic band. Leave in a draught-free place to stand overnight.

3 Rinse the beans, lentils or grains gently but thoroughly three times a day, for 2–4 days. Make sure they are drained thoroughly to prevent them from turning mouldy. Remove the sprouts from the jar, rinse well and remove any ungerminated beans.

HOW TO USE SPROUTS

• Try combining different types of sprouted beans and grains for a range of textures and flavours. They add a crunchy texture to salads and sandwich fillings.
• Mung beansprouts are often used in Oriental food, particularly stir-fries, and require little cooking.
• Alfalfa sprouts, which derive from a seed, are another popular sprout. They have tiny, wispy white sprouts and a mild nutty flavour.

• Sprouted grains are good in breads, adding a pleasant crunchy texture. Knead them in after the first rising, before shaping the loaf.
• Use chickpea and lentil sprouts in casseroles and bakes.

Right: Wheat berry sprouts.

Right: Chickpea sprouts.

Right: Lentil sprouts.

Right: Aduki bean sprouts.

TIPS ON SPROUTING

• If you are growing your own sprouts, it's important to buy beans, lentils or grains that are specifically for sprouting, rather than cooking.
• Use whole beans, lentils and grains as split or processed ones will not germinate.
• Regular rinsing with fresh water and thorough draining is essential when sprouting to prevent the beans from turning rancid and mouldy.
• Cover the sprouting jar with muslin to allow air to circulate and to let water in and out.
• After two or three days, the jar can be placed near sunlight (but not hot sun) to encourage the green pigment chlorophyll and increase the sprout's magnesium and fibre content.
• Soya beans and chickpea sprouts need to be rinsed four times a day.
• Keen sprouters may wish to invest in a special sprouting container that comes with a number of holes in the base for easy draining.
• The soaking water is said to be very nutritious and can be drunk, if liked.

Below: Germinating sprouts.

WHEAT GRAINS

GRAINS HAVE BEEN CULTIVATED THROUGHOUT THE WORLD FOR CENTURIES. THE SEEDS OF CEREAL GRASSES, THEY ARE PACKED WITH CONCENTRATED GOODNESS AND ARE AN IMPORTANT SOURCE OF COMPLEX CARBOHYDRATES, PROTEIN, VITAMINS AND MINERALS. THE MOST POPULAR TYPES OF GRAIN, SUCH AS WHEAT, RICE, OATS, BARLEY AND CORN OR MAIZE, COME IN VARIOUS FORMS, FROM WHOLE GRAINS TO FLOURS. INEXPENSIVE AND READILY AVAILABLE, GRAINS ARE INCREDIBLY VERSATILE AND SHOULD FORM A MAJOR PART OF OUR DIET.

WHEAT

The largest and most important grain crop in the world, there are said to be more than 30,000 varieties of wheat. Present day wheat varieties are believed to have derived from a hybrid wild wheat that grew in the Middle East about 10,000 years ago. The wheat kernel comprises three parts: bran, germ and endosperm. Wheat bran is the outer husk, while wheat germ is the nutritious seed from which the plant grows.

Sprouted wheat is an excellent food, often recommended in cancer-prevention diets. The endosperm, the inner part of the kernel, is full of starch and protein, and forms the basis of wheat flour. In addition to flour, wheat comes in various other forms.

Wheat Berries

These are whole wheat grains with the husks removed and they can be bought in health food shops. Wheat berries may be used to add a sweet, nutty flavour and chewy texture to breads, soups and stews, or can be combined with rice or other grains. Wheat berries must be soaked overnight, then cooked in boiling water until tender. If they are left to germinate, the berries sprout into wheatgrass, a powerful detoxifier and cleanser (see below).

Wheat Bran

The outer husk of the wheat kernel is known as wheatbran and is a by-product of white flour production. It is very high in insoluble dietary fibre, which absorbs water and promotes healthy bowel activity. Wheat bran makes a healthy addition to bread doughs, breakfast cereals, cakes, muffins and biscuits (cookies), and it can be used to add substance to stews and bakes.

Above: Wholewheat berries.

Below: Wheatgrass.

WHEATGRASS – A NATURAL HEALER

Grown from the whole wheat grain, wheatgrass has been recognized for centuries for its general healing qualities. When juiced, it is a powerful detoxifier and cleanser and is a rich source of B vitamins and vitamins A, C and E, as well as all the known minerals and phyto-nutrients. It is also a complete source of protein. Its vibrant green colour comes from chlorophyll (known as "nature's healer"), which works directly on the liver to eliminate harmful toxins. It is also reputed to have anti-ageing capabilities. Once it is juiced, wheatgrass must be consumed within 15 minutes, preferably on an empty stomach. Some people may experience nausea or dizziness when drinking the juice for the first time, but this will soon pass.

Wheat Flakes

Steamed and softened berries that have been rolled and pressed are known as wheat flakes or rolled wheat. They are best used on their own or mixed with other flaked grains in porridge, as a base for muesli, or to add nutrients and substance to breads and cakes.

Wheat Germ

The nutritious heart of the whole wheat berry, wheat germ is a rich source of protein, vitamins B and E, and iron. It is used in much the same way as wheat bran and lends a pleasant, nutty flavour to breakfast cereals and porridge. It is available toasted or untoasted. Store wheat germ in an airtight container in the refrigerator as it can become rancid if kept at room temperature.

Cracked Wheat

This is made from crushed wheat berries and retains all the nutrients of whole-wheat. Often confused with bulgur wheat, cracked wheat can be used in the same way as wheat berries (although it cooks in less time), or as an alternative to rice and other grains. When cooked, it has a slightly sticky texture and pleasant crunchiness. Serve it as an accompani-ment, or use in salads and pilaffs.

Bulgur Wheat

Unlike cracked wheat, this grain is made from cooked wheat berries with the bran removed, and then dried and crushed. This light, nutty grain is simply soaked in water for 20 minutes, then drained – some manufacturers specify cold water but boiling water produces a softer grain. It can also be cooked in boiling water until tender. Bulgur wheat is the main ingredient in the Middle Eastern salad, tabbouleh, where it is combined with chopped parsley, mint, tomatoes, cucumber and onion, and dressed with lemon juice and olive oil. It can also be used as an alternative to couscous.

Right: Wheat germ.

Right: Wheat flakes.

Right: Bulgur wheat.

COOKING WHEAT BERRIES

Wheat berries make a delicious addition to salads, and they can also be used to add a pleasant texture to breads and stews.

1 Place the wheat berries in a bowl and cover with cold water. Soak overnight, then rinse thoroughly and drain well.

2 Place the wheat berries in a pan with water. Bring to the boil, then cover and simmer for 1–2 hours until tender, replenishing the water when necessary.

Semolina

Made from the endosperm of durum wheat, semolina can be used to make a hot milk pudding or it can be added to cakes, biscuits and breads to give them a pleasant grainy texture.

Couscous

Although this looks like a grain, couscous consists of coarsely ground wheat semolina. It can also be made with corn, millet, freekah or sorghum. Couscous is popular in North Africa, where it forms

Above: Semolina.

the basis of a national dish of the same name. Individual grains are moistened by hand, passed through a sieve and then steamed in a couscousière, suspended over a bubbling vegetable stew, until light and fluffy. Nowadays, the couscous that is generally available is the instant variety, which simply needs soaking in boiling water, although it can also be steamed or baked. Couscous has a fairly bland flavour, which makes it a good foil for spicy dishes.

Wheat Flour

This is ground from the whole grain and may be wholemeal (whole-wheat), brown or wholemeal, or white, depending on the degree of processing. Hard, or strong flour is high in a protein called gluten, which makes it ideal for bread making, while soft flour is lower in gluten but higher in starch and is better for light cakes and pastries. Durum wheat flour comes from one of the hardest varieties of wheat and is used to make pasta. Most commercial white flour is a combination of soft and hard wheat, which produces an "all-purpose" flour.

Since the refining process robs many flours (white and lower extraction-rate types) of most of their nutrients, the lost vitamins and minerals are replaced with supplements. Unbleached and organically produced flours have fewer chemical additives. Nutritionally, stone-ground wholemeal or whole-wheat flour is the best buy because it is largely unprocessed and retains all the valuable nutrients. It produces slightly heavier breads, cakes and pastries than white flour, but can be combined with white flour to make lighter versions, although, of course, the nutritional value will not be as high.

Farro

This is another type of ancient wheat that is becoming increasingly fashionable. It is grown in certain parts of Italy, where it is turned into various forms, including whole, pearled, cracked or flour. Farro can be used in soups or to make risottos or pilafs.

Freekah

Pronounced "freeka", this traditional grain is processed from durum wheat and harvested while young and green. The grains are then roasted and dried. It has a nutty, crunchy texture and is an excellent alternative to rice. Freekah has a low glycaemic index (GI) and four times the fibre of brown rice. It also has a high protein content and is rich in iron, calcium and zinc. As with the other traditional forms of wheat, freekah, is said to be tolerated by those with a wheat allergy.

Kamut

An ancient relative of durum wheat, this grain has long, large, brown kernels with a creamy, nutty flavour. It is as versatile as wheat and, when ground into flour, can be used to make pasta, breads, cakes and pastry. Puffed kamut cereals

Above: Couscous.

COOKING COUSCOUS

Traditionally, the preparation of couscous is a time-consuming business, requiring lengthy steaming. The couscous found in most shops nowadays, however, is precooked, which cuts the preparation time drastically.

1 Place the couscous in a large bowl, add enough boiling water to cover and leave for 10 minutes or until all the water has been absorbed. Separate the grains, season and mix in a knob of butter.

2 Alternatively, moisten the grains and place in a muslin-lined steamer. Steam for 15 minutes or until the grains are tender and fluffy.

SEITAN

Used as a meat replacement, seitan is made from wheat gluten and has a firm, chewy texture. It can be found in the chiller cabinet of health food shops. Seitan has a neutral flavour that benefits from marinating. Slice or cut into chunks and stir-fry, or add to stews and pasta sauces during the last few minutes of cooking time. Seitan does not need to be cooked for long, just heated through.

Wheat flour (below) and malted brown flour, which contains flour from malted wheat grains. Stoneground versions are available.

and kamut crackers are available in health food shops. Kamut has a higher nutritional value than wheat and is easier to digest. Although it contains gluten, people suffering from coeliac disease have found that they can tolerate the grain if eaten in moderation.

Spelt

This is one of the most ancient cultivated wheats and, because of its high nutritional value, is becoming more widely available. Spelt grain looks very similar to wheat and the flour can be substituted for wheat flour in bread. However, it is richer in vitamins and minerals than wheat, and in a more readily digestible form. Although spelt contains

gluten, it usually can be tolerated in moderate amounts by people suffering from coeliac disease.

Buying and Storing Wheat Grains: Buy wheat-based foods from shops with a high turnover of stock. Wheat berries can be kept for around 6 months, but wholewheat flour should be used within 3 months, as its oils turn rancid. Always decant grains into airtight containers and store in a cool, dark place. Wheat germ deteriorates very quickly at room temperature and should be stored in an airtight container in the refrigerator for no more than a month.

Health Benefits of Wheat Grains: Wheat is most nutritious when it is unprocessed and in its whole form. (When milled into

white flour, wheat loses a staggering 80 per cent of its nutrients.) Wheat is an excellent source of dietary fibre, the B vitamins and vitamin E, as well as iron, selenium and zinc. Fibre is the most discussed virtue of whole wheat and most of this is concentrated in the bran. Eating one or more spoonfuls of bran a day is recommended to relieve constipation. Numerous studies show fibre to be effective in inhibiting colon and rectal cancer, varicose veins, haemorrhoids and obesity. Phytoestrogens found in whole grains may also ward off breast cancer. On the negative side, wheat is also a well-known allergen and triggers coeliac disease, a gluten intolerance, although varieties of wheat, such as spelt and kamut, have been found to be tolerated by some coeliacs if eaten in moderation.

COELIAC DISEASE
This is caused by an allergy to gluten, a substance found in bread, cakes, pastries and cereals. It is estimated that thousands of people suffer from the disease, many without diagnosis. Symptoms may include anaemia, weight loss, fatigue, depression and diarrhoea. Wheat, rye, barley and oats are the main culprits and sufferers are usually advised to remove these completely from their diet. Rice, soya, buckwheat, quinoa, millet and corn are gluten-free substitutes.

Left: Seitan.

OTHER GRAINS

WHEAT IS THE MOST FAMILIAR AND WIDELY USED GRAIN, YET DON'T FORGET THE WEALTH OF OTHER GRAINS THAT ARE AVAILABLE, INCLUDING OATS, RYE, CORN, QUINOA AND BARLEY.

OATS

Available whole, rolled, flaked, as oatmeal or oatbran, oats are warming and sustaining when cooked. Like rye, oats are popular in northern Europe, particularly Scotland. They are commonly turned into porridge, oatcakes and pancakes, and used raw in muesli.

Whole oats are unprocessed with the nutritious bran and germ remaining intact. Oat groats are the hulled, whole kernel, while rolled oats are made from groats that have been heated and pressed flat. Quick-cooking rolled oats have been pre-cooked in water and then dried, which diminishes their nutritional value. Medium oatmeal is best in cakes and breads, while fine is ideal in pancakes, and fruit and milk drinks. Oatmeal and oat flour contain very little gluten so should be mixed with wheat flour to make leavened bread. Oat bran can be sprinkled over breakfast cereals and mixed into plain or fruit yogurt.

Below. Clockwise from top left: rolled oats, oatmeal, whole oats and bran.

Health Benefits of Oats: Oats are perhaps the most nutritious of all the grains. Recent research has focused on the ability of oat bran to reduce blood cholesterol (sometimes with dramatic results), while beneficial HDL cholesterol levels increase. For best results, oat bran should be eaten daily at regular intervals.

High in soluble fibre (especially uncooked), oats are an effective laxative and also feature protease inhibitors, a combination that has been found to inhibit certain cancers. Oats also contain vitamin E and some B vitamins, as well as iron, calcium, magnesium, phosphorus and potassium.

RYE

The most popular grain for bread-making in Eastern Europe, Scandinavia and Russia, rye flour produces a dark, dense and dry loaf that keeps well. It is a hardy grain, which grows where most others fail – hence its popularity in colder climates. Rye is low in gluten and so rye flour is often mixed with high-gluten wheat flours to create lighter textured breads, the colour of which is sometimes intensified using molasses. The whole grain can be soaked overnight, then cooked in boiling water until tender, but the flour, with its robust, full flavour and greyish colour, is the most commonly used form. The flour ranges from dark to light, depending on whether the bran and germ have been removed.

Below: Rye grain and flour.

Health Benefits of Rye: Rye is a good source of vitamin E and some B vitamins, as well as protein, calcium, iron, phosphorus and potassium. It is also high in fibre, and is used in natural medicine to help to strengthen the digestive system.

CORN

Although we are familiar with yellow corn or maize, blue, red, black and even multi-coloured varieties can also be found. Corn is an essential store-cupboard ingredient in the USA, the Caribbean and Italy, and comes in many forms.

Masa Harina

Maize meal, or masa harina, comes from the cooked whole grain, which is ground into flour and commonly used to make the Mexican flat bread, tortilla.

Cornmeal

The most popular culinary uses for cornmeal are cornbread, a classic, southern American bread, and polenta, which confusingly is both the Italian name for cornmeal as well as a dish made with the grain. Polenta (the cooked dish), or mamaliga as it is known in Romania, is a thick, golden porridge, characteristic of northern Italian cooking. It is often flavoured with butter and cheese, such as Gorgonzola, or chopped herbs. Once cooked, polenta can also be left to cool, then cut into slabs and fried, barbecued or griddled until golden brown. It is delicious with roasted vegetables. Ready made polenta, sold in blocks and ready-to-slice, is available from some supermarkets.

Polenta grain comes in various grades, ranging from fine to coarse. You can buy polenta that takes 40–45 minutes to cook or an "instant" part-cooked version that can be cooked in less than 5 minutes.

In the Caribbean, cornmeal is used to make puddings and dumplings.

MAKING POLENTA

Polenta makes an excellent alternative to mashed potato or rice. It needs plenty of seasoning and is even better with a knob of butter and cheese, such as Parmesan, Gorgonzola or Taleggio. Serve with stews or casseroles.

1 Pour 1 litre/1¾ pints/4 cups water into a heavy pan and bring to the boil. Remove from the heat.

2 In a steady stream, gradually add 185g/6½oz/1½ cups instant polenta and stir constantly with a balloon whisk to avoid any lumps forming and until incorporated.

3 Return the pan to the heat and cook, stirring continuously with a wooden spoon, until the polenta is thick and creamy and starts to come away from the sides of the pan – this will only take a few minutes if you are using instant polenta.

4 Season to taste, then add a generous knob of butter and mix well. Remove from the heat and stir in the cheese, if using, until melted. The polenta can be served in its soft form or omit the cheese and spoon on to a wet work surface and spread out until 1cm/½in thick. Leave to cool, then cut into slices.

Right. Clockwise from top left: Blue and yellow cornmeal, cornflour, popcorn, masa harina and polenta.

Cornflour

This fine white powder, also known as cornstarch, is a useful thickening agent for sauces, soups and casseroles. It can also be added to cakes.

Hominy

These are the husked whole grains of corn. They should be cooked in boiling water until softened, then used in stews and soups, or added to cakes and muffins. They are, however, most commonly eaten ground, as grits, in cereals.

Grits

Coarsely ground, dried yellow or white corn is known as grits. Use for porridge and pancakes or add to baked goods.

Popcorn

This is a separate strain of corn that is grown specifically to make the popular snack food. The kernel's hard outer casing explodes when heated. Popcorn can easily be made at home and flavoured sweet or savoury according to taste. The shop-bought types are often high in salt or sugar.

Health Benefits of Corn: In American folk medicine, corn is considered a diuretic and a mild stimulant. Corn is said to prevent cancer of the colon, breast and prostate and to lower the risk of heart disease. It is believed to be the only grain that contains vitamin A as well as some of the B vitamins and iron.

Right:
Quinoa.

BARLEY

Believed to be the oldest cultivated grain, barley is still a fundamental part of the everyday diet in Eastern Europe, the Middle East and Asia.

Pearl barley, the most usual form, is husked, steamed and then polished to give it its characteristic cream-coloured appearance. It has a mild, sweet flavour and chewy texture, and can be added to soups, stews and bakes. It is also used to make traditional barley water.

Pot barley is the whole grain with just the inedible outer husk removed. It takes much longer to cook than pearl barley. Barley flakes, which make a satisfying porridge, barley couscous and barley flour are also available.

Health Benefits of Barley: Pot barley is more nutritious than pearl barley, because it contains extra fibre, calcium, phosphorus, iron, magnesium and B vitamins. Barley was once used to increase potency and boost physical strength. More recently, studies have shown that its fibre content may help to prevent constipation and other digestive problems, as well as heart disease and certain cancers. In addition, the protease inhibitors in barley have been found to suppress cancer of the intestines, and eating barley regularly may also reduce the amount of harmful cholesterol produced by the liver.

QUINOA

Hailed as the supergrain of the future, quinoa (pronounced "keen-wa") is a grain of the past. It was called "the mother grain" by the Incas, who cultivated it for hundreds of years, high in the Andes, solely for their own use.

Nowadays, quinoa is widely available. Although we tend to see the creamy coloured variety in shops, it's also available in red, black, green and pink. The tiny, bead-shaped grains have a mild,

Above: Clockwise from top left: pot barley, barley flakes and pearl barley.

LEMON BARLEY WATER

INGREDIENTS
225g/8oz/1 cup pearl barley
1.75 litres/3 pints/7½ cups water
grated rind of 1 lemon
50g/2oz/¼ cup golden caster
  (superfine) sugar
juice of 2 lemons

1 Rinse the barley thoroughly in cold water, then place it in a large pan and cover with the water. Bring to the boil, then reduce the heat and simmer gently for 20 minutes, skimming off any scum that rises to the surface from time to time. Remove the pan from the heat.

2 Add the lemon rind and sugar to the pan, stir well and leave to cool. Strain, and add the lemon juice.

3 Taste the lemon barley water and add more sugar, if necessary. Serve chilled with ice and slices of lemon.

slightly bitter taste and firm texture. It is cooked in the same way as rice, but the grains quadruple in size, becoming translucent with an unusual white outer ring. Quinoa is useful for making stuffings, pilaffs, salads, bakes and breakfast cereals.

Health Benefits of Quinoa: Quinoa's supergrain status hails from its rich nutritional value. Unlike most other grains, quinoa is a complete protein because it contains all eight essential amino acids. It is an excellent source of calcium, potassium and zinc as well as iron, magnesium and B vitamins. It is particularly valuable for people with coeliac disease as it is gluten-free.

MILLET

Although millet is usually associated with bird food, it is a highly nutritious grain. It once rivalled barley as the main food of Europe and remains a staple ingredient in many parts of the world, including Africa, China and India. Its mild flavour makes it an ideal

accompaniment to spicy stews and curries, and it can be used as a base for pilaffs or milk puddings. The tiny, firm grains can also be flaked or ground into flour. Millet is gluten-free, so it is a useful food for people with coeliac disease. The flour can be used for baking, but needs to be combined with high-gluten flours to make leavened bread.

Health Benefits of Millet: Millet is an easily digestible grain. It contains more iron than other grains and is a good source of zinc, calcium, manganese and B vitamins. It is believed to be beneficial to those suffering from candidiasis, a fungal infection caused by the yeast *Candida albicans.*

Above: Millet.

Above: Amaranth.

AMARANTH

This plant, which is native to Mexico, is unusual in that it can be eaten as both a vegetable and a grain. Like quinoa, amaranth is considered a supergrain due to its excellent nutritional content. The tiny pale seed or "grain" has a strong and distinctive, peppery flavour. It is best used in stews and soups, or it can be ground into flour to make bread, pastries and biscuits. The flour is gluten-free and has to be mixed with wheat or another flour that contains gluten to make leavened bread. Amaranth leaves are similar to spinach and can be cooked or eaten raw in salads.

Health Benefits of Amaranth: Although its taste may take some getting used to, the nutritional qualities of amaranth more than make up for it. It has more protein than pulses and is rich in amino acids, particularly lysine. Amaranth is also high in iron and calcium.

SORGHUM

This grain is best known for its thick sweet syrup, which is used in cakes and desserts. The grain is similar to millet and is an important, extremely nutritious staple food in Africa and India. It can be used much like rice, and when ground into flour is used to make unleavened bread.

Health Benefits of Sorghum: Sorghum is a useful source of calcium, iron and B vitamins.

Left to right: Plain buckwheat, buckwheat flour and toasted buckwheat.

BUCKWHEAT

In spite of its name, buckwheat is not a type of wheat, but is actually related to the rhubarb family. Available plain or toasted, it has a nutty, earthy flavour. It is a staple food in Eastern Europe as well as Russia, where the triangular grain is milled into a speckled-grey flour and used to make blini. The flour is also used in Japan for soba noodles and in Italy for pasta. Buckwheat pancakes are popular in parts of the USA and France. The whole grain, which is also known as kasha, makes a fine porridge or a creamy pudding.

Health Benefits of Buckwheat:
Buckwheat is a complete protein. It contains all eight essential amino acids as well as rutin, which aids circulation and helps treat high blood pressure. It is an excellent, sustaining cereal, rich in iron and some of the B complex vitamins. It is also reputed to be good for the lungs, the kidneys and the bladder. Buckwheat is gluten-free, and so is useful for people who suffer from coeliac disease.

TRITICALE

A hybrid of wheat and rye, triticale was created by Swedish researchers in 1875. It has a sweet, nutty taste and chewy texture and can be used in the same way as rice, and is ground into flour. It contains more protein than wheat but has less gluten and may need to be mixed with other flours when baking. Triticale flakes can be used in breakfast cereals and crumbles.

Health Benefits of Triticale: Triticale contains significant amounts of calcium, iron and B vitamins. It is particularly rich in lysine an essential amino acid that must be taken in through the diet.

TEFF

An important grain in Ethiopia, teff is nutritionally similar to millet. This tiny grain is gluten-free and is therefore suitable for those with coeliac disease. Teff is an ancient grain and seeds were even found in a pyramid dating back to 3359BC.

Health Benefits of Teff: Teff is a complete protein since it contains all eight essential amino acids and is rich in calcium, iron, phosphorus and thiamine.

Buying and Storing: Buy grains in small quantities from a shop with a high turnover of stock. Grains can be affected by heat and moisture, and easily become rancid. Store in a dry, cool, dark place.

Right: Spelt grain and flour.

HOW TO COOK GRAINS

All grains can be simply boiled in water to cook them, but, to enhance their flavour, first cook them in a little oil for a few minutes. When they are well coated in oil, add two or three times their volume of water or stock. Bring to the boil, then simmer, covered, until the water is absorbed and the grains are tender. Do not disturb the grains while they are cooking. Other flavourings, such as chopped herbs and whole or ground spices, can be added to the cooking liquid.

Above: Kamut.

FABULOUS FIBRE

Whole grains are one of the few food groups to contain both soluble and insoluble fibre. The former is prevalent in oats and rye, while wheat, rice and corn contain insoluble fibre. Both are fundamental to good health and may prevent constipation, ulcers, colitis, colon and rectal cancer, heart disease, diverticulitis and irritable bowel syndrome. Soluble fibre slows down the absorption of energy from the gut, which means there are no sudden demands on insulin, making it especially important for diabetics as well as those following a low GI diet.

RICE

Throughout Asia, a meal is considered incomplete without rice. It is a staple food for over half the world's population, and almost every culture has its own repertoire of rice dishes, ranging from risottos to pilaffs. What's more, this valuable food provides a good source of vitamins and minerals, as well as a steady supply of energy.

Below: White and brown long grain rice.

Below: Jasmine fragrant rice.

Long Grain Rice

The most widely used type of rice is long grain rice, where the grain is five times as long as it is wide. Long grain brown rice has had its outer husk removed, leaving the bran and germ intact, which gives it a chewy, nutty flavour. It takes longer to cook than white rice but contains more fibre, vitamins and minerals. Long grain white rice has had its husk, bran and germ removed, taking most of the nutrients with them and leaving a mild-tasting rice that is light and fluffy when cooked. It is often whitened with chalk, talc or other preservatives, so rinsing is essential. Easy-cook long grain white rice, sometimes called parboiled or converted rice, has been steamed under pressure. This process hardens the grain and makes it difficult to overcook, and some nutrients are transferred from the bran and germ into the kernel during this process. Easy-cook brown rice cooks more quickly than normal brown rice.

Jasmine Rice

This rice has a soft, sticky texture and a delicious, mildly perfumed flavour – which accounts for its other name, fragrant rice. It is a long grain rice that is widely used in Thai cooking, where its delicate flavour tempers strongly spiced food.

COOKING LONG GRAIN BROWN RICE

There are many methods and opinions on how to cook perfect, light fluffy rice. The absorption method is one of the simplest and retains valuable nutrients, which would otherwise be lost in cooking water that is drained away.

Different types of rice have different powers of absorption. However, the general rule of thumb for long grain rice is to use double the volume of water to rice. For example, use 1 cup of rice to 2 cups of water. 200g/7oz/1 cup long grain rice is sufficient to feed about four people as a side dish.

1 Rinse the rice in a sieve under cold, running water. Place in a heavy pan and add the measured cold water. Bring to the boil, uncovered, then reduce the heat and stir the rice. Add salt, to taste, if you wish.

2 Cover the pan. Simmer over a very low heat for 25–35 minutes, without removing the lid, until the water is absorbed and the rice tender. Remove from the heat and leave to stand, covered, for 5 minutes before serving.

Basmati Rice

This is a slender, long grain rice, which is grown in the foothills of the Himalayas. It is aged for a year after harvest, giving it a characteristic light, fluffy texture and aromatic flavour. Its name means "fragrant".

White and brown types of basmati rice are available. Brown basmati contains more nutrients, and has a slightly nuttier flavour than the white variety. Widely used in Indian cooking, basmati rice has a cooling effect on hot and spicy curries. It is also excellent for biryanis and for rice salads, when you want very light, fluffy separate grains.

Red Rice

This rice comes from the Camargue in France and has a distinctive chewy texture and a nutty flavour. It is an unusually hard grain, which although it takes almost an hour to cook, retains its shape. Cooking intensifies its red colour, making it a distinctive addition to salads and stuffings.

Wild Rice

This is not a true rice but an aquatic grass grown in North America. It has dramatic, long, slender brown-black grains that have a nutty flavour and chewy texture. It takes longer to cook than most types of rice – from 35–60 minutes, depending on whether you like it chewy or tender – but you can reduce the cooking time by soaking it in water overnight. Wild rice is extremely nutritious. It contains all eight essential amino acids and is particularly rich in lysine. It is a good source of fibre, low in calories and gluten free. Use in stuffings, serve plain or mix with other rices in pilaffs and rice salads.

QUICK WAYS TO FLAVOUR RICE

• Cook brown rice in vegetable stock with sliced dried apricots. Sauté an onion in a little oil and add ground cumin, coriander and fresh chopped chilli, then mix in the cooked rice.

• Add raisins and toasted almonds to saffron-infused rice.

Above: Red rice.

Above: Wild rice.

Above: White and brown basmati rice.

Right:
Calasparra rice.

Calasparra Rice

Traditionally used for making Spanish paella, this short grain rice is not as sturdy as risotto rice and needs to be handled with care because it breaks down easily. The best way of cooking paella is to leave the rice unstirred once all the ingredients have been added to the pan.

Risotto Rice

To make Italian risotto, it is essential that you use a special, fat, short grain rice. Arborio rice, which originates from the Po Valley region in Italy, is the most widely sold variety of risotto rice, but you may also find varieties such as carnaroli and vialone nano. It is best to add the cooking liquid gradually and allow it to be absorbed before adding the next ladleful. When cooked, most rice absorbs around three times its weight in water, but risotto rice can absorb nearly five times its weight, and the result is a creamy grain that retains a slight bite.

QUICK WAYS TO FLAVOUR RISOTTO

• When making risotto, replace a quarter of the vegetable stock with red or white wine.

• Add a bay leaf, the juice and rind of a lemon, or a lemon grass stalk, and cardamom pods to the cooking water.
• Saffron adds a yellow colour to risotto rice. Add a few threads to the vegetable stock.

Above: Clockwise from left: arborio, carnaroli and vialone nano risotto rice.

MAKING A SIMPLE RISOTTO

A good risotto – creamy and moist with tender grains that retain a slight bite – is easy to make. The secrets are to use the correct type of rice (arborio, carnaroli, or vialone nano); to add the cooking liquid gradually – it should be completely absorbed by the rice before the next ladleful is added; and to stir the risotto frequently to prevent the grains from sticking to the pan.

SERVES FOUR

INGREDIENTS

15ml/1 tbsp olive oil
small knob (pat) of butter
1 onion, finely chopped
350g/12oz/1¾ cups risotto rice
1.2 litres/2 pints stock, simmering
50g/2oz/⅔ cup freshly grated
  Parmesan cheese
salt and ground black pepper

VARIATIONS

• Add finely chopped cooked (not pickled) beetroot towards the end of cooking to give the rice a vibrant pink colour and slight sweetness.
• To make mushroom and broccoli risotto, sauté 175g/6oz/2 cups sliced flat mushrooms with the onion. Blanch 225g/8oz/2 cups broccoli florets for 3 minutes until tender, and add towards the end of cooking time.

1 Heat the oil and butter in a large, heavy pan, then cook the onion for 7 minutes until soft, stirring occasionally. Add the rice and stir to coat the grains in the hot oil and butter.

2 Add a quarter of the stock and cook over a low-medium heat, stirring until the liquid is absorbed. Add more stock, a little at a time, stirring, until all the liquid is added and absorbed.

3 After about 20 minutes, the grains will be creamy but still retain a bite. Turn off the heat, stir in the Parmesan and check the seasoning. Add salt and pepper to taste and serve immediately.

JAPANESE RICE PRODUCTS

The Japanese are extremely resourceful when it comes to exploiting the vast potential of rice.

Sake: This spirit is Japan's national drink and comes in various grades. It can be used in cooking, especially to tenderize meat.

Mirin: Sweet rice wine that is delicious in marinades and savoury dishes, and is a key ingredient in teriyaki.

Rice vinegar: Popular throughout Asia, this ranges in colour from white to brown. Japanese rice vinegar has a mild, mellow flavour. The Chinese version is much harsher.

Amasake: A healthful rice drink made by adding enzymes from fermented rice to wholegrain pudding rice. It has a similar consistency to soya "milk" and can be flavoured. Amasake can be used for baking or to make creamy desserts. It is also an excellent and easily digestible weaning food.

Above: Clockwise from top left: Amasake, mirin, rice vinegar and sake.

Pudding Rice

This rounded, short grain rice is suitable for milk puddings and rice desserts. The grains swell and absorb a great deal of milk during cooking, which gives the pudding a soft, creamy consistency. Brown pudding rice is also available.

Glutinous Rice

This rice is almost round in shape and has a slightly sweet flavour. Despite its name, the rice is gluten-free. The grains stick together when cooked due to their high starch content, making the rice easier to eat with chopsticks. Glutinous rice, which can be either white, black or purple, is used in many South-east Asian countries to make sticky, creamy puddings. In China, white glutinous rice is often wrapped in lotus leaves and steamed to make a popular dim sum dish.

Right: White and black glutinous rice.

Japanese Sushi Rice

Similar to glutinous rice, this is mixed with a rice vinegar dressing to make sushi. Most sushi rice eaten in the West is grown in California.

Left: Pudding rice.

Buying and Storing Rice: To ensure freshness, always buy rice from shops that have a regular turnover of stock. Store in an airtight container in a cool, dry, dark place to keep out moisture and insects. Wash before use to remove any impurities. Cooked rice should be cooled quickly, then chilled and reheated thoroughly before serving.

Health Benefits of Rice: Rice is a valuable source of complex carbohydrates and fibre. In its whole form it is a good source of B vitamins. White rice is deprived of much of its nutrients because the bran and germ have been removed. The starch in brown rice is absorbed slowly, keeping blood sugar levels on an even keel and making it a useful food for diabetics. Research shows that rice may benefit sufferers of psoriasis. It can also be used to treat digestive disorders, calm the nervous system, prevent kidney stones and reduce the risk of bowel cancer. However, the phytates found in brown rice can inhibit the absorption of iron and calcium.

Above: Sushi rice.

QUICK IDEAS FOR RICE
Rice can be served plain, but it is also good in one-dish meals, marrying well with a host of exotic flavourings and simple store-cupboard ingredients.
• To make a Middle-Eastern inspired rice dish, cook long grain brown rice in vegetable stock, then stir in some toasted flaked almonds, chopped dried dates and figs, cooked chickpeas, and chopped fresh mint.
• For a simple pilao, gently fry a finely chopped onion in sunflower oil with cardamom pods, a cinnamon stick and cloves, then stir in basmati rice. Add water, infused with a pinch of saffron, and cook until tender. Towards the end of the cooking time, add sultanas (golden raisins) and cashew nuts, then garnish with fresh coriander (cilantro).

RICE PRODUCTS
Rice flakes: These are made by steaming and rolling whole or white grains. They are light and quick-cooking, and can be added raw to muesli or used to make porridge, creamy puddings, bread, biscuits and cakes.
Rice bran: Like wheat and oat bran, rice bran comes from the husk of the grain kernel. It is high in soluble fibre and useful for adding texture and substance to bread, cakes and biscuits, and stews.
Rice flour: Often used to make sticky Asian cakes and sweets, rice flour can also be used to thicken sauces. Because rice flour does not contain gluten, cakes made with it are rather flat. It can be combined with wheat flour to make cakes and bread, but produces a crumbly loaf. Rice powder is a very fine rice flour, found in Asian shops.

Right: Clockwise from top left: rice bran, rice flour, rice powder and rice flakes.

SOYA BEAN PRODUCTS

Soya beans are incredibly versatile and are used to make an extensive array of by-products, including tofu, tempeh, textured vegetable protein (TVP), flour, miso, and a variety of sauces. The soya bean is the most nutritious of all beans. Rich in high-quality protein, it is one of the few vegetarian foods that contains all eight essential amino acids that cannot be synthesized in the body and are vital for the renewal of cells and tissues.

TOFU

Also known as beancurd, tofu is made in a similar way to soft cheese. The beans are boiled, mashed and sieved to make soya "milk", and the "milk" is then curdled using a coagulant. The resulting curds are drained and pressed to make tofu, and there are several different types to choose from.

Firm Tofu

This type of tofu is sold in blocks and can be cubed or sliced and used in vegetable stir-fries, kebabs, salads, soups and casseroles. Alternatively, firm tofu can be mashed and used in bakes and burgers. The mild flavour of firm tofu is improved by marinating, since its porous texture readily absorbs flavours and seasonings.

Silken Tofu

Soft blocks with a silky, smooth texture, this type of tofu is ideal for use in sauces, dressings, dips and soups. It is a useful dairy-free alternative to cream, soft cheese or yogurt, and can be used to make creamy desserts.

OTHER FORMS OF TOFU

Smoked, marinated and deep-fried tofu are all readily available in health food stores and some supermarkets.

Deep-fried tofu is often used in Chinese dishes. It puffs up during cooking and, underneath the golden, crisp coating the tofu is white and soft, and easily absorbs the flavour of other ingredients. It can be used in much the same way as firm tofu and, as it has been fried in vegetable oil, it is suitable for vegetarian cooking.

Buying and Storing Tofu: All types of fresh tofu can be kept in the refrigerator for up to one week. Firm tofu should be kept covered in water, which must be changed regularly. Freezing tofu is not recommended, because it alters its texture. Silken tofu is often available in long-life vacuum packs, which do not have to be kept in the refrigerator and have a much longer shelf life.

TEMPEH

This Indonesian speciality is made by fermenting cooked soya beans with a cultured starter. Tempeh is similar to tofu but has a nuttier, more savoury flavour and a firmer texture. It can be used in the same way as firm tofu and also benefits from marinating. While some types of tofu are regarded as a dairy replacement, the firmer texture of tempeh means that it can be used instead of meat in pies and casseroles.

Buying and Storing Tempeh: Tempeh is available chilled or frozen in health food stores and oriental shops, and can be ready marinated. Chilled tempeh can be stored in the refrigerator for up to a week. Frozen tempeh can be left in the freezer for one month; defrost before use.

BEANCURD SKINS AND STICKS

Made from soya "milk", dried beancurd skins and sticks, like fresh beancurd, have neither aroma nor flavour until they are cooked, when they will rapidly absorb the flavour of seasonings and

Above: Clockwise from left: silken tofu, beancurd skins, firm tofu and deep fried tofu.

Left: Tempeh.

TVP

Textured vegetable protein, or TVP, is a useful meat replacement and is usually bought in dry chunks or as mince. Made from processed soya beans, TVP is very versatile and readily absorbs the strong flavours of ingredients such as herbs, spices and vegetable stock. It is inexpensive and is a convenient store-cupboard item. TVP needs to be rehydrated in boiling water or vegetable stock, and can be used in stews and curries, or as a filling for pies.

other ingredients. Beancurd skins and sticks are used in Chinese cooking and need to be soaked until pliable before use. Beancurd skins should be soaked in cold water for an hour or two and can be used to wrap a variety of fillings.

Beancurd sticks need to be soaked for several hours or overnight. They can be chopped and added to soups, stir-fries and casseroles.

TOFU FRUIT FOOL

1 Place a packet of silken tofu in the bowl of a food processor. Add some soft fruit, such as berries – for example, strawberries, raspberries or blackberries.

2 Process the mixture to form a smooth purée, then sweeten to taste with a little honey, maple syrup or maize malt syrup.

MARINATED TOFU KEBABS

Tofu is relatively tasteless but its great advantage is that it readily takes on other flavours. It is at its best when marinated in aromatic oils, soy sauce, Asian pastes or sauces, spices and herbs.

1 Cut a block of tofu into 1cm/½in cubes and marinate in a mixture of groundnut (peanut) oil, sesame oil, soy sauce, crushed garlic, grated fresh root ginger and honey for at least 1 hour.

2 Carefully thread the cubes of tofu on to skewers with chunks of courgettes (zucchini), onions and mushrooms. Brush with the marinade and grill (broil) or barbecue until golden, turning occasionally.

Left: Soya flour.

SOYA FLOUR

This is a finely ground, high-protein flour, which is also gluten-free. It is often mixed with other flours in bread and pastries, adding a pleasant nuttiness, or it can be used as a thickener in sauces.

Buying and Storing TVP and Soya Flour: Store TVP and soya flour in an airtight container in a cool, dry, dark place.

Soy Sauce

This soya by-product originated more than 2,000 years ago and the recipe has changed little since then. It is made by combining crushed soya beans with wheat, salt, water and a yeast-based culture called koji. The mixture is left to ferment for between 6 months and 3 years.

There are two basic types of soy sauce: light and dark. Light soy sauce is slightly thinner in consistency but it is saltier. It is used in dressings, soups and stir-fries. Dark soy sauce is heavier and sweeter, with a more rounded flavour, and is used in marinades, stir-fries and sauces. Try to buy naturally brewed soy sauce as many other kinds are now chemically prepared to hasten the fermentation process, and may contain flavourings and colourings.

Shoyu

Made in Japan, shoyu is aged for 1–2 years to produce a full-flavoured sauce that can be used in the same way as dark soy sauce. You can buy it in health food stores and oriental shops.

Tamari

This form of soy sauce is a natural by-product of making miso, although it is often produced in the same way as soy sauce. Most tamari is made without wheat, which means that it is gluten-free. It has a rich, dark, robust flavour and is used in cooking or as a condiment.

Buying and Storing Soy Sauce, Shoyu and Tamari: Keep soy sauce, shoyu and tamari in a cool, dark place.

MISO

This thick paste is made from a mixture of cooked soya beans, rice, wheat or barley, salt and water. Miso is then left to ferment for up to 3 years. It can be used to add a savoury flavour to soups, stocks, stir-fries and noodle dishes, and is a staple food in Asia. There are three main types: kome, or white miso, is the lightest and sweetest; medium-strength

SOYA BEAN SAUCES

Black bean sauce: Made from fermented black soya beans, this has a rich, thick consistency and a salty, full flavour. It should always be heated before use to bring out the flavour. Fermented black beans, which Chinese cooks use to make home-made black bean sauce, can be bought in vacuum-packs or cans from oriental shops. They need rinsing before use.

Yellow bean sauce: Produced from fermented yellow soya beans, this sauce has an intense flavour.

Hoisin sauce: A thick red-brown sauce made from soya beans, flour, garlic, chilli, sesame oil and vinegar. Mainly intended as a marinade, it can also be used as a dipping sauce.

Kecap manis: An Indonesian-style dark, sweet soy sauce, which can be found in oriental shops.

Above: Minced and cubed textured vegetable protein (TVP).

mugi miso, which has a mellow flavour and is preferred for everyday use; and hacho miso, which is dark chocolate in colour, has a thick texture and a strong flavour.

Buying and Storing Miso: Miso keeps well and can be stored for several months, but should be kept in the refrigerator once it has been opened.

Health Benefits of Soya Products: Soya is often hailed for its health benefits. Rich in minerals, particularly iron and calcium, it is also low in saturated fat and is cholesterol-free. Some soya products are thought to help reduce osteoporosis, blood pressure and blood cholesterol, and there is evidence to suggest that it can help reduce the risk of cancer.

Japanese women (whose diets include soya) have a lower incidence of breast cancer than women who consume a typical Western diet. Likewise, Japanese men have a lower incidence of prostate cancer than Western men. This is thought to be because soya contains hormone-like substances called phytoestrogens.

Studies have also shown that eating miso on a regular basis can increase the body's natural resistance to radiation. Additionally, miso is said to help prevent cancer of the liver, and it can also help to expel toxins from the body.

Right: Light soy sauce (below) and dark soy sauce.

WATCH POINT
Although soya beans and products are nutritionally beneficial, they are also common allergens and can provoke reactions such as headaches and digestive problems. Avoid eating excessive amounts of soya, and always cook sprouted soya beans before use.

Left: Mugi miso (left) and hacho miso.

Above: Tamari (left) and shoyu.

PASTA

PASTA, MEANING "DOUGH", IS ONE OF THE OLDEST "MANUFACTURED" FOODS, DATING BACK MORE THAN 1,000 YEARS, THAT IS STILL POPULAR TODAY. TOP-QUALITY PASTA IS MADE FROM DURUM WHEAT AND WATER, OR EGG, WHICH GIVES THE PASTA A RICHER FLAVOUR AND GOLDEN COLOUR. THE VARIETY OF SHAPES IS ALMOST ENDLESS, FROM THE MYRIAD TINY SOUP PASTAS TO LARGE SHELLS USED FOR STUFFING. LOW IN FAT AND HIGH IN COMPLEX CARBOHYDRATES, IT PROVIDES PLENTY OF LONG-TERM ENERGY.

Durum Wheat Pasta

When buying pasta look for one that is made with durum wheat. This hard, high-protein wheat produces a fine semolina flour that is called "00" in Italy. The pasta may then include egg or not. Egg pasta, because it is more delicate, is often packed in nests or compressed into waves. Lasagne can be made with either plain or egg pasta. At one time, almost all short pasta shapes were made from plain pasta, but shapes made with egg pasta are now readily available. Pasta made with egg has several advantages over plain pasta: it has a higher protein content and many people consider it to have a superior, richer flavour.

Wholewheat Pasta

This substantial pasta is made using wholemeal (whole wheat) flour and it contains more fibre than plain durum wheat pasta. It has a slightly chewy texture and nutty flavour and takes longer to cook. Wholewheat spaghetti (bigoli), a traditional Italian variety that comes from the area around Venice known as the Veneto, can be found in

Right: Spaghetti, linguine and tagliatelle.

good delicatessens, and in health food shops and supermarkets. There is an increasing range of wholewheat shapes, from tiny soup pastas to rotelle (wheels) and lasagne.

Below: Buckwheat pasta spirals and short cut pasta.

Buckwheat Pasta

Pasta made from buckwheat flour has a nutty taste and is darker in colour than wholewheat pasta. Pizzoccheri from Lombardy is the classic shape. These thin, flat noodles are traditionally sold in nests like tagliatelle (although pizzoccheri are about half the length), but they are also available cut into short strips.

Other buckwheat pasta shapes are available in health food shops and supermarkets. Buckwheat pasta is gluten-free and suitable for people who are intolerant to gluten or wheat. It is also very nutritious, containing all eight amino acids, calcium, zinc and B vitamins.

Corn Pasta

This pasta, made with corn or maize flour, is gluten-free and a good alternative for people who cannot tolerate gluten or wheat. It is made in a wide range of shapes, including spaghetti, fusilli (spirals) and conchiglie (shells), as well as more unusual varieties. Plain corn pasta is a sunshine-yellow colour, or may be flavoured with spinach or tomato. It is cooked and used in the same way as wheat pasta and is available from many health food stores.

Coloured and Flavoured Pasta

A variety of ingredients can be added to the pasta dough to give it both flavour and colour. The most common additions are tomato and spinach, but beetroot, saffron, fresh herbs such as basil, and even chocolate are used. Mixed bags of pasta are also available – the traditional

combination of plain and spinach-flavoured pasta is called *paglia e fieno*, which means straw and hay. But there are many other mixtures, some having as many as seven different flavours and colours of pasta.

Rice Pasta

Like pasta made with corn and buckwheat, rice pasta is gluten-free. It also comes in a range of shapes.

Left: Corn or maize pasta can be bought in a wide variety of shapes from simple elbow macaroni to fusilli and three coloured radiatori.

Above: Pasta can be coloured and flavoured in a variety of ways, but plain, spinach and tomato varieties are the most common.

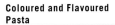

QUICK IDEAS FOR PASTA

• To make a richly flavoured tomato sauce: place some plum or cherry tomatoes in a baking dish and drizzle with a little olive oil. Roast in a hot oven for 15 minutes, then add two peeled garlic cloves and continue roasting for 10 minutes more. Transfer to a food processor and blend with basil leaves. Season and stir into cooked pasta.

• Toss cooked pasta in a little chilli oil, scatter over rocket leaves and pine nuts and serve with finely grated Parmesan cheese.

• Stir a spoonful of black olive tapenade into cooked pasta, then scatter a few lightly toasted walnuts on top.

• Roast a head of garlic, then squeeze out the pulpy cloves and mix with olive oil. Toss with cooked pasta and sprinkle over plenty of fresh, chopped parsley.

• Olives, mushrooms, aubergines (eggplant) and artichokes bottled in olive oil make quick and delicious additions to pasta.

• Combine cooked pasta with small chunks of mozzarella cheese, sliced sun-dried tomatoes, chopped fresh mint and a splash of olive oil.

PASTA SHAPES

Many different shapes of pasta are available and all are suitable for serving with different types of pasta sauces.

Long Pasta

Dried long pasta in the form of spaghetti is probably the best known shape, but there are many other varieties, from fine vermicelli to pappardelle – broad ribbon noodles. Tagliatelle, the most common form of ribbon noodles, is usually sold coiled into nests. Long pasta is best served with a thin sauce, made with olive oil, butter, cream, eggs, grated cheese or chopped fresh herbs. When vegetables are added to the sauce, they should be finely chopped.

Short Pasta

There are hundreds of different short dried pasta shapes, which may be made with plain pasta dough or the egg pasta. Conchiglie (shells) is one of the most useful shapes because it is concave and traps virtually any sauce. Fusilli (spirals) is good with thick tomato-based sauces and farfalle (butterflies) can be served with creamy sauces, but is very versatile and works equally well with tomato- or olive oil-based sauces. Macaroni used to be the most common short shape and, being hollow, it is good for most sauces and baked dishes. However, penne (quills) have become more popular, per-haps because the hollow tubes with diag-onally cut ends go well with virtually any sauce. They are particularly good with chunky vegetable sauces or baked with cheese sauce.

Below: Spinach and wholewheat lasagne and plain cannelloni.

Flat Pasta

Lasagne is designed to be baked between layers of sauce, or cooked in boiling water, then layered, or rolled around a filling to make cannelloni. Lasagne is made from plain or egg pasta and both fresh and dried versions are available. The pasta sheets may be flavoured with tomato or spinach, or made with wholewheat flour.

Stuffed Pasta

The most common stuffed pasta shapes are ravioli, tortellini (little pies) and cappelletti (little hats), athough there are other less common shapes available from Italian delicatessens. Plain, spinach and tomato doughs are the most usual, and there is a wide range of vegetarian fillings such as spinach and ricotta, sun-dried tomatoes, mushroom or pumpkin.

Right: Large and small conchiglie shells.

COOKING PASTA

Pasta should be cooked in a large pan of salted boiling water to allow the strands or shapes to expand, and stirred occasionally to prevent them from sticking together. Do not add oil to the cooking water as it makes the pasta slippery and pre-vents it from absorbing the sauce. Cooking instructions are given on the packaging but always taste just before the end of the given time to prevent overcooking. Dried pasta should be *al dente*, or firm to the bite, while fresh pasta should be just tender.

Bring a large pan of salted water to the boil. For shapes, tip in the pasta and then cover the pan. Bring quickly back to the boil and remove the lid. Reduce the heat slightly, then stir the pasta and cook accord-ing to the instructions on the packet. For long straight pasta, such as spaghetti, coil the pasta into the water as it softens.

Pasta for Soup

These tiny shapes are mostly made from plain durum wheat pasta, though you may find them with egg. There are hundreds of different ones, from tiny risi, which look like grains of rice, to alfabeti (alphabet shapes), which are popular with children. Slightly larger shapes such as farfallini (little bows) and tubetti (little tubes), the more substantial conchigliette (little shells) and farfallini (little butterflies) go well in hearty vegetable soup, such as minestrone.

Right: Fresh tortellini.

Buying and Storing Pasta: The quality of pasta varies tremendously – choose good-quality Italian brands of pasta made from 100 per cent durum wheat, and visit your local Italian delicatessen to buy fresh pasta, rather than buying pre-packed pasta from the supermarket. Dried pasta will keep almost indefinitely, but if you decant the pasta into a storage jar, it is a good idea to use up the remaining pasta before adding any from a new packet. Fresh pasta from a delicatessen is usually sold loose and is best cooked the same day, but can be kept in the refrigerator for a day or two. Fresh pasta from a supermarket is likely to be packed in plastic packs and bags, and these will keep for 3–4 days in the refrigerator. Fresh pasta freezes well and should be cooked from frozen. Packs and bags of supermarket pasta have the advantage of being easy to store in the freezer.

Health Benefits of Pasta: Pasta provides the body with fuel for all kinds of physical activity, from walking to the bus stop to running a marathon. High in complex carbohydrates, pasta is broken down slowly, providing energy over a long period of time. Wholewheat pasta is the most nutritious, containing a richer concentration of vitamins, minerals and fibre. Nevertheless, all pasta is a useful source of protein, as well as being low in fat. Buckwheat is very nutritious; it contains all eight essential amino acids, making it a complete protein. It is also particularly high in fibre.

CHOOSING THE RIGHT SHAPE

- Long pasta shapes, such as spaghetti, linguine, tagliatelle and fettuccine, suit smooth cream, or olive oil-based sauces, or vegetable sauces in which the ingredients are very finely chopped.
- Hollow shapes, such as penne (quills), fusilli (spirals) and macaroni, all work well with more robust sauces, such as cheese, tomato and vegetable.
- Stuffed pasta shapes, such as ravioli and cappelletti, are good with simple sauces made with butter, extra virgin olive oil or tomatoes.
- Delicate small shapes, risi (rice), orzi (barley) and quadrucci (squares), suit lighter broths.

Above: Tiny soup pasta is available in hundreds of different shapes.

NOODLES

*THE FAST FOOD OF THE EAST, NOODLES CAN BE MADE FROM WHEAT FLOUR, RICE, BUCKWHEAT FLOUR
OR MUNG BEAN FLOUR. BOTH FRESH AND DRIED NOODLES ARE READILY AVAILABLE IN HEALTH FOOD
STORES AND ASIAN SHOPS AS WELL AS SUPERMARKETS. LIKE PASTA, NOODLES ARE LOW IN FAT AND
HIGH IN COMPLEX CARBOHYDRATES, SO PROVIDE LONG-TERM ENERGY.*

Wheat Noodles

There are two main types of noodle: plain
and egg. Plain noodles are made from
strong flour and water, they can be flat or
round and come in various thicknesses.

Udon Noodles

These thick Japanese noodles can be
round or flat and are available fresh,
pre-cooked or dried. Wholewheat udon
noodles have a more robust flavour.

Somen Noodles

Usually sold in bundles, held together by
a paper band, these thin, white noodles
are available from oriental stores.

Egg Noodles

These noodles are sold both fresh
and dried. The Chinese type come in
various thicknesses. Very fine egg
noodles, which resemble vermicelli, are
usually sold in coils. Wholewheat egg
noodles are widely available from
larger supermarkets.

Ramen Noodles

These Japanese egg noodles are also
sold in coils and are often cooked and
served in a broth.

Left: Rice noodles.

Rice Noodles

These fine, delicate noodles are made
from rice and are opaque-white in
colour. Like wheat noodles, they come in
various widths, from the very thin
strands known as rice vermicelli, which
are popular in Thailand and southern
China, to the thicker rice sticks, which
are used more in Vietnam and Malaysia.
A huge range of rice noodles is available

dried from oriental grocers. Fresh noodles are occasionally found in the chiller
cabinets. Since all rice noodles are
pre-cooked, they need only to be soaked
in hot water for a few minutes to soften
them. Drain well and rinse under cold
running water before use in stir-fries
and salads.

*Left: Udon noodles
(above) and cellophane
noodles (below).*

Cellophane Vermicelli and Noodles

Made from mung bean starch, these
translucent noodles, also known as bean
thread vermicelli and glass noodles,
come in a variety of thicknesses and are
only available dried. Although very fine,
the strands are firm and fairly tough.
Cellophane noodles don't need to be
boiled, and are simply soaked in boiling
water for 10–15 minutes. They have a
firm texture, which they retain when
cooked, never becoming soggy.
Cellophane noodles are almost tasteless
unless combined with other strongly
flavoured foods and seasonings. They

are never eaten on their own, but used as an ingredient. They are good in vegetarian dishes, and as an ingredient in spring rolls.

Soba Noodles

The best-known type of buckwheat noodle is the soba noodle. They are much darker in colour than wheat noodles – almost brownish grey. In Japan, soba noodles are traditionally served in soups or stir-fries with a variety of sauces.

Above: Dried and fresh egg noodles.

QUICK IDEAS FOR NOODLES
• To make a broth, dissolve mugi miso in hot water, add cooked soba noodles; sprinkle with chilli flakes and sliced spring onions (scallions).

• Cook ramen noodles in vegetable stock, then add a splash of dark soy sauce, shredded spinach and grated ginger. Sprinkle with sesame seeds and fresh coriander (cilantro).

• Stir-fry sliced shiitake and oyster mushrooms in garlic and ginger, then toss with rice or egg noodles (above). Sprinkle with fresh chives and a little roasted sesame oil.
• In a food processor, blend together some lemon grass, chilli, garlic, ginger, kaffir lime leaves and fresh coriander (cilantro). Fry the paste in sunflower oil and combine with cooked ribbon noodles. Sprinkle on top fresh basil and chopped spring onions (scallions) before serving.

Buying and Storing Noodles: Packets of fresh noodles are found in the chiller cabinets of Asian shops. They usually carry a use-by date and must be stored in the refrigerator. Dried noodles will keep for many months if stored in an air-tight container in a cool, dry place.

Health Benefits of Noodles: Wholewheat noodles are high in complex carbohydrates, which are broken down slowly, providing energy over a long period of time. They are also the most nutritious, containing a richer concentration of vitamins, minerals and fibre. Nevertheless, some noodles are a useful source of protein, as well as being low in fat. Buckwheat noodles are made from buckwheat flour, which contains all eight essential amino acids, making it a complete protein. It is also particularly high in fibre. Cellophane noodles are made from mung bean starch, which is reputed to be one of the most effective detoxifiers.

COOKING WHEAT NOODLES

Wheat noodles are very easy to cook. Both dried and fresh noodles are cooked in a large pan of boiling water; how long depends on the type of noodle and the thickness of the strips. Dried noodles need about 3 minutes cooking time, while fresh ones will often be ready in less than a minute. Fresh noodles may need to be rinsed quickly in cold water to prevent them from overcooking.

Below: Wholewheat egg noodles.

BREAKFAST

*The most important meal of the day, breakfast
replenishes energy and nutrients depleted
overnight. Grains, especially the wholegrain
variety, are complex carbohydrates and
provide plenty of long-term energy, while pulses
and legumes are a valuable source of protein,
which are said to satisfy the appetite for
sustained periods.*

WHEAT BRAN SMOOTHIE

EASY TO PREPARE AND EVEN EASIER TO DRINK, THIS ENERGY-PACKED SMOOTHIE MAKES A GREAT START TO THE DAY. WHEAT BRAN AND BANANAS PROVIDE THE PERFECT FUEL IN THE FORM OF SLOW-RELEASE CARBOHYDRATE THAT WILL KEEP YOU GOING ALL MORNING, WHILE FRESH AND ZESTY ORANGE JUICE AND SWEET, SCENTED MANGO WILL PROVIDE VALUABLE VITAMINS.

MAKES TWO GLASSES

INGREDIENTS
 ½ mango
 1 banana
 1 large orange
 30ml/2 tbsp wheat bran
 15ml/1 tbsp sesame seeds
 10–15ml/2–3tsp honey

COOK'S TIP
Mango juice is naturally very sweet so you may wish to add less honey or leave it out altogether. Taste the drink to decide how much you need.

1 Using a small, sharp knife, skin the mango, then slice the flesh off the stone (pit). Peel the banana and break it into short lengths, then place it in a blender or food processor with the mango.

2 Squeeze the juice from the orange and add to the blender or food processor along with the bran, sesame seeds and honey. Whizz until the mixture is smooth and creamy, then pour into glasses and serve.

Energy 172kcal/726kJ; Protein 4.9g; Carbohydrate 27.6g, of which sugars 23.1g; Fat 5.5g, of which saturates 0.9g; Cholesterol 0mg; Calcium 102mg; Fibre 8.5g; Sodium 11mg.

MUESLI SMOOTHIE

THIS STORE-CUPBOARD SMOOTHIE IS PACKED WITH HEALTHY INGREDIENTS AND IS AN INNOVATIVE WAY OF USING MUESLI. ANY EXTRA DRINK CAN BE STORED OVERNIGHT IN THE REFRIGERATOR, ALTHOUGH YOU'LL PROBABLY NEED TO ADD MORE MILK IN THE MORNING AS IT WILL UNDOUBTEDLY THICKEN ON STANDING.

MAKES TWO GLASSES

INGREDIENTS
1 piece preserved stem ginger, plus 30ml/2 tbsp syrup from the ginger jar
50g/2oz/¼ cup ready-to-eat dried apricots, halved or quartered
40g/1½oz/scant ½ cup natural muesli (granola)
about 200ml/7fl oz/scant 1 cup semi-skimmed (low-fat) milk

COOK'S TIP
Apricot and ginger are perfect partners in this divine drink. It makes an incredibly healthy, tasty breakfast, but is so delicious and indulgent that you could even serve it as a dessert after a summer meal.

1 Chop the preserved ginger and put it in a blender or food processor with the syrup, apricots, muesli and milk.

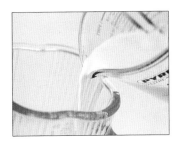

2 Process until smooth, adding more milk if necessary. Serve in wide glasses.

COOK'S TIP
Choose unsulphured dried apricots for the healthiest choice of dried fruit.

Energy 204kcal/865kJ; Protein 6.6g; Carbohydrate 39.1g, of which sugars 28.8g; Fat 3.4g, of which saturates 1.4g; Cholesterol 6mg; Calcium 150mg; Fibre 3.1g; Sodium 97mg.

RASPBERRY AND OATMEAL SMOOTHIE

JUST A SPOONFUL OR SO OF HIGH-FIBRE OATMEAL GIVES SUBSTANCE TO THIS TANGY, INVIGORATING DRINK. IF YOU CAN, PREPARE IT AHEAD OF TIME BECAUSE SOAKING THE RAW OATS HELPS TO BREAK DOWN THE STARCH INTO NATURAL SUGARS, MAKING THE DRINK EASIER TO DIGEST. THE SMOOTHIE WILL THICKEN UP IN THE REFRIGERATOR SO YOU MIGHT NEED TO STIR IN A LITTLE EXTRA MILK OR FRUIT JUICE JUST BEFORE SERVING.

MAKES ONE LARGE GLASS

INGREDIENTS

    25ml/1½ tbsp medium oatmeal
    150g/5oz/scant 1 cup raspberries
    5–10ml/1–2 tsp clear honey
    45ml/3 tbsp natural (plain) yogurt

1 Spoon the oatmeal into a heatproof bowl. Pour in 120ml/4fl oz/½ cup boiling water and leave to stand for about 10 minutes.

2 Put the soaked oats in a blender or food processor and add all but two or three of the raspberries, the honey and about 30ml/2 tbsp of the yogurt. Process until smooth, scraping down the side of the bowl if necessary.

3 Pour the raspberry and oatmeal smoothie into a large glass, swirl in the remaining yogurt and top with the reserved raspberries.

COOK'S TIPS
• If you don't like raspberry pips (seeds) in your smoothies, press the fruit through a sieve with the back of a wooden spoon to make a smooth purée, then process with the oatmeal and yogurt as before.
• Alternatively, try using redcurrants or strawberries instead of the raspberries.
• Although a steaming bowl of porridge can't be beaten as a winter warmer, this smooth, oaty drink makes a great, light alternative in warmer months. It is a good way to make sure you get your fill of wholesome oats for breakfast.

Energy 192kcal/817kJ; Protein 7.5g; Carbohydrate 36.1g, of which sugars 17.9g; Fat 3.1g, of which saturates 0.4g; Cholesterol 1mg; Calcium 137mg; Fibre 5.5g; Sodium 51mg.

TOFU AND STRAWBERRY CREAM

This energizing blend is simply bursting with goodness — just what you need when the morning has got off to a slow start. Not only is tofu a perfect source of protein, it is also rich in minerals and nutrients. Blended with seeds and vitamin-rich strawberries, this creamy blend should see you through until lunchtime. Store any leftovers in the regrigerator for later in the day or the following morning.

MAKES TWO GLASSES

INGREDIENTS
250g/9oz firm tofu
200g/7oz/1¾ cups strawberries
45ml/3 tbsp pumpkin or sunflower
    seeds, plus extra for sprinkling
30–45ml/2–3 tbsp clear honey
juice of 2 large oranges
juice of 1 lemon

1 Roughly chop the tofu, then hull and roughly chop the strawberries. Reserve a few strawberry chunks.

2 Put all the ingredients in a blender or food processor and blend until completely smooth, scraping the mixture down from the side of the bowl, if necessary.

3 Pour into tumblers and sprinkle with extra seeds and strawberry chunks.

COOK'S TIP
Almost any other fruit can be used instead of the strawberries. Those that blend well, such as mangoes, bananas, peaches, plums and raspberries, make an excellent substitute.

Energy 310kcal/1296kJ; Protein 15.7g; Carbohydrate 26.9g, of which sugars 22.6g; Fat 16.1g, of which saturates 1.7g; Cholesterol 0mg; Calcium 684mg; Fibre 2.5g; Sodium 19mg.

BEANSPROUT AND GRAPE JUICE

BEANSPROUTS ARE A HIGHLY NUTRITIOUS FOOD, BURSTING WITH VITAMINS B, C AND E, AND THEY ARE ONE OF THE FEW INGREDIENTS THAT ACTUALLY INCREASE IN GOODNESS AFTER THEY ARE SPROUTED. ALTHOUGH MILD IN FLAVOUR, THEIR JUICINESS WORKS WELL IN ANY NOURISHING JUICE. MIXED WITH BROCCOLI, ANOTHER SUPERFOOD, AND NATURALLY SWEET FRUITS, THIS BLEND IS A REAL TONIC FOR YOUR SKIN, HAIR AND GENERAL HEALTH.

MAKES ONE LARGE OR TWO
SMALL GLASSES

INGREDIENTS
90g/3½oz broccoli
1 large pear
90g/3½oz/scant ½ cup beansprouts
200g/7oz green grapes
ice cubes and sliced green
  grapes, to serve

COOK'S TIPS
• When juicing always use the freshest ingredients you can find; that way the juice will have maximum flavour and you'll get additional health benefits. If at all possible, use organic produce.
• Beansprouts are sprouted mung beans and have a crunchy texture and delicate flavour. In Chinese medicine they are praised for their cleansing properties.

1 Using a small, sharp knife, cut the broccoli into pieces small enough to fit through a juicer funnel.

2 Quarter the pear and carefully remove the core, then roughly chop the flesh into small chunks.

3 Push all the ingredients through the juicer. Pour into glasses and serve with ice cubes and sliced green grapes.

Energy 119kcal/505kJ; Protein 3.9g; Carbohydrate 25.5g, of which sugars 24.6g; Fat 0.8g, of which saturates 0.2g; Cholesterol 0mg; Calcium 56mg; Fibre 4.2g; Sodium 10mg.

WHEATGRASS TONIC

THE NUTRITIONAL BENEFITS OF WHEATGRASS ARE ENORMOUS. IT IS GROWN FROM WHOLEWHEAT GRAIN AND IS A CONCENTRATED SOURCE OF CHLOROPHYLL, WHICH IS A POWERFUL DETOXIFIER, AND ALSO PROVIDES ENZYMES, VITAMINS AND MINERALS. IT HAS A DISTINCTIVE FLAVOUR SO IN THIS JUICE IT IS BLENDED WITH MILD WHITE CABBAGE, BUT IT IS JUST AS TASTY COMBINED WITH OTHER VEGETABLES INSTEAD. ONCE MADE, THIS JUICE SHOULD BE DRUNK WITHIN 15 MINUTES.

MAKES ONE SMALL GLASS

INGREDIENTS
  50g/2oz white cabbage
  90g/3½oz wheatgrass

1 Using a small, sharp knife, roughly shred the cabbage.

2 Push through a juicer with the wheatgrass. Pour the juice into a small glass and serve immediately.

Energy 36kcal/149kJ; Protein 3.2g; Carbohydrate 3.9g, of which sugars 3.8g; Fat 0.8g, of which saturates 0.1g; Cholesterol 0mg; Calcium 178mg; Fibre 2.9g; Sodium 130mg.

TRADITIONAL PORRIDGE

PORRIDGE REMAINS A FAVOURITE WAY TO START THE DAY, ESPECIALLY DURING WINTER. OATMEAL IS RICH IN FIBRE, AND OATS IN GENERAL HAVE BEEN FOUND TO REDUCE HARMFUL BLOOD CHOLESTEROL LEVELS. A SPOONFUL OF BROWN SUGAR OR HONEY AND CREAM ARE ADDITIONAL TREATS.

SERVES FOUR

INGREDIENTS
1 litre/1¾ pints/4 cups water
115g/4oz/1 cup pinhead oatmeal
good pinch of salt

VARIATION
Rolled oats can be used, in the proportion of 115g/4oz/1 cup rolled oats to 750ml/1¼ pints/3 cups water, plus a sprinkling of salt. This cooks more quickly than pinhead oatmeal. Simmer, stirring to prevent the porridge from sticking, for about 5 minutes. Either type of oatmeal can be left to cook overnight in the slow oven of a range.

1 Put the water, pinhead oatmeal and salt into a heavy pan and bring to the boil over a medium heat, stirring with a wooden spatula. When the porridge is smooth and beginning to thicken, reduce the heat to a simmer.

2 Cook gently for about 25 minutes, stirring occasionally, until the oatmeal is cooked and the consistency smooth.

3 Serve hot with cold milk and extra salt, if required.

Energy 115kcal/488kJ; Protein 3.6g; Carbohydrate 20.9g, of which sugars 0g; Fat 2.5g, of which saturates 0g; Cholesterol 0mg; Calcium 16mg; Fibre 2g; Sodium 304mg.

OATMEAL PANCAKES WITH BACON

THESE OATY PANCAKES HAVE A SPECIAL AFFINITY WITH GOOD BACON, MAKING AN INTERESTING BASE FOR AN ALTERNATIVE TO THE BIG TRADITIONAL FRY-UP. SERVE WITH SAUSAGES, FRIED OR POACHED EGGS AND COOKED TOMATOES FOR A HEARTY BREAKFAST.

MAKES EIGHT PANCAKES

INGREDIENTS
115g/4oz/1 cups wholemeal (whole-wheat) flour
25g/1oz/¼ cup fine pinhead oatmeal
pinch of salt
2 eggs
about 300ml/½ pint/1¼ cups buttermilk
butter or oil, for greasing
8 bacon rashers (strips)

COOK'S TIP
When whole oats are chopped into pieces they are called pinhead or coarse oatmeal. They take longer to cook than rolled oats and have a chewier texture.

1 Mix the flour, oatmeal and salt in a bowl or food processor, beat in the eggs and add enough buttermilk to make a creamy batter of the same consistency as ordinary pancakes.

2 Thoroughly heat a griddle or cast-iron frying pan over a medium-hot heat. When very hot, grease lightly with butter or oil.

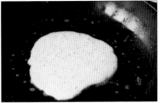

3 Pour in the batter, about a ladleful at a time. Tilt the pan around to spread the batter evenly and cook for about 2 minutes on the first side, or until set and the underside is browned. Turn over and cook for 1 minute until browned. Fry the bacon and roll in the cooked pancakes.

Energy 202kcal/845kJ; Protein 11.9g; Carbohydrate 17.8g, of which sugars 2g; Fat 11.8g, of which saturates 4.8g; Cholesterol 87mg; Calcium 59mg; Fibre 1.5g; Sodium 654mg.

LUXURY MUESLI

COMMERCIALLY MADE MUESLI REALLY CAN'T COMPETE WITH THIS HOME-MADE VERSION. THIS COMBINATION OF SEEDS, GRAINS, NUTS AND DRIED FRUITS WORKS PARTICULARLY WELL, BUT YOU CAN ALTER THE BALANCE OF INGREDIENTS, OR SUBSTITUTE OTHERS, IF YOU LIKE.

SERVES FOUR

INGREDIENTS
    50g/2oz/½ cup sunflower seeds
    25g/1oz/¼ cup pumpkin seeds
    115g/4oz/1 cup rolled oats
    115g/4oz/heaped 1 cup wheat flakes
    115g/4oz/heaped 1 cup barley flakes
    115g/4oz/1 cup raisins
    115g/4oz/1 cup chopped hazelnuts,
      roasted
    115g/4oz/½ cup unsulphured dried
      apricots, chopped
    50g/2oz/2 cups dried apple
      slices, halved
    25g/1oz/⅓ cup desiccated (dry,
      unsweetened shredded) coconut

1 Put the sunflower and pumpkin seeds in a dry frying pan and cook over a medium heat for 3 minutes until golden, tossing the seeds regularly to prevent them from burning.

2 Mix the toasted seeds with the remaining ingredients and leave to cool. Store in an airtight container.

Energy 787kcal/3310kJ; Protein 20g; Carbohydrate 104.4g, of which sugars 38.7g; Fat 35.1g, of which saturates 5.7g; Cholesterol 0mg; Calcium 137mg; Fibre 14g; Sodium 60mg.

GRANOLA

HONEY-COATED NUTS, SEEDS AND OATS, COMBINED WITH SWEET DRIED FRUITS, MAKE AN EXCELLENT AND NUTRITIOUS START TO THE DAY — WITHOUT THE ADDITIVES OFTEN FOUND IN PRE-PACKED CEREALS. SERVE THE GRANOLA WITH SEMI-SKIMMED MILK OR NATURAL LIVE YOGURT AND FRESH FRUIT.

SERVES FOUR

INGREDIENTS
    115g/4oz/1 cup rolled oats
    115g/4oz/1 cup jumbo oats
    50g/2oz/½ cup sunflower seeds
    25g/1oz/2 tbsp sesame seeds
    50g/2oz/½ cup hazelnuts, roasted
    25g/1oz/¼ cup almonds, roughly
      chopped
    50ml/2fl oz/¼ cup sunflower oil
    50ml/2fl oz/¼ cup clear honey
    50g/2oz/½ cup raisins
    50g/2oz/½ cup dried sweetened
      cranberries

1 Preheat the oven to 140°C/275°F/ Gas 1. Mix together the oats, seeds and nuts in a bowl.

COOK'S TIPS
• Try varying the grains, nuts, seeds and dried fruit in this recipe, depending on personal taste.
• For a delicious dessert, serve the granola layered in a glass with fresh fruit and fromage frais or yogurt.

2 Heat the oil and honey in a large pan until melted, then remove the pan from the heat. Add the oat mixture and stir well. Spread out on one or two baking sheets.

3 Bake for about 40–50 minutes until crisp, stirring occasionally to prevent the mixture from sticking. Remove from the oven and mix in the raisins and cranberries. Leave to cool, then store in an airtight container.

Energy 614kcal/2573kJ; Protein 14.4g; Carbohydrate 72.3g, of which sugars 27.9g; Fat 31.6g, of which saturates 2.6g; Cholesterol 0mg; Calcium 132mg; Fibre 6.9g; Sodium 39mg.

WHOLEMEAL BREAKFAST SCONES

THESE UNUSUALLY LIGHT SCONES, MADE FROM A COMBINATION OF WHITE AND WHOLEMEAL FLOUR, ARE VIRTUALLY FAT-FREE SO THEY MUST BE EATEN VERY FRESH — WARM FROM THE OVEN IF POSSIBLE, BUT DEFINITELY ON THE DAY OF BAKING. SERVE WITH HIGH-QUALITY BUTTER.

MAKES ABOUT SIXTEEN

INGREDIENTS
- 225g/8oz/2 cups plain (all-purpose) flour
- 2.5ml/½ tsp bicarbonate of soda (baking soda)
- 2.5ml/½ tsp salt
- 225g/8oz/2 cups wholemeal (whole-wheat) flour
- about 350ml/12fl oz/1½ cups buttermilk or sour cream and milk mixed
- topping (optional): egg wash (1 egg yolk mixed with 15ml/1 tbsp water), or a little grated cheese

VARIATION
For a traditional scone mixture that keeps longer, rub 50g/2oz/¼ cup butter into the dry ingredients. Increase the proportion of the soda to 5ml/1 tsp, as the scones will not be as light.

1 Preheat the oven to 220°C/425°F/Gas 7. Oil and flour a baking tray. Sift the plain flour, bicarbonate of soda and salt in a bowl, add the wholemeal flour and mix. Make a well in the centre, pour in almost all the liquid and mix, adding the remaining liquid as needed to make a soft, moist dough. Do not overmix.

2 Lightly dust a work surface with flour, turn out the dough and dust the top with flour; press out evenly to a thickness of 4cm/1½in. Cut out about 16 scones with a 5cm/2in fluted pastry (cookie) cutter. Place on the baking tray and then brush the tops with egg wash, or sprinkle with a little grated cheese, if using.

3 Bake for about 12 minutes until well risen and golden brown.

Energy 117Kcal/493kJ; Protein 3.8g; Carbohydrate 20.9g, of which sugars 1.5g; Fat 2.6g, of which saturates 1.4g; Cholesterol 6mg; Calcium 49mg; Fibre 1.7g; Sodium 72mg.

WHOLEWHEAT FRUITY BREAKFAST BARS

INSTEAD OF BUYING FRUIT AND CEREAL BARS FROM THE SUPERMARKET, TRY MAKING THIS QUICK AND EASY VERSION — THEY ARE MUCH TASTIER AND SINCE THEY ARE MADE WITH WHOLEMEAL FLOUR, THEY ARE FULL OF FIBRE AND OTHER BENEFICIAL NUTRIENTS. STORE IN AN AIRTIGHT CONTAINER.

MAKES TWELVE

INGREDIENTS
270g/10oz jar apple sauce
115g/4oz/½ cup ready-to-eat dried
  apricots, chopped
115g/4oz/¾ cup raisins
50g/2oz/¼ cup demerara (raw) sugar
50g/2oz/⅓ cup sunflower seeds
25g/1oz/2 tbsp sesame seeds
25g/1oz/¼ cup pumpkin seeds
75g/3oz/scant 1 cup rolled oats
75g/3oz/⅔ cup self-raising
  (self-rising) wholemeal (whole-
  wheat) flour
50g/2oz/⅔ cup desiccated (dry
  unsweetened shredded) coconut
2 eggs, beaten

COOK'S TIP
Allow the baking parchment to hang over the edges of the tin; this makes the baked bars easier to remove.

1 Preheat the oven to 200°C/400°F/Gas 6. Grease a 20cm/8in square shallow baking tin (pan) and line with baking parchment.

2 Put the apple sauce in a large bowl with the apricots, raisins, sugar and the sunflower, sesame and pumpkin seeds. Stir together with a wooden spoon until thoroughly mixed.

3 Add the oats, flour, coconut and eggs to the fruit mixture and gently stir together until evenly combined.

4 Turn the mixture into the tin and spread to the edges in an even layer. Bake for about 25 minutes or until golden and just firm to the touch.

5 Leave to cool in the tin, then lift out on to a board and cut into bars.

Energy 207kcal/871kJ; Protein 4.9g; Carbohydrate 29.6g, of which sugars 19.3g; Fat 8.5g, of which saturates 3g; Cholesterol 32mg; Calcium 67mg; Fibre 2.8g; Sodium 46mg.

BASMATI RICE KEDGEREE

This classic dish originated in India. It is best made with basmati rice, which goes well with the mild curry flavour, but long grain rice will do. For a colourful garnish, add some finely sliced red onion and a little red onion marmalade.

SERVES FOUR

INGREDIENTS

450g/1lb undyed smoked
 haddock fillet
750ml/1¼ pints/3 cups milk
2 bay leaves
½ lemon, sliced
50g/2oz/¼ cup butter
1 onion, chopped
2.5ml/½ tsp ground turmeric
5ml/1 tsp mild Madras curry powder
2 green cardamom pods, split
350g/12oz/1¾ cups basmati or long
 grain rice, washed and drained
4 hard-boiled eggs (not *too* hard),
 roughly chopped
150ml/¼ pint/⅔ cup single (light)
 cream or Greek (US strained plain)
 yogurt
30ml/2 tbsp chopped fresh parsley
salt and ground black pepper

1 Put the haddock in a shallow pan and add the milk, bay leaves and lemon slices. Poach gently for 8–10 minutes, until the haddock flakes easily when tested with the tip of a sharp knife. Strain the milk into a jug, discarding the bay leaves and lemon slices. Remove the skin from the flesh of the haddock, and flake the flesh into large pieces. Keep hot until required.

2 Melt the butter in the pan, add the onion and cook over a low heat for about 3 minutes, until softened. Stir in the turmeric, the curry powder and cardamom pods and fry for 1 minute.

3 Add the rice, stirring to coat it well with the butter. Pour in the reserved milk, stir and bring to the boil. Lower the heat and simmer the rice for 10–12 minutes, until all the milk has been absorbed and the rice is tender. Season to taste.

4 Gently stir in the fish and hard-boiled eggs, with the cream or yogurt, if using. Sprinkle with the parsley and serve.

VARIATION
Use smoked or poached fresh salmon for a delicious change from haddock.

Energy 582kcal/2431kJ; Protein 34.7g; Carbohydrate 71.4g, of which sugars 1.2g; Fat 17.1g, of which saturates 8.2g; Cholesterol 257mg; Calcium 101mg; Fibre 0.8g; Sodium 1005mg.

KITCHIRI

THIS SPICY LENTIL AND RICE DISH IS A DELICIOUS VARIATION OF THE ORIGINAL INDIAN VERSION OF KEDGEREE. SERVE IT AS IT IS, OR TOPPED WITH QUARTERED HARD-BOILED EGGS IF YOU'D LIKE TO ADD MORE PROTEIN. IT IS ALSO DELICIOUS SERVED ON GRILLED, LARGE FIELD MUSHROOMS.

SERVES FOUR

INGREDIENTS
- 50g/2oz/¼ cup dried red lentils, rinsed
- 1 bay leaf
- 225g/8oz/1 cup basmati rice, rinsed
- 4 cloves
- 50g/2oz/4 tbsp butter
- 5ml/1 tsp curry powder
- 2.5ml/½ tsp mild chilli powder
- 30ml/2 tbsp chopped flat leaf parsley
- salt and ground black pepper
- 4 hard-boiled eggs, quartered, to serve (optional)

1 Put the lentils in a pan, add the bay leaf and cover with cold water. Bring to the boil, skim off any foam, then reduce the heat. Cover and simmer for 25–30 minutes, until tender. Drain, then discard the bay leaf.

2 Meanwhile, place the rice in a pan and cover with 475ml/16fl oz/2 cups boiling water. Add the cloves and a generous pinch of salt. Cook, covered, for 10–15 minutes, until all the water is absorbed and the rice is tender. Discard the cloves.

3 Melt the butter in a large frying pan over a gentle heat, then add the curry and chilli powders and cook for 1 minute.

4 Stir in the lentils and rice and mix well until they are coated in the spiced butter. Season and cook for 1–2 minutes until heated through. Stir in the parsley and serve with the hard-boiled eggs, if using.

Energy 339kcal/1414kJ; Protein 7.6g; Carbohydrate 52.4g, of which sugars 0.7g; Fat 10.9g, of which saturates 6.5g; Cholesterol 27mg; Calcium 44mg; Fibre 1.3g; Sodium 85mg.

HERRINGS IN OATMEAL WITH BACON

THIS DELICIOUS DISH IS CHEAP AND NUTRITIOUS. FOR EASE OF EATING, BONE THE HERRINGS BEFORE COATING THEM IN THE OATMEAL. IF YOU DON'T LIKE HERRINGS, USE TROUT OR MACKEREL INSTEAD. FOR EXTRA COLOUR AND FLAVOUR, SERVE WITH GRILLED TOMATOES.

SERVES FOUR

INGREDIENTS

115–150g/4–5oz/1–1¼ cups
   medium oatmeal
10ml/2 tsp mustard powder
4 herrings, about 225g/8oz each,
   cleaned, boned, heads and
   tails removed
30ml/2 tbsp sunflower oil
8 rindless streaky (fatty) bacon
   rashers (strips)
salt and ground black pepper
lemon wedges, to serve

COOK'S TIPS
• Use tongs to turn the herrings so as
not to dislodge the oatmeal.
• Cook the herrings two at a time.
• Don't overcrowd the frying pan.

1 In a shallow dish, mix together the oatmeal and mustard powder with salt and pepper. Press the herrings into the mixture one at a time to coat them thickly on both sides. Shake off the excess oatmeal mixture and set the herrings aside.

2 Heat the oil in a large frying pan and fry the bacon until crisp. Drain on kitchen paper and keep hot.

3 Put the herrings into the pan and fry them for 3–4 minutes on each side, until crisp and golden brown. Serve the herrings with the streaky bacon rashers and lemon wedges.

Energy 700kcal/2917kJ; Protein 51.9g; Carbohydrate 20.9g, of which sugars 0g; Fat 46g, of which saturates 11.2g; Cholesterol 139mg; Calcium 153mg; Fibre 2g; Sodium 1050mg.

SPANISH-STYLE BEAN OMELETTE

ALMOST REGARDED AS THE NATIONAL DISH OF SPAIN, THE TRADITIONAL SPANISH OMELETTE CONSISTS SIMPLY OF POTATOES, ONIONS AND EGGS. THIS ONE HAS CANNELLINI BEANS, TOO, AND MAKES A VERY SUBSTANTIAL VEGETARIAN BREAKFAST.

SERVES SIX

INGREDIENTS
    30ml/2 tbsp olive oil, plus extra
        for drizzling
    1 Spanish onion, chopped
    1 small red (bell) pepper, seeded
        and diced
    2 celery sticks, chopped
    225g/8oz potatoes, peeled, diced
        and cooked
    400g/14oz can cannellini
        beans, drained and rinsed
    8 eggs
    salt and ground black pepper
    sprigs of oregano, to garnish
    green salad and olives, to serve

1 Heat the olive oil in a frying pan. Add the onion, red pepper and celery, and cook for 3–5 minutes until the vegetables are soft, but not coloured.

2 Add the potatoes and beans, and cook for several minutes.

3 In a small bowl, beat the eggs with a fork, then season well and pour over the ingredients in the pan.

4 Stir the egg mixture with a wooden spatula until it begins to thicken, then allow it to cook over a low heat for about 8 minutes. The omelette should be firm, but still moist in the middle.

5 Cool slightly then invert on to a serving plate. Cut the omelette into thick wedges. Serve warm or cool with a green salad and olives and a little olive oil. Garnish with oregano.

Energy 252kcal/1055kJ; Protein 14.5g; Carbohydrate 23.8g, of which sugars 7.6g; Fat 11.8g, of which saturates 2.7g; Cholesterol 254mg; Calcium 107mg; Fibre 5.8g; Sodium 366mg.

APPETIZERS

The selection of recipes in this chapter traverse
the globe, from a healthy Moroccan Broad Bean
Dip and Eastern European Cornmeal Balls to
Italian Polenta Fritters and Japanese Simple
Rolled Sushi. Many of the appetizers would
work equally well served as a snack, light lunch
or as part of a buffet or mezze meal.

BROAD BEAN DIP WITH PAPRIKA

THIS GARLICKY BROAD BEAN DIP IS ENJOYED THROUGHOUT MOROCCO. SPRINKLED WITH PAPRIKA OR DRIED THYME, IT MAKES A TASTY APPETIZER SERVED WITH FLAT BREAD.

SERVES FOUR

INGREDIENTS

350g/12oz/1¾ cups dried broad
  (fava) beans, soaked overnight
4 garlic cloves
10ml/2 tsp cumin seeds
60–75ml/4–5 tbsp olive oil
salt
paprika or dried thyme, to garnish

COOK'S TIP
Broad (fava) beans are a popular
ingredient in North African cooking. They
change colour from green to brown when
dried and have a tough outer skin which
is best removed after soaking or cooking.

1 Drain the beans, remove their wrinkly skins and place them in a large pan with the garlic and cumin seeds. Add enough water to cover the beans and bring to the boil. Boil for 10 minutes, then reduce the heat, cover the pan and simmer gently for about 1 hour, or until the beans are tender.

2 When cooked, drain the beans and, while they are still warm, pound or process them with the olive oil until the mixture forms a smooth dip. Season to taste with salt and serve warm or at room temperature, sprinkled with paprika or thyme. Alternatively, simply drizzle with a little olive oil.

Energy 344kcal/1449kJ; Protein 20.3g; Carbohydrate 40.6g, of which sugars 2.4g; Fat 12.3g, of which saturates 1.8g; Cholesterol 0mg; Calcium 90mg; Fibre 14.3g; Sodium 16mg.

HUMMUS

BLENDING CHICKPEAS WITH GARLIC AND OIL MAKES A SURPRISINGLY CREAMY PURÉE THAT IS DELICIOUS AS A DIP WITH VEGETABLES OR SPREAD OVER PITTA BREAD.

SERVES FOUR TO SIX

INGREDIENTS

150g/5oz/¾ cup dried chickpeas
juice of 2 lemons
2 garlic cloves, sliced
30ml/2 tbsp olive oil
pinch of cayenne pepper
150ml/¼ pint/⅔ cup tahini paste
salt and ground black pepper
extra olive oil and cayenne pepper,
  for sprinkling
flat leaf parsley, to garnish

1 Put the chickpeas in a bowl with plenty of cold water and leave to soak overnight.

2 Drain the chickpeas and cover with fresh water in a pan. Bring to the boil and boil rapidly for 10 minutes. Reduce the heat and simmer gently for about 1 hour until soft. Drain.

3 Put the chickpeas in a blender or food processor and process to a coarse purée. Add the lemon juice, garlic, olive oil, cayenne pepper and tahini and blend until smooth and creamy, scraping the mixture down from the sides of the bowl.

4 Season the purée with salt and pepper and transfer to a serving dish. Sprinkle with oil and cayenne pepper and serve garnished with a few parsley sprigs.

COOK'S TIPS
• For convenience, canned chickpeas can be used instead. Allow two 400g/14oz cans and drain and rinse them thoroughly.
• Tahini paste can now be purchased from most supermarkets or health food shops.
• Add a handful of chopped black olives to the purée.

Energy 202Kcal/845kJ; Protein 11.9g; Carbohydrate 13.1g, of which sugars 2g; Fat 11.8g, of which saturates 4.8g; Cholesterol 87mg; Calcium 59mg; Fibre 1.5g; Sodium 654mg.

CANNELLINI BEAN DIP

SPREAD THIS SOFT BEAN DIP OR PÂTÉ ON WHEATEN CRACKERS OR TOASTED MUFFINS. ALTERNATIVELY, IT CAN BE SERVED WITH WEDGES OF TOMATO AND A FRESH GREEN SALAD.

2 Use a potato masher to roughly purée the beans, then stir in the lemon rind and juice and olive oil.

3 Stir in the garlic and parsley. Add Tabasco sauce and salt and pepper.

4 Spoon the dip into a bowl and dust lightly with cayenne pepper. Chill until ready to serve.

VARIATION
Other beans can be used for this dish, if preferred, for example, butter beans or kidney beans.

SERVES FOUR

INGREDIENTS
    400g/14oz can cannellini beans
    grated rind and juice of 1 lemon
    30ml/2 tbsp olive oil
    1 garlic clove, finely chopped
    30ml/2 tbsp chopped fresh parsley
    red Tabasco sauce, to taste
    cayenne pepper
    salt and ground black pepper

1 Drain the cannellini beans in a sieve and rinse them well under cold running water. Transfer to a shallow bowl.

Energy 155kcal/650kJ; Protein 7.4g; Carbohydrate 18.4g, of which sugars 3.9g; Fat 6.3g, of which saturates 0.9g; Cholesterol 0mg; Calcium 96mg; Fibre 6.9g; Sodium 394mg.

MUSHROOM AND BEAN PÂTÉ

THIS LIGHT AND TASTY PÂTÉ IS DELICIOUS SERVED ON WHOLEMEAL TOAST OR WITH CRUSTY FRENCH BREAD AND MAKES AN EXCELLENT VEGETARIAN APPETIZER OR LIGHT LUNCH SERVED WITH SALAD.

SERVES EIGHT

INGREDIENTS
30ml/2 tbsp vegetable stock
1 onion, finely chopped
2 garlic cloves, crushed
1 red (bell) pepper, seeded and diced
450g/1lb/6 cups mushrooms, sliced
30ml/2 tbsp dry white wine
400g/14oz can red kidney beans,
  drained and rinsed
1 egg, beaten
50g/2oz/1 cup fresh wholemeal
  (whole-wheat) breadcrumbs
10ml/2 tsp chopped fresh thyme
10ml/2 tsp chopped fresh rosemary
salt and ground black pepper
salad leaves, fresh herbs and tomato
  wedges, to garnish

1 Heat the stock in a pan. Add the onion, garlic and pepper, and cook for 15 minutes, stirring occasionally, until softened but not browned.

2 Add the mushrooms. Stir well, cover and cook gently for 15 minutes, until the mushrooms are reduced slightly. Add the wine, stir and then simmer, uncovered, for a further 15 minutes, until the excess liquor has evaporated.

3 Tip the mushroom mixture into a food processor or blender and add the rinsed kidney beans. process to make a smooth purée, stopping the machine once or twice to scrape down the sides.

4 Add the egg to the processor and blend briefly. Finally, add the breadcrumbs, thyme, rosemary and seasoning. Pulse briefly to mix, taking care not to overprocess the mixture.

5 Preheat the oven to 180°C/350°F/gas 4. Line a 450g/1lb loaf tin (pan) with greaseproof (waxed) paper and grease well.

6 Turn the mixture into the prepared tin and press down well. Cover with greaseproof paper and foil, folding it around the edges of the tin.

7 Bake for about 1¼ hours, until the pâté is just firm. Leave to cool completely and then chill for several hours or overnight.

8 To serve, turn the pâté out of the tin, peel off the lining paper and cut into slices. Serve with Melba toast and salad leaves.

VARIATION
To make a lighter, milder-tasting pâté, use cannellini or flageolet beans in place of the kidney beans.

Energy 104kcal/440kJ; Protein 6.6g; Carbohydrate 16.4g, of which sugars 4g; Fat 1.6g, of which saturates 0.3g; Cholesterol 24mg; Calcium 67mg; Fibre 4.7g; Sodium 257mg.

POLENTA FRITTERS

These stuffed polenta fritters come from the Jewish community of Italy. Two rounds of polenta are sandwiched together with a filling of rosemary, tomatoes and Italian cheeses, then fried to make a delicous appetizer or light lunch.

SERVES SIX

INGREDIENTS

250g/9oz/1½ cups polenta
30–45ml/2–3 tbsp tomato
  purée (paste)
30–45ml/2–3 tbsp diced ripe fresh or
  canned chopped tomatoes
30ml/2 tbsp chopped fresh rosemary
30–45ml/2–3 tbsp freshly grated
  Parmesan or Pecorino cheese
130g/4½oz mozzarella, Gorgonzola
  or Fontina cheese, finely chopped
half vegetable and half olive oil,
  for deep-frying
1–2 eggs, lightly beaten
plain (all-purpose) flour, for dusting
salt
diced red (bell) pepper, shredded
  lettuce and rosemary sprigs, to garnish

COOK'S TIPS

• If the polenta is too thin the fritters will fall apart; if too thick they will be heavy.
• Do not use instant polenta as the sandwiches will fall apart on cooking.
• The fritters can be cooked ahead of time and reheated in the oven at 200°C/400°F/Gas 6 for 5–10 minutes.

1 In a large pan, combine the polenta with 250ml/8fl oz/1 cup cold water and stir. Add 750ml/1¼ pints/3 cups boiling water and cook, stirring constantly, for about 30 minutes until the mixture is very thick and no longer grainy. If the mixture is thick but still not cooked through, stir in a little more boiling water and simmer until soft. Season.

2 Pour the mixture into an oiled baking dish, forming a layer about 1cm/½in thick. Lightly cover, then cool and chill.

3 Using a 6–7.5cm/2½–3in plain pastry (cookie) cutter or the rim of a glass, cut the polenta into rounds.

4 In a small bowl, combine the tomato purée with the diced tomatoes. Spread a little of the mixture on the soft, moist side of a polenta round, sprinkle with rosemary and a little of the grated and chopped cheeses, then top with another round of polenta, the moist soft side against the filling. Press the edges together to seal the sandwiches. Fill the remaining polenta rounds in the same way.

5 Heat the oil in a wide, deep frying pan, to a depth of about 5cm/2in, until it is hot enough to brown a cube of bread in 30 seconds.

6 Dip a sandwich into the beaten egg, then coat in the flour. Gently lower it into the hot oil and fry for 4–5 minutes, turning once. Drain on kitchen paper. Cook the remaining polenta sandwiches in the same way. Serve warm, garnished with pepper, lettuce and rosemary.

COOK'S TIP

Polenta makes the basis of a very filling meal. Serve with a light salad for a lunchtime dish or appetizer.

Energy 136Kcal/573kJ; Protein 9.8g; Carbohydrate 16g, of which sugars 0.9g; Fat 4.1g, of which saturates 2.6g; Cholesterol 13mg; Calcium 34mg; Fibre 1.4g; Sodium 97mg

CANNELLINI BEAN BRUSCHETTA

MORE BRUNCH THAN BREAKFAST, THIS DISH IS A SOPHISTICATED VERSION OF BEANS ON TOAST. CANNELLINI BEANS HAVE A DELICATE FLAVOUR AND SOFT TEXTURE THAT MELDS WELL WITH MORE INTENSE INGREDIENTS SUCH AS SUN-DRIED TOMATOES, GARLIC AND BASIL.

SERVES FOUR

INGREDIENTS

150g/5oz/²⁄₃ cup dried cannellini
  beans
5 fresh tomatoes
45ml/3 tbsp olive oil, plus extra
  for drizzling
2 sun-dried tomatoes in oil, drained
  and finely chopped
2 garlic cloves
30ml/2 tbsp chopped fresh rosemary
salt and ground black pepper
a handful of fresh basil leaves,
  to garnish
12 slices Italian-style bread, such
  as ciabatta

1 Place the beans in a large bowl and cover with water. Leave to soak overnight. Drain and rinse the beans, then place in a pan and cover with fresh water. Bring to the boil and boil rapidly for 10 minutes. Reduce the heat and simmer for 50–60 minutes or until tender. Drain and set aside.

2 Meanwhile, place the tomatoes in a bowl, cover with boiling water, leave for 30 seconds, then peel, seed and chop the flesh. Heat the oil in a frying pan, add the fresh and sun-dried tomatoes. Crush 1 garlic clove into the pan and add the rosemary. Cook for 2 minutes until the tomatoes begin to break down and soften.

3 Add the tomato mixture to the cannellini beans, season to taste and mix well. Reheat gently.

COOK'S TIP
Canned beans can be used instead of dried; use 275g/10oz/2 cups drained and rinsed canned beans and add to the tomato mixture in step 3.

4 Cut the remaining garlic clove in half. Rub the cut sides of the bread slices with the garlic clove, then toast lightly. Spoon the cannellini bean mixture on top of the toast. Sprinkle with basil leaves and drizzle with a little extra olive oil before serving.

Energy 479kcal/2026kJ; Protein 19.9g; Carbohydrate 74.8g, of which sugars 10.3g; Fat 13.3g, of which saturates 2g; Cholesterol 0mg; Calcium 173mg; Fibre 10.2g; Sodium 563mg.

FALAFEL

THESE SPICY FRITTERS CAN BE MADE USING DRIED BROAD BEANS, BUT CHICKPEAS ARE MUCH EASIER TO BUY. THEY ARE LOVELY SERVED WITH GARLICKY YOGURT OR STUFFED INTO WARMED PITTA BREAD, WITH SALAD, HUMMUS AND CHILLI SAUCE.

SERVES FOUR

INGREDIENTS

150g/5oz/³⁄₄ cup dried chickpeas
1 large onion, roughly chopped
2 garlic cloves, roughly chopped
60ml/4 tbsp roughly chopped parsley
5ml/1 tsp cumin seeds, crushed
5ml/1 tsp coriander seeds, crushed
2.5ml/¹⁄₂ tsp baking powder
vegetable oil, for deep-frying
salt and ground black pepper
pitta bread, salad and yogurt,
 to serve

1 Put the chickpeas in a bowl with plenty of cold water. Leave to soak overnight.

2 Drain the chickpeas and cover with water in a pan. Bring to the boil. Boil rapidly for 10 minutes. Reduce the heat and simmer for about 1 hour until soft. Drain.

3 Place the chickpeas in a food processor with the onion, garlic, parsley, cumin, coriander and baking powder. Add salt and pepper to taste. Process until the mixture forms a firm paste.

4 Shape the mixture into walnut-size balls and flatten them slightly. In a deep pan, heat 5cm/2in oil until a little of the mixture sizzles on the surface. Fry the falafel in batches until golden. Drain on kitchen paper and keep hot while frying the remainder. Serve warm in pitta bread, with salad and yogurt.

Energy 249kcal/1041kJ; Protein 9.2g; Carbohydrate 24.8g, of which sugars 5.4g; Fat 13.3g, of which saturates 1.5g; Cholesterol 0mg; Calcium 99mg; Fibre 5.6g; Sodium 20mg.

MAMALIGA BALLS

THE MAMALIGA BALLS IN THIS RECIPE CONTAIN BITE-SIZED PIECES OF SALAMI, BUT CHUNKS OF SMOKED HAM OR CHEESE ARE EQUALLY SUITABLE. MAMALIGA IS A THICK CORNMEAL PORRIDGE-LIKE DISH WHICH CAN BE SERVED AS IS OR TURNED INTO BALLS, AS HERE.

SERVES SIX TO EIGHT

INGREDIENTS

   250g/9oz/generous 2 cups fine
      cornmeal
   600ml/1 pint/2½ cups lightly
      salted water
   generous knob (pat) of butter
   115g/4oz/1 cup salami,
      roughly chopped
   vegetable oil, for deep-frying
   pan-fried tomatoes and fresh herbs,
      to serve

1 Stir the cornmeal and water together in a heavy pan. Bring to the boil and, stirring continuously, cook for 12 minutes, or until suitable for rolling into balls. Stir in the butter.

COOK'S TIP

Mamaliga is available in several grades, from coarse to fine. Coarse stoneground is often the best type for cooking.

2 When cool, with lightly floured hands, roll the mixture into balls double the size of a walnut. Press a piece of salami into the middle and neatly roll again.

3 Heat the oil to 180–190°C/ 350–375°F and fry the balls for 2–3 minutes or until golden brown. Drain well on kitchen paper. Serve with fried tomatoes and chopped herbs.

Energy 246kcal/1022kJ; Protein 6g; Carbohydrate 22.9g, of which sugars 0.1g; Fat 14.2g, of which saturates 4g; Cholesterol 17mg; Calcium 3mg; Fibre 0.7g; Sodium 274mg.

BLACK BEAN SALSA

THIS SALSA HAS A VERY STRIKING APPEARANCE, COMBINING DISTINCTIVE BLACK BEANS WITH RED CHILLIES, RED ONION AND FRESH CORIANDER. LIKE OTHER MEMBERS OF THE KIDNEY BEAN FAMILY, THEY HAVE A SUCCULENT TEXTURE AND SLIGHT SWEETNESS.

SERVES FOUR

INGREDIENTS

130g/4½oz/generous ½ cup black beans, soaked overnight in water to cover
1 pasado chilli
2 fresh red Fresno chillies
1 red onion
grated rind and juice of 1 lime
30ml/2 tbsp Mexican beer (optional)
15ml/1 tbsp olive oil
small bunch of fresh coriander, (cilantro) chopped
salt

1 Drain the beans and put them in a large pan. Pour in water to cover and bring to the boil and boil for 10 minutes. Reduce the heat, cover and simmer for about 40 minutes or until tender. They should still have a little bite and should not have begun to disintegrate. Drain, rinse under cold water, then drain again and leave the beans until cold.

2 Soak the pasado chilli in hot water for about 10 minutes until softened. Drain, remove the stalk, then slit the chilli and scrape out the seeds with a small sharp knife. Chop the flesh finely.

3 Spear the Fresno chillies on a long-handled metal skewer and roast them over the flame of a gas burner until the skins blister and darken. Do not let the flesh burn. Alternatively, dry-fry them in a griddle pan until the skins are scorched. Then place the roasted chillies in a strong plastic bag and tie the top to keep the steam in. Set aside for 20 minutes.

4 Meanwhile, chop the red onion finely. Remove the chillies from the bag and peel off the skins. Slit them, remove the seeds and chop them finely.

5 Tip the beans into a bowl and add the onion and both types of chilli. Stir in the lime rind and juice, beer, oil and coriander. Season with salt and mix well. Chill for a few hours before serving to allow the flavours to merge.

Energy 121kcal/510kJ; Protein 7.7g; Carbohydrate 15.9g, of which sugars 2g; Fat 3.4g, of which saturates 0.5g; Cholesterol 0mg; Calcium 61mg; Fibre 6g; Sodium 11mg.

PINTO BEAN SALSA

THESE BEANS HAVE A PRETTY, SPECKLED APPEARANCE AND ARE MOST COMMONLY USED TO MAKE THE TRADITIONAL MEXICAN DISH OF REFRIED BEANS. THE SMOKY FLAVOUR OF THE CHIPOTLE CHILLIES AND THE HERBY TASTE OF THE PASILLA CHILLI CONTRAST WELL WITH THE TART TOMATILLOS.

SERVES FOUR

INGREDIENTS

130g/4½oz/generous ½ cup pinto
  beans, soaked overnight in water
  to cover
2 chipotle chillies
1 pasilla chilli
2 garlic cloves, peeled
½ onion
200g/7oz fresh tomatillos
salt

1 Drain the beans and put them in a large pan. Pour in water to cover and place the lid on the pan. Bring to the boil, lower the heat slightly and simmer the beans for 45–50 minutes or until tender. They should still have a little bite and should not have begun to disintegrate. Drain, rinse under cold water, then drain again and tip into a bowl. Leave the beans until cold.

2 Soak the chipotle and pasilla chillies in hot water for about 10 minutes until softened. Drain, reserving the soaking water. Remove the stalks, then slit each chilli and scrape out the seeds with a small sharp knife. Chop the flesh finely and mix it to a smooth paste with a little of the soaking water.

COOK'S TIP
Canned tomatillos can be used instead, but to keep a clean, fresh flavour add a little lime juice.

3 Roast the garlic in a dry frying pan over a medium heat for a few minutes until the cloves start to turn golden. Crush them and add them to the beans.

4 Chop the onion and tomatillos and stir them into the beans. Add the chilli paste and mix well. Add salt to taste, cover and chill before serving.

Energy 104kcal/444kJ; Protein 7.9g; Carbohydrate 17.7g, of which sugars 3.8g; Fat 0.7g, of which saturates 0.2g; Cholesterol 0mg; Calcium 42mg; Fibre 6.2g; Sodium 12mg.

SMOKED TROUT ON RYE WITH BEETROOT

THIS DELICIOUS APPETIZER, ALSO SUITABLE FOR A LIGHT LUNCH, IS MADE OF INGREDIENTS THAT EACH HAVE STRONG AND DISTINCTIVE FLAVOURS. WHAT'S MORE, IT'S QUICK TO MAKE FOR A LUNCHTIME ON THE MOVE. THE DRY TEXTURE OF RYE BREAD IS A GOOD FOIL FOR THE FILLING.

SERVES FOUR

INGREDIENTS
  30ml/2 tbsp horseradish sauce
  15ml/1 tbsp sour cream
  2 cooked beetroots (beets) (not in
    vinegar), diced
  4 smoked trout fillets,
    halved crossways
  4 slices rye bread, halved crossways
  salt and ground black pepper
  wedges of lemon, to serve

1 To make the beetroot cream, mix together the horseradish sauce and sour cream, season and gently stir in the beetroot.

2 Arrange the trout fillets on the slices of rye bread, top with a spoonful of the beetroot cream and a sprig of dill. Serve with wedges of lemon.

Energy 193kcal/812kJ; Protein 22.1g; Carbohydrate 14.4g, of which sugars 3g; Fat 5.6g, of which saturates 0.6g; Cholesterol 3mg; Calcium 40mg; Fibre 1.7g; Sodium 283mg.

PASTRAMI ON RYE OPEN SANDWICH

*NEW YORK WOULDN'T BE NEW YORK WITHOUT PASTRAMI ON RYE. DARK AND DENSELY TEXTURED RYE
BREAD IS USED HERE BUT YOU COULD ALSO TRY LIGHT RYE BREAD. THE PASTRAMI IS TOPPED WITH A
SPOONFUL OF RED ONION MARMALADE AND CRÈME FRAÎCHE.*

SERVES FOUR

INGREDIENTS
    45ml/3 tbsp olive oil
    3 red onions, papery skin removed
    60ml/4 tbsp sherry vinegar
    90ml/6 tbsp caster (superfine) sugar,
      or to taste
    4 slices rye bread, halved crossways
    8 slices pastrami
    20ml/4 tsp crème fraîche (optional)

1 Preheat the oven to 180°C/350°F/
Gas 4. Put 15ml/1tbsp of the olive oil in
a roasting pan. Place the onions in the
pan and roll them around until they are
coated in the oil, then roast them for
45 minutes until tender when pierced
with a skewer.

2 Leave the onions until cool enough
to handle then peel off the tough
outer layer and slice the onions. Put
them in a pan with the sherry vinegar,
remaining olive oil and sugar. Bring to
the boil and allow to bubble until the
liquid becomes syrupy.

3 Transfer the onions to a bowl, taste
for sweetness and add more sugar, if
necessary. Leave this onion marmalade
to cool before serving.

4 Arrange the rye bread on a serving
platter. Top each piece with a slice of
pastrami, half a teaspoonful of crème
fraîche, if using, and a spoonful of the
red onion marmalade.

COOK'S TIP
Rye bread is made with rye flour and
contains more fibre than bread made
with wheat flour.

Energy 271kcal/1142kJ; Protein 7.7g; Carbohydrate 41.2g, of which sugars 28.4g; Fat 9.7g, of which saturates 1.5g; Cholesterol 15mg; Calcium 53mg; Fibre 2.2g; Sodium 449mg.

STUFFED VINE LEAVES

STUFFED VINE LEAVES ARE A CLASSIC GREEK DISH. HERE THEY ARE FILLED WITH A FLAVOURSOME COMBINATION OF HERBS, YELLOW SPLIT PEAS AND LAMB.

SERVES FOUR TO SIX

INGREDIENTS
250g/9oz vine leaves
30ml/2 tbsp olive oil
1 large onion, finely chopped
250g/9oz minced (ground) lamb
50g/2oz/¼ cup yellow split peas
75g/3oz/½ cup cooked rice
30ml/2 tbsp chopped fresh parsley
30ml/2 tbsp chopped fresh mint
30ml/2 tbsp chopped fresh chives
3–4 spring onions (scallions),
    finely chopped
juice of 2 lemons
30ml/2 tbsp tomato purée (paste)
30ml/2 tbsp sugar
salt and ground black pepper
yogurt and pitta bread, to serve

1 Blanch fresh vine leaves, if using, in boiling water for 1–2 minutes to soften them, or rinse preserved, bottled or canned vine leaves under cold water.

2 Heat the olive oil in a large frying pan and fry the onion for a few minutes until slightly softened. Add the minced lamb and fry over a medium heat until well browned, stirring frequently. Season with salt and pepper and remove from the heat.

3 Place the split peas in a small pan with enough water to cover and bring to the boil. Cover the pan and simmer gently over a low heat for 12–15 minutes, until soft. Drain the split peas if necessary.

4 Stir the split peas, cooked rice, chopped herbs, spring onions, and the juice of one of the lemons into the meat. Add the tomato purée and then knead until thoroughly blended.

5 Place each vine leaf on a chopping board with the vein side up. Place 15ml/1 tbsp of the meat mixture on each leaf and fold the stem end over the meat. Fold the sides in towards the centre and then roll into a neat parcel.

6 Line the base of a large pan with unstuffed leaves and arrange the rolled leaves in layers on top. Stir the remaining lemon juice and sugar into 150ml/¼ pint/⅔ cup water and pour over the leaves. Place a heatproof plate over the stuffed vine leaves.

7 Cover the pan and cook over a very low heat for 2 hours, checking occasionally and adding extra water if necessary. Serve with yogurt and bread.

COOK'S TIP
If using preserved vine leaves, soak them overnight in cold water and then rinse several times before use.

Energy 319Kcal/1336kJ; Protein 18.4g; Carbohydrate 29.8g, of which sugars 16.2g; Fat 14.8g, of which saturates 4.8g; Cholesterol 48mg; Calcium 117mg; Fibre 4.2g; Sodium 98mg.

BLACK-EYED BEAN FRITTERS

THESE BLACK-EYED BEAN FRITTERS ARE MADE IN MUCH THE SAME WAY AS FALAFEL. THE MIXTURE CAN BE MADE THE DAY BEFORE COOKING AND REFRIGERATED.

SERVES FOUR

INGREDIENTS
225g/8oz/1¼ cups dried
  black-eyed beans (peas)
1 onion, chopped
1 fresh red chilli, halved, with seeds
  removed (optional)
about 150ml/¼ pint/⅔ cup water
salt and ground black pepper
vegetable oil, for deep-frying

1 Soak the black-eyed beans in plenty of cold water for 6–8 hours or overnight. Drain the beans and then briskly rub them between the palms of your hands to remove the skins.

2 Return the beans to a bowl, top up with water and the skins will float to the surface. Discard the skins and soak the beans again for 2 hours.

3 Place the beans in a blender or food processor with the onion, chilli (if using), and a little water. Process to make a thick paste. Season with salt and pepper. Pour the mixture into a large bowl and whisk for a few minutes.

4 Heat the oil in a large, heavy pan and fry spoonfuls of the mixture for 4 minutes, until golden brown. Serve.

Energy 254kcal/1066kJ; Protein 12.6g; Carbohydrate 26g, of which sugars 2.3g; Fat 11.8g, of which saturates 1.4g; Cholesterol 0mg; Calcium 60mg; Fibre 9.1g; Sodium 11mg.

TORTILLA WRAP <u>WITH</u> TABBOULEH

TO BE SUCCESSFUL THIS CLASSIC MIDDLE EASTERN BULGUR WHEAT SALAD NEEDS SPRING ONIONS, LEMON JUICE, PLENTY OF FRESH HERBS AND LOTS OF FRESHLY GROUND BLACK PEPPER. IT IS BEST SERVED AT ROOM TEMPERATURE AND GOES SURPRISINGLY WELL WITH THE GUACAMOLE.

SERVES FOUR TO SIX

INGREDIENTS
175g/6oz/1 cup bulgur wheat
30ml/3 tbsp chopped fresh mint
30ml/3 tbsp chopped fresh flat
    leaf parsley
1 bunch spring onions (scallions)
    (about 6), sliced
½ cucumber, diced
50ml/2fl oz/¼ cup extra virgin
    olive oil
juice of 1 large lemon
salt and ground black pepper
flat leaf parsley, to garnish (optional)
4 wheat tortillas, to serve
For the guacamole
1 ripe avocado, stoned (pitted),
    peeled and diced
juice of ½ lemon
½ red chilli, seeded and sliced
1 garlic clove, crushed
½ red (bell) pepper, seeded and
    finely diced

1 To make the tabbouleh, place the bulgur wheat in a large heatproof bowl and pour over enough boiling water to cover.

2 Leave for 30 minutes until the grains are tender but still retain a little resistance to the bite. Drain thoroughly in a sieve, then tip back into the bowl.

3 Add the mint, parsley, spring onions and cucumber to the bulgur wheat and mix thoroughly. Blend together the olive oil and lemon juice and pour over the tabbouleh, season to taste and toss well to mix. Chill for 30 minutes to allow the flavours to mingle.

4 To make the guacamole, place the avocado in a bowl and add the lemon juice, chilli and garlic. Season to taste and mash with a fork to form a smooth purée. Stir in the red pepper.

5 Warm the tortillas in a dry frying pan and serve either flat, folded or rolled up with the tabbouleh and guacamole. Garnish with parsley, if using.

COOK'S TIP
The soaking time for bulgur wheat can vary. For the best results, follow the instructions on the packet and taste the grain every now and again to check whether it is tender enough.

Energy 259kcal/1081kJ; Protein 5.1g; Carbohydrate 35g, of which sugars 1.9g; Fat 11.5g, of which saturates 1.9g; Cholesterol 0mg; Calcium 55mg; Fibre 1.7g; Sodium 52mg.

POLENTA CHIP DIPPERS

THESE TASTY PARMESAN-FLAVOURED BATONS ARE MADE USING INSTANT POLENTA WHICH COOKS A LOT QUICKER THAN OTHER TYPES OF CORNMEAL. THEY ARE BEST SERVED WARM FROM THE OVEN WITH A SPICY, TANGY DIP — A BOWL OF CREAMY, CHILLI-SPIKED GUACAMOLE IS PERFECT.

MAKES ABOUT EIGHTY

INGREDIENTS
  1.5 litres/2½ pints/6¼ cups water
  10ml/2 tsp salt
  375g/13oz/3¼ cups instant polenta
  150g/5oz/1½ cups freshly grated
    Parmesan cheese
  90g/3½oz/scant ½ cup butter
  10ml/2 tsp cracked black pepper
  olive oil, for brushing
  salt

1 Pour the water into a large heavy pan and bring to the boil over a high heat. Reduce the heat, add the salt and pour in the polenta in a steady stream, stirring constantly with a wooden spoon. Cook over a low heat, stirring constantly, until the mixture thickens and starts to come away from the sides of the pan – this will take about 5 minutes.

2 Remove the pan from the heat and add the cheese, butter, pepper and salt to taste. Stir well until the butter has completely melted and the mixture is smooth.

3 Pour on to a smooth surface, such as a marble slab or a baking sheet. Spread the polenta out using a palette knife (metal spatula) to a thickness of 2cm/¾in and shape into a rectangle. Leave for at least 30 minutes to become quite cold. Meanwhile preheat the oven to 200°C/400°F/Gas 6 and lightly oil two or three baking sheets with some olive oil.

COOK'S TIP
The unbaked dough can be made a day ahead, then wrapped in clear film (plastic wrap) and kept in the refrigerator until ready to bake.

4 Cut the polenta slab in half, then carefully cut into even-size strips using a sharp knife.

5 Bake the polenta chips for about 40–50 minutes until they are dark golden brown and crunchy. Turn them over from time to time during cooking. Serve warm.

Energy 39kcal/162kJ; Protein 1.2g; Carbohydrate 3.4g, of which sugars 0g; Fat 2.2g, of which saturates 1g; Cholesterol 4mg; Calcium 23mg; Fibre 0.1g; Sodium 76mg.

STEAMED RICE BALLS WITH SPICY SAUCE

BITESIZE BALLS OF STEAMED PORK AND MUSHROOMS ROLLED IN JASMINE RICE MAKE A FABULOUS
SNACK TO SERVE WITH PRE-DINNER DRINKS, OR AS PART OF A SELECTION OF DIM SUM. THE
DIPPING SAUCE HAS A SWEET-AND-SOUR FLAVOUR.

SERVES FOUR

INGREDIENTS
30ml/2 tbsp oil
200g/7oz/scant 3 cups finely
  chopped shiitake mushrooms
400g/14oz minced (ground) pork
4 spring onions (scallions), chopped
2 garlic cloves, crushed
15ml/1 tbsp fish sauce
15ml/1 tbsp soy sauce
15ml/1 tsp grated fresh root ginger
60ml/4 tbsp finely chopped
  coriander (cilantro)
1 egg, lightly beaten
salt and ground black pepper
200g/7oz/1 cup jasmine rice
For the dipping sauce
120ml/4fl oz/½ cup sweet
  chilli sauce
105ml/7 tbsp soy sauce
15ml/1 tbsp Chinese rice wine
5–10ml/1–2 tsp chilli oil

1 Heat the oil in a large wok, then add the mushrooms and stir-fry over a high heat for 2–3 minutes. Transfer to a food processor with the pork, spring onions, garlic, fish sauce, soy sauce, ginger, coriander and beaten egg. Process for 30–40 seconds, transfer to a bowl and combine well by hand. Cover and chill in the refrigerator for 3–4 hours or overnight.

2 To cook, place the rice in a bowl. With wet hands, divide the mushroom mixture into 20 portions and roll each one into a firm ball. Roll each ball in the rice then arrange the balls, spaced apart, in two baking parchment-lined tiers of a bamboo steamer.

3 Cover the steamer and place over a wok of simmering water. Steam for 1 hour 15 minutes. (Check the water often, replenishing when necessary.)

4 Meanwhile, combine all the dipping sauce ingredients in a small bowl.

5 When the balls are cooked, remove from the steamer and serve warm or at room temperature with the bowl of spicy dipping sauce.

COOK'S TIP
Jasmine rice has a soft, sticky texture that forms a casing around these Thai-style balls. You could also try sushi rice.

Energy 428kcal/1790kJ; Protein 28.9g; Carbohydrate 50.1g, of which sugars 9.7g; Fat 12.4g, of which saturates 2.7g; Cholesterol 111mg; Calcium 61mg; Fibre 1.6g; Sodium 1296mg.

LETTUCE PARCELS WITH NOODLES

KNOWN AS SANG CHOY IN HONG KONG, THIS IS A POPULAR "ASSEMBLE-IT-YOURSELF" TREAT.
CHICKEN, CELLOPHANE NOODLES AND CHINESE VEGETABLES ARE ENCLOSED IN A LETTUCE LEAF TO
MAKE A WRAP. THE FINE NOODLES TAKE A MATTER OF SECONDS TO COOK.

SERVES SIX

INGREDIENTS

2 boneless chicken breasts, total
  weight about 350g/12oz
4 Chinese dried mushrooms, soaked
  for 30 minutes in warm water
  to cover
30ml/2 tbsp vegetable oil
2 garlic cloves, crushed
6 canned water chestnuts, drained
  and thinly sliced
30ml/2 tbsp light soy sauce
5ml/1 tsp Sichuan peppercorns, dry-
  fried and crushed
4 spring onions (scallions),
  finely chopped
5ml/1 tsp sesame oil
vegetable oil, for deep-frying
50g/2oz fine cellophane noodles
salt and ground black pepper
  (optional)
1 crisp lettuce and 60ml/4 tbsp
  hoisin sauce, to serve

3 Add the sliced mushrooms, water chestnuts, soy sauce and peppercorns. Toss for 2–3 minutes, then season, if needed. Stir in half of the spring onions, then the sesame oil. Remove from the heat and set aside.

5 Crush the noodles and put in a serving dish. Top with the chicken skin, chicken mixture and the remaining spring onions. Wash the lettuce leaves, pat dry and arrange on a large platter.

1 Remove the skin from the chicken breasts, pat dry and set aside. Chop the chicken into thin strips. Drain the soaked mushrooms. Cut off and discard the mushroom stems; slice the caps finely and set aside.

2 Heat the oil in a wok or large frying pan. Add the garlic, then add the chicken and stir-fry until the pieces are cooked through and no longer pink.

4 Heat the oil for deep frying to 190°C/375°F. Cut the chicken skin into strips, deep-fry until very crisp and drain on kitchen paper. Add the noodles to the hot oil, deep-fry until crisp. Transfer to a plate lined with kitchen paper.

6 Toss the chicken and noodles to mix. Invite guests to take one or two lettuce leaves, spread the inside with hoisin sauce and add a spoonful of filling, turning in the sides of the leaves and rolling them into a parcel. The parcels are traditionally eaten in the hand.

Energy 237kcal/984kJ; Protein 15.3g; Carbohydrate 7.6g, of which sugars 1.1g; Fat 16.1g, of which saturates 2g; Cholesterol 41mg; Calcium 24mg; Fibre 0.6g; Sodium 41mg.

SPICED NOODLE PANCAKES

THE DELICATE RICE NOODLES PUFF UP IN THE HOT OIL TO GIVE A WONDERFULLY CRUNCHY BITE THAT MELTS IN THE MOUTH. FOR MAXIMUM ENJOYMENT, SERVE THE GOLDEN PANCAKES AS SOON AS THEY ARE COOKED AND SAVOUR THE SUBTLE BLEND OF SPICES AND WONDERFULLY CRISP TEXTURE.

SERVES FOUR

INGREDIENTS
150g/5oz dried vermicelli rice
    noodles
1 red chilli, finely diced
10ml/2 tsp garlic salt
5ml/1 tsp ground ginger
¼ small red onion, very finely diced
5ml/1 tsp finely chopped lemon grass
5ml/1 tsp ground cumin
5ml/1 tsp ground coriander
large pinch of ground turmeric
salt
vegetable oil, for frying
bottled sweet chilli sauce, for dipping

1 Roughly break up the noodles and place in a large bowl. Pour over enough boiling water to cover and soak for 4–5 minutes. Drain and rinse under cold water. Dry on kitchen paper.

2 Transfer the noodles to a bowl and add the chilli, garlic salt, ground ginger, red onion, lemon grass, ground cumin, coriander and turmeric. Toss well to mix and season with salt.

3 Heat 5–6cm/2–2½in oil in a wok. Working in batches, drop tablespoons of the noodle mixture into the oil. Flatten using the back of a skimmer or metal spatula and cook for 1–2 minutes on each side until crisp and golden.

4 Drain on kitchen paper and serve with the chilli sauce.

Energy 248kcal/1031kJ; Protein 2.4g; Carbohydrate 32.7g, of which sugars 0.9g; Fat 11.5g, of which saturates 1.3g; Cholesterol 0mg; Calcium 32mg; Fibre 1.1g; Sodium 22mg.

SIMPLE ROLLED SUSHI

MAKING THESE SIMPLE ROLLS IS AN EXCELLENT WAY OF LEARNING THE ART OF ROLLING SUSHI.
JAPANESE SUSHI RICE STICKS TOGETHER WHEN COOKED DUE TO ITS HIGH STARCH CONTENT. THIS
QUALITY MAKES IT PERFECT FOR SUSHI. YOU WILL NEED A BAMBOO MAT FOR THE ROLLING PROCESS.

MAKES 12 ROLLS OR 72 SLICES

INGREDIENTS
    400g/14oz/2 cups sushi rice, soaked
      for 20 minutes in water to cover
    55ml/3½ tbsp rice vinegar
    15ml/1 tbsp sugar
    2.5ml/½ tsp salt
    6 sheets yaki-nori seaweed
    200g/7oz tuna, in one piece
    200g/7oz salmon, in one piece
    wasabi paste
    ½ cucumber, quartered lengthways
      and seeded
    pickled ginger, to garnish (optional)
    Japanese soy sauce, to serve

1 Drain the rice, then put in a pan with 525ml/18fl oz/2¼ cups water. Bring to the boil, then lower the heat, cover and simmer for 20 minutes, or until all the liquid has been absorbed. Meanwhile, heat the vinegar, sugar and salt, stir well and cool. Add to the hot rice, then remove the pan from the heat and allow to stand (covered) for 20 minutes.

2 Cut the yaki-nori sheets in half lengthways. Cut each of the tuna and salmon into four long sticks, about the same length as the long side of the yaki-nori, and about 1cm/½in square if viewed from the end.

3 Place a sheet of yaki-nori, shiny side down, on a bamboo mat. Divide the rice into 12 portions. Spread one portion over the yaki-nori, leaving a 1cm/½in clear space at the top and bottom.

4 Spread a little wasabi paste in a horizontal line along the middle of the rice and place one or two sticks of tuna on this.

5 Holding the mat and the edge of the yaki-nori nearest to you, roll up the yaki-nori and rice into a cylinder with the tuna in the middle. Use the mat as a guide – do not roll it into the food. Roll the rice tightly so that it sticks together and encloses the filling firmly.

6 Carefully roll the sushi off the mat. Make 11 more rolls in the same way, four for each filling ingredient, but do not use wasabi with the cucumber. Use a wet knife to cut each roll into six slices and stand them on a platter. Garnish with pickled ginger, if you wish, and serve with soy sauce.

Energy 31kcal/128kJ; Protein 1.7g; Carbohydrate 4.8g, of which sugars 0.3g; Fat 0.5g, of which saturates 0.1g; Cholesterol 2mg; Calcium 4mg; Fibre 0.1g; Sodium 3mg.

SOUPS

*Pulses, legumes and grains lend themselves
particularly well to soups, whether it be a
hearty farmhouse Beef and Barley Soup or
Ribollita, or a lighter, fragrant Spicy Couscous
and Shellfish Broth or nutritious Miso Soup.
Many of the soups in this chapter are a complete
meal in themselves, while others are best served
as the first course.*

SPICED RED LENTIL AND COCONUT SOUP

HOT, SPICY AND RICHLY FLAVOURED, THIS SUBSTANTIAL SOUP IS ALMOST A MEAL IN ITSELF. IF YOU ARE REALLY HUNGRY, SERVE WITH CHUNKS OF WARMED NAAN BREAD OR THICK SLICES OF TOAST.

SERVES FOUR

INGREDIENTS
    30ml/2 tbsp sunflower oil
    2 red onions, finely chopped
    1 birds' eye chilli, seeded and
        finely sliced
    2 garlic cloves, chopped
    2.5cm/1in piece fresh lemon grass,
        outer layers removed and inside
        finely sliced
    200g/7oz/scant 1 cup red
        lentils, rinsed
    5ml/1 tsp ground coriander
    5ml/1 tsp paprika
    400ml/14fl oz/1⅔ cups
        coconut milk
    900ml/1½ pints/3¾ cups water
    juice of 1 lime
    3 spring onions (scallions), chopped
    20g/¾oz/scant 1 cup fresh coriander
        (cilantro), finely chopped
    salt and ground black pepper

1 Heat the oil in a large pan and add the onions, chilli, garlic and lemon grass. Cook for 5 minutes or until the onions have softened but not browned, stirring occasionally.

2 Add the lentils and spices. Pour in the coconut milk and water, and stir until well mixed. Bring to the boil, stir, then reduce the heat and simmer for 40–45 minutes or until the lentils are soft and mushy.

3 Pour in the lime juice and add the spring onions and fresh coriander, reserving a little of each for the garnish. Season, then ladle into bowls. Garnish with the reserved spring onions and coriander.

Energy 263kcal/1109kJ; Protein 13.6g; Carbohydrate 39.5g, of which sugars 10.8g; Fat 6.8g, of which saturates 1g; Cholesterol 0mg; Calcium 96mg; Fibre 4.1g; Sodium 134mg.

LENTIL SOUP

THE SECRET OF A GOOD LENTIL SOUP IS TO BE GENEROUS WITH THE OLIVE OIL. THE SOUP IS SERVED AS A MAIN MEAL, ACCOMPANIED BY OLIVES, BREAD AND CHEESE.

SERVES FOUR

INGREDIENTS
275g/10oz/1¼ cups brown or green lentils, preferably the small variety
150ml/¼ pint/⅔ cup extra virgin olive oil
1 onion, thinly sliced
2 garlic cloves, sliced into thin batons
1 carrot, sliced into thin discs
400g/14oz can chopped tomatoes
15ml/1 tbsp tomato purée (paste)
2.5ml/½ tsp dried oregano
1 litre/1¾ pints/4 cups hot water
salt and ground black pepper
30ml/2 tbsp roughly chopped fresh herb leaves, to garnish

1 Rinse the lentils, drain them and put them in a large pan with cold water to cover. Bring to the boil and boil for 3–4 minutes. Strain, discarding the liquid, and set the lentils aside.

2 Wipe the pan clean, heat the olive oil in it, then add the onion and sauté until translucent. Stir in the garlic, then, as soon as it becomes aromatic, return the lentils to the pan. Add the carrot, tomatoes, tomato purée and oregano. Stir in the hot water and a little pepper to taste.

3 Bring to the boil, then lower the heat, cover the pan and cook gently for 20–30 minutes until the lentils feel soft but have not begun to disintegrate. Add salt and the chopped herbs just before serving.

Energy 463kcal/1937kJ; Protein 17.9g; Carbohydrate 40.4g, of which sugars 7.2g; Fat 26.7g, of which saturates 3.9g; Cholesterol 0mg; Calcium 67mg; Fibre 8g; Sodium 33mg.

MIXED BEAN SOUP

THIS CLASSIC VEGETARIAN SOUP, BETTER KNOWN AS PISTOU, HAS A MIXED BEAN BASE AND IS RICHLY FLAVOURED WITH A HOME-MADE GARLIC, FRESH BASIL AND PARMESAN PISTOU SAUCE.

SERVES FOUR TO SIX

INGREDIENTS
150g/5oz/scant 1 cup dried haricot (navy) beans, soaked overnight in cold water
150g/5oz/scant 1 cup dried flageolet or cannellini beans, soaked overnight in cold water
1 onion, chopped
1.2 litres/2 pints/5 cups hot vegetable stock
2 carrots, roughly chopped
225g/8oz Savoy cabbage, shredded
1 large potato, about 225g/8oz, roughly chopped
225g/8oz French (green) beans, chopped
salt and ground black pepper
basil leaves, to garnish
For the pistou
4 garlic cloves
8 large basil sprigs
90ml/6 tbsp olive oil
60ml/4 tbsp freshly grated Parmesan cheese

1 Soak a bean pot in cold water for 20 minutes then drain. If you don't have a bean pot use a large casserole dish, but you do not need to soak it. Drain the soaked haricot and flageolet or cannellini beans and place in the bean pot or casserole dish. Add the onion and pour over sufficient cold water to come 5cm/2in above the beans. Cover and place the pot in an unheated oven.

2 Set the oven to 200°C/400°F/Gas 6 and cook for about 1½ hours, or until the beans are tender.

3 Drain the beans and onions. Place half the beans and onions in a food processor or blender and process to a paste. Return the drained beans and the bean paste to the bean pot or casserole. Add the hot vegetable stock.

4 Add the chopped carrots, shredded cabbage, chopped potato and French beans to the bean pot or casserole. Season with salt and pepper, cover and return the pot to the oven. Reduce the oven temperature to 180°C/350°F/Gas 4 and cook for 1 hour, or until all the vegetables are cooked right through.

5 Meanwhile make the pistou: place the garlic and basil in a mortar and pound with a pestle, then gradually beat in the oil. Stir in the grated Parmesan. Stir half the pistou into the soup and then ladle it into warmed soup bowls. Top each bowl of soup with a spoonful of the remaining pistou and serve garnished with basil.

Energy 338kcal/1416kJ; Protein 17.2g; Carbohydrate 34.6g, of which sugars 7.5g; Fat 15.5g, of which saturates 3.8g; Cholesterol 10mg; Calcium 215mg; Fibre 10.8g; Sodium 133mg.

LENTIL AND PASTA SOUP

THIS RUSTIC VEGETARIAN SOUP MAKES A HEARTY AND WARMING WINTER MEAL AND GOES ESPECIALLY WELL WITH GRANARY OR CRUSTY ITALIAN BREAD.

SERVES FOUR TO SIX

INGREDIENTS

175g/6oz/3/4 cup brown lentils
3 garlic cloves, unpeeled
1 litre/13/4 pints/4 cups water
45ml/3 tbsp olive oil
25g/1oz/2 tbsp butter
1 onion, finely chopped
2 celery sticks, finely chopped
30ml/2 tbsp sun-dried tomato
   purée (paste)
1.75 litres/3 pints/71/2 cups
   vegetable stock
a few fresh marjoram leaves
a few fresh basil leaves
leaves from 1 fresh thyme sprig
50g/2oz/1/2 cup dried small pasta
   shapes, such as macaroni or tubetti
salt and ground black pepper
tiny fresh herb leaves, to garnish

1 Put the lentils in a large pan. Smash one of the garlic cloves using the blade of a large knife (there's no need to peel it first), then add it to the lentils. Pour in the water and bring to the boil. Simmer for about 20 minutes, or until the lentils are tender. Drain the lentils in a sieve, remove the garlic and set it aside. Rinse the lentils under the cold tap and leave to drain.

2 Heat 30ml/2 tbsp of the oil with half the butter in the pan. Add the onion and celery and cook gently for 5 minutes.

3 Crush the remaining garlic, then peel and mash the reserved garlic. Add to the pan with the remaining oil, the tomato purée and the lentils. Stir, then add the stock, herbs and salt and pepper. Bring to the boil, stirring. Simmer for 30 minutes, stirring occasionally.

4 Add the pasta and bring the soup back to the boil, stirring. Reduce the heat and simmer until the pasta is just tender. Add the remaining butter to the pan and stir until melted. Taste the soup for seasoning, then serve hot in warmed bowls, sprinkled with the fresh herb leaves.

Energy 179kcal/753kJ; Protein 8.4g; Carbohydrate 24.2g, of which sugars 2.3g; Fat 6.1g, of which saturates 0.9g; Cholesterol 0mg; Calcium 25mg; Fibre 2.1g; Sodium 29mg.

CANNELLINI BEAN SOUP

THIS SUBSTANTIAL BEAN SOUP IS SO POPULR IN GREECE THAT IT COULD ALMOST BE CALLED A NATIONAL FAVOURITE. IT IS ALWAYS SERVED WITH BREAD AND OLIVES, AND PERHAPS RAW ONION QUARTERS. IT HAS A HEARTY QUALITY AND FLAVOURFUL INGREDIENTS.

SERVES FOUR

INGREDIENTS

275g/10oz/1½ cups dried cannellini
    beans, soaked overnight in
    cold water
1 large onion, thinly sliced
1 celery stick, sliced
2–3 carrots, sliced in discs
400g/14oz can tomatoes
15ml/1 tbsp tomato purée (paste)
150ml/¼ pint/⅔ cup extra virgin
    olive oil
5ml/1 tsp dried oregano
30ml/2 tbsp finely chopped fresh
    flat leaf parsley
salt and ground black pepper

1 Drain the beans, rinse them under cold water and drain them again. Tip them into a large pan, pour in enough water to cover and bring to the boil. Cook for about 3 minutes, then drain.

2 Return the beans to the pan, pour in fresh water to cover them by about 3cm/1¼in, then add the onion, celery, carrots and tomatoes, and stir in the tomato purée, olive oil and oregano. Season with a little pepper, but don't add salt at this stage, as it would toughen the skins of the beans.

3 Bring to the boil, lower the heat and cook for about 1 hour, until the beans are just tender. Season with salt, stir in the parsley and serve.

Energy 460kcal/1922kJ; Protein 16.8g; Carbohydrate 41.1g, of which sugars 11.8g; Fat 26.5g, of which saturates 3.9g; Cholesterol 0mg; Calcium 103mg; Fibre 14g; Sodium 54mg.

CHICKPEA SOUP

COMPARED TO OTHER SOUPS BASED ON PULSES, WHICH ARE OFTEN VERY HEARTY, THIS HAS A UNIQUE LIGHTNESS IN TERMS OF BOTH FLAVOUR AND TEXTURE. WITH FRESH BREAD AND FETA CHEESE, IT MAKES A DELICIOUS, HEALTHY MEAL.

SERVES FOUR

INGREDIENTS

150ml/¼ pint/⅔ cup extra virgin olive oil, plus extra for serving
1 large onion, chopped
350g/12oz/1¾ cups dried chickpeas, soaked in cold water overnight
15ml/1 tbsp plain (all-purpose) flour
juice of 1 lemon, or more if needed
45ml/3 tbsp chopped fresh flat leaf parsley
salt and ground black pepper

1 Heat the olive oil in a heavy pan, add the onion and sauté until it starts to colour. Meanwhile, drain the chickpeas, rinse them under cold water and drain them again. Shake the colander or sieve to dry the chickpeas as much as possible, then add them to the pan. Turn them with a spatula for a few minutes to coat them well in the oil, then pour in enough hot water to cover them by about 4cm/1½in.

2 Bring to the boil. Skim off any white froth that rises to the surface, using a slotted spoon. Lower the heat, add some pepper, cover and cook for 1–1¼ hours or until the chickpeas are soft.

3 Put the flour in a cup and stir in the lemon juice with a fork. When the chickpeas are perfectly soft, add this mixture to them. Mix well, then add salt and pepper to taste. Cover the pan and cook gently for 5–10 minutes more, stirring occasionally.

4 To thicken the soup slightly, take out about two cupfuls of the chickpeas and put them in a food processor. Process briefly so that the chickpeas are broken up, but remain slightly rough. Stir into the soup and mix well. Add the parsley, then taste the soup. If it seems a little bland, add more lemon juice. Serve in heated bowls and offer extra olive oil at the table, for drizzling on top of the soup.

Energy 557kcal/2330kJ; Protein 20.5g; Carbohydrate 54.5g, of which sugars 8.2g; Fat 30.1g, of which saturates 4g; Cholesterol 0mg; Calcium 193mg; Fibre 11.5g; Sodium 41mg.

BRAISED BEAN AND WHEAT SOUP

*THIS DISH IS WONDERFULLY EASY TO MAKE, BUT IT IS VITAL THAT YOU START SOAKING THE PULSES
AND WHEAT THE DAY BEFORE YOU WANT TO SERVE IT. OFFER SOME TASTY EXTRA VIRGIN OLIVE OIL AT
THE TABLE, SO GUESTS CAN DRIZZLE A LITTLE OIL OVER THEIR FOOD.*

SERVES FOUR

INGREDIENTS

200g/7oz/1¼ cups mixed beans
   and lentils
25g/1oz/2 tbsp whole wheat grains
150ml/¼ pint/⅔ cup extra virgin
   olive oil
1 large onion, finely chopped
2 garlic cloves, crushed
5–6 fresh sage leaves, chopped
juice of 1 lemon
3 spring onions (scallions),
   thinly sliced
60–75ml/4–5 tbsp chopped fresh dill
salt and ground black pepper

1 Put the pulses and wheat in a large
bowl and cover with cold water. Leave to
soak overnight.

2 Next day, drain the pulse mixture,
rinse it under cold water and drain
again. Put the mixture in a large pan.
Cover with plenty of cold water and
cook for about 1½ hours, by which time
all the ingredients will be quite soft.

3 Strain the bean mixture, reserving
475ml/16fl oz/2 cups of the cooking
liquid. Return the bean mixture to the
clean pan.

4 Heat the oil in a frying pan and fry
the onion until light golden. Add the
garlic and sage. As soon as the garlic
becomes aromatic, add the mixture to
the beans. Stir in the reserved liquid,
add plenty of seasoning and simmer for
about 15 minutes, or until the pulses
are piping hot. Stir in the lemon juice,
then spoon into serving bowls, top with
a sprinkling of spring onions and dill
and serve.

Energy 442kcal/1844kJ; Protein 14.1g; Carbohydrate 39.2g, of which sugars 5.9g; Fat 26.5g, of which saturates 3.7g; Cholesterol 0mg; Calcium 76mg; Fibre 4.7g; Sodium 27mg.

BEAN RIBOLLITA

ORIGINATING FROM TUSCANY, THE NAME RIBOLLITA OR "RE-BOILED" DERIVES FROM THE FACT THAT THE SOUP TASTES BETTER THE DAY AFTER IT HAS BEEN MADE. TRADITIONALLY IT IS SERVED LADLED OVER BREAD AND A DARK GREEN VEGETABLE, ALTHOUGH YOU COULD OMIT THIS FOR A LIGHTER VERSION.

SERVES SIX TO EIGHT

INGREDIENTS
  45ml/3 tbsp olive oil
  2 onions, chopped
  2 carrots, sliced
  4 garlic cloves, crushed
  2 celery sticks, thinly sliced
  1 fennel bulb, trimmed and chopped
  2 large courgettes (zucchini),
    thinly sliced
  400g/14oz can chopped tomatoes
  30ml/2 tbsp home-made or
    bought pesto
  900ml/1½ pints/3¾ cups
    vegetable stock
  400g/14oz can haricot (navy) or
    borlotti beans, drained
  salt and ground black pepper
To serve
  450g/1lb young spinach
  15ml/1 tbsp extra virgin olive oil,
    plus extra for drizzling
  6–8 slices white bread
  Parmesan cheese shavings

1 Heat the oil in a large pan. Add the onions, carrots, garlic, celery and fennel, and fry gently for 10 minutes. Add the courgettes and fry for a further 2 minutes.

VARIATION
Use other beans such as chickpeas or cannellini, or dark greens, such as chard or cabbage, instead of the spinach.

2 Add the chopped tomatoes, pesto, stock and beans, and bring to the boil. Reduce the heat, cover and simmer gently for 25–30 minutes, until the vegetables are completely tender. Season with salt and pepper to taste.

3 To serve, fry the spinach in the oil for 2 minutes or until wilted. Spoon over the bread in soup bowls, then ladle the soup over the spinach. Serve with extra olive oil for drizzling on to the soup and Parmesan cheese to sprinkle on top.

Energy 227kcal/952kJ; Protein 10.5g; Carbohydrate 28.9g, of which sugars 11.2g; Fat 8.5g, of which saturates 1.8g; Cholesterol 4mg; Calcium 245mg; Fibre 7.9g; Sodium 444mg.

TOMATO SOUP WITH ISRAELI COUSCOUS

ISRAELI COUSCOUS IS A TOASTED ROUND PASTA, WHICH IS MUCH LARGER THAN REGULAR COUSCOUS. IT MAKES A WONDERFUL ADDITION TO THIS WARM AND COMFORTING SOUP. IF YOU LIKE YOUR SOUP REALLY GARLICKY, ADD AN EXTRA CLOVE OF CHOPPED GARLIC JUST BEFORE SERVING.

SERVES FOUR TO SIX

INGREDIENTS
    30ml/2 tbsp olive oil
    1 onion, chopped
    1–2 carrots, diced
    400g/14oz can chopped tomatoes
    6 garlic cloves, roughly chopped
    1.5 litres/2½ pints/6¼ cups
      vegetable or chicken stock
    200–250g/7–9oz/1–1½ cups
      Israeli couscous
    2–3 mint sprigs, chopped, or several
      pinches of dried mint
    1.5ml/¼ tsp ground cumin
    ¼ bunch fresh coriander (cilantro),
      or about 5 sprigs, chopped
    cayenne pepper, to taste
    salt and ground black pepper

1 Heat the oil in a large pan, add the onion and carrots and cook gently for about 10 minutes until softened. Add the tomatoes, half the garlic, the stock, couscous, mint, ground cumin, coriander, and cayenne pepper, salt and pepper to taste.

2 Bring the soup to the boil, add the remaining chopped garlic, then reduce the heat slightly and simmer gently for 7–10 minutes, stirring occassionally, or until the couscous is just tender. Serve piping hot, ladled into individual serving bowls.

Energy 130kcal/541kJ; Protein 2.6g; Carbohydrate 21.3g, of which sugars 3.9g; Fat 4.3g, of which saturates 0.6g; Cholesterol 0mg; Calcium 19mg; Fibre 1.3g; Sodium 11mg.

BLACK-EYED BEAN SOUP

THIS DELICIOUS ISRAELI BLACK-EYED BEAN AND TURMERIC-TINTED TOMATO BROTH, IS FLAVOURED WITH TANGY LEMON AND SPECKLED WITH CHOPPED FRESH CORIANDER. IT'S A FILLING SOUP THAT IS IDEAL FOR LUNCH OR SERVED AS A LIGHT SUPPER DISH.

SERVES FOUR

INGREDIENTS

175g/6oz/1 cup black-eyed
   beans (peas)
15ml/1 tbsp olive oil
2 onions, chopped
4 garlic cloves, chopped
1 medium-hot or 2–3 mild fresh
   chillies, chopped
5ml/1 tsp ground cumin
5ml/1 tsp ground turmeric
250g/9oz fresh or canned
   tomatoes, diced
600ml/1 pint/2½ cups chicken,
   beef or vegetable stock
25g/1oz fresh coriander (cilantro)
   leaves, roughly chopped
juice of ½ lemon
pitta bread, to serve

1 Put the beans in a pan, cover with cold water, bring to the boil, then cook for 5 minutes. Remove from the heat, cover and leave to stand for 2 hours.

2 Heat the oil in a pan, add the onions, garlic and chilli and cook for 5 minutes, or until the onion is soft. Stir in the cumin, turmeric, tomatoes, stock, half the coriander and the beans and simmer for 20–30 minutes. Stir in the lemon juice and remaining coriander and serve at once with pitta bread.

Energy 167kcal/706kJ; Protein 10.9g; Carbohydrate 24g, of which sugars 5g; Fat 3.8g, of which saturates 0.6g; Cholesterol 0mg; Calcium 81mg; Fibre 8.6g; Sodium 19mg.

MEAT, BEAN AND LENTIL SOUP

*THIS IS A HEARTY MEAT, BEAN AND LENTIL SOUP, KNOWN AS HARIRA, AND TRADITIONAL TO MOROCCO.
THE LAMB AND LENTILS ARE SIMMERED GENTLY WITH WARMING SPICES.*

SERVES FOUR

INGREDIENTS

450g/1lb well-flavoured tomatoes
225g/8oz lamb, cut into
   1cm/¹/₂in pieces
2.5ml/¹/₂ tsp ground turmeric
2.5ml/¹/₂ tsp ground cinnamon
25g/1oz/2 tbsp butter
60ml/4 tbsp chopped fresh
   coriander (cilantro)
30ml/2 tbsp chopped fresh parsley
1 onion, chopped
50g/2oz/¹/₄ cup split red lentils
75g/3oz/¹/₂ cup dried chickpeas,
   soaked overnight and drained
4 baby onions or small
   shallots, peeled
25g/1oz/¹/₄ cup soup noodles
salt and ground black pepper
chopped fresh coriander (cilantro),
   lemon slices and ground cinnamon,
   to garnish

1 Plunge the tomatoes into boiling water for 30 seconds, then rinse in cold water. Peel, seed and roughly chop.

2 Put the lamb, turmeric, cinnamon, butter, coriander, parsley and onion into a large pan, and cook over a moderate heat, stirring, for 5 minutes. Add the chopped tomatoes and continue to cook for 10 minutes.

3 Rinse the lentils and add to the pan with the chickpeas and 600ml/1 pint/2¹/₂ cups water. Bring to the boil, cover, and simmer gently for 1 hour. Add the baby onions and continue to cook for a further 30 minutes.

4 Add the soup noodles about 5 minutes before the end of the cooking time. Season to taste. Garnish with the coriander, lemon slices and cinnamon.

Energy 297kcal/1248kJ; Protein 19.6g; Carbohydrate 26.4g, of which sugars 5.4g; Fat 13.1g, of which saturates 6.4g; Cholesterol 56mg; Calcium 75mg; Fibre 4.5g; Sodium 113mg.

SPICY PEANUT SOUP

THIS DISTINCTIVE SOUP IS MADE WITH AN UNUSUAL COMBINATION OF INGREDIENTS. IT HAS A RICH
PEANUT AND CHILLI FLAVOUR AND A THICK TEXTURE MAKING IT A GOOD FILLING AUTUMNAL CHOICE.

SERVES SIX

INGREDIENTS
  30ml/2 tbsp oil
  1 large onion, finely chopped
  2 garlic cloves, crushed
  5ml/1 tsp mild chilli powder
  2 red (bell) peppers, seeded and
    finely chopped
  225g/8oz carrots, finely chopped
  225g/8oz potatoes, peeled and cubed
  3 celery sticks, sliced
  900ml/1½ pints/3¾ cups
    vegetable stock
  90ml/6 tbsp crunchy peanut butter
  115g/4oz/⅔ cup corn
  salt and ground black pepper
  roughly chopped unsalted roasted
    peanuts, to garnish

1 Heat the oil in a large pan and
cook the onion and garlic for about
3 minutes. Add the chilli powder and
cook for a further 1 minute.

2 Add the peppers, carrots, potatoes
and celery to the pan. Stir well,
then cook for a further 4 minutes,
stirring occasionally.

3 Stir in the stock, peanut butter and
corn until combined.

4 Season well. Bring to the boil,
cover and simmer for 20 minutes, or
until all the vegetables are tender.
Adjust the seasoning before serving,
and sprinkle with the chopped roasted
peanuts, to garnish.

Energy 222kcal/925kJ; Protein 6g; Carbohydrate 23.4g, of which sugars 12.1g; Fat 12.2g, of which saturates 2.6g; Cholesterol 0mg; Calcium 41mg; Fibre 4g; Sodium 130mg.

SPINACH AND RISOTTO RICE SOUP

USE VERY FRESH, YOUNG SPINACH LEAVES TO PREPARE THIS LIGHT AND FRESH-TASTING SOUP. RISOTTO RICE HAS A SOFT, CREAMY TEXTURE WHICH HELPS TO MAKE A COMFORTING FILLING SOUP.

SERVES FOUR

INGREDIENTS
  675g/1½lb fresh spinach, washed
  45ml/3 tbsp extra virgin olive oil
  1 small onion, finely chopped
  2 garlic cloves, finely chopped
  1 small fresh red chilli, seeded and
    finely chopped
  115g/4oz/generous 1 cup risotto rice
  1.2 litres/2 pints/5 cups
    vegetable stock
  60ml/4 tbsp grated Pecorino cheese
  salt and ground black pepper

1 Place the spinach in a large pan with just the water that clings to its leaves after washing. Add a large pinch of salt. Heat gently until the spinach has wilted, then remove from the heat and drain, reserving any liquid.

2 Either chop the spinach finely using a large knife or place in a food processor and process to a fairly coarse purée.

3 Heat the oil in a large pan and gently cook the onion, garlic and chilli for 4–5 minutes until softened. Stir in the rice until well coated, then pour in the stock and reserved spinach liquid. Bring to the boil, lower the heat and simmer for 10 minutes.

4 Add the spinach, with salt and pepper to taste. Cook for 5–7 minutes more, until the rice is tender. Check the seasoning and serve with the Pecorino cheese.

Energy 279kcal/1157kJ; Protein 11.4g; Carbohydrate 25.9g, of which sugars 2.5g; Fat 14.2g, of which saturates 4.4g; Cholesterol 15mg; Calcium 381mg; Fibre 2.6g; Sodium 322mg.

CHICKEN, LEEK AND BARLEY SOUP

THIS RECIPE IS BASED ON THE TRADITIONAL SCOTTISH SOUP, COCK-A-LEEKIE. THE UNUSUAL COMBINATION OF LEEKS AND PRUNES IS SURPRISINGLY DELICIOUS.

SERVES SIX

INGREDIENTS

115g/4oz/²⁄₃ cup pearl barley
1 chicken, weighing about 2kg/4¹⁄₄lb
900g/2lb leeks
1 fresh bay leaf
a few fresh parsley stalks and
   thyme sprigs
1 large carrot, thickly sliced
2.4 litres/4 pints/10 cups chicken
   or beef stock
400g/14oz ready-to-eat prunes
salt and ground black pepper
chopped fresh parsley, to garnish

1 Rinse the pearl barley thoroughly in a sieve under cold running water, then cook it in a large pan of boiling water for about 10 minutes. Drain the barley, rinse well again and drain thoroughly. Set aside in a cool place.

2 Cut the breast portions off the chicken and set aside, then place the remaining chicken carcass in the pan. Cut half the leeks into 5cm/2in lengths and add them to the pan. Tie the herbs together into a bouquet garni and add to the pan with the carrot and stock.

3 Bring the stock to the boil, then reduce the heat and cover the pan. Simmer gently for 1 hour. Skim off any scum when the water first starts to boil and occasionally during simmering.

4 Add the chicken breasts to the pan and continue to cook for another 30 minutes until they are just cooked. Leave until cool enough to handle.

5 Strain the stock. Reserve the chicken breast portions and the meat from the carcass. Discard all the skin, bones, cooked vegetables and herbs. Skim as much fat as you can from the stock, then return it to the pan.

6 Add the pearl barley to the stock. Bring to the boil over a medium heat, then lower the heat and cook very gently for 15–20 minutes, until the barley is just cooked and tender. Season the soup with 5ml/1 tsp each salt and ground black pepper.

7 Add the ready-to-eat prunes to the pan, then thinly slice the remaining leeks and add them to the pan. Bring to the boil, then cover the pan and simmer gently for about 10 minutes, or until the leeks are just cooked.

8 Slice the chicken breast portions and then add them to the soup with the remaining chicken meat from the carcass, sliced or cut into neat pieces. Reheat the soup, if necessary, then ladle it into warm, deep soup plates and sprinkle with plenty of chopped parsley to garnish.

Energy 326kcal/1383kJ; Protein 33.7g; Carbohydrate 44.4g, of which sugars 27.2g; Fat 2.7g, of which saturates 0.5g; Cholesterol 82mg; Calcium 73mg; Fibre 7.5g; Sodium 85mg.

BEEF AND BARLEY SOUP

This farmhouse soup, combining sustaining barley, split peas and beef, makes a
wonderfully restorative dish on a cold day. The flavours develop particularly well
if it is made a day in advance and reheated to serve.

2 Meanwhile, trim any fat or gristle from the meat and cut into small pieces. Chop the remaining onions finely. Drain the stock from the bones, make it up with water to 2 litres/ 3½ pints/9 cups, and return to the rinsed pan with the meat, onions, barley and split peas.

3 Season, bring to the boil, and skim if necessary. Reduce the heat, cover and simmer for about 30 minutes.

4 Add the rest of the vegetables and simmer for 1 hour, or until the meat is tender. Check the seasoning. Serve in large warmed bowls, generously sprinkled with parsley.

COOK'S TIP
Other grains and beans can be used in this soup. Try cannellini or haricot beans combined with freekah or spelt grains.

SERVES SIX TO EIGHT

INGREDIENTS
450–675g/1–1½lb rib steak, on
    the bone
2 large onions
50g/2oz/¼ cup pearl barley
50g/2oz/¼ cup green split peas
3 large carrots, chopped
2 white turnips, chopped
3 celery stalks, chopped
1 large or 2 medium leeks,
    thinly sliced
sea salt and ground black pepper
chopped fresh parsley, to serve

1 Bone the meat, put the bones and half an onion, roughly sliced, into a large pan. Cover with cold water, season and bring to the boil. Skim, then simmer for 1–1½ hours, until required.

Energy 194kcal/814kJ; Protein 16.7g; Carbohydrate 19.6g, of which sugars 9g; Fat 6g, of which saturates 2.2g; Cholesterol 33mg; Calcium 62mg; Fibre 3.9g; Sodium 61mg.

BEAN AND HOCK SOUP

THIS CLASSIC GALICIAN SOUP FEATURES SALT PORK AND HARICOT BEANS WITH YOUNG TURNIPS.
GALICIA IS A REGION IN THE NORTH-WEST CORNER OF SPAIN AND IS RENOWNED FOR ITS HEARTY FARE.
YOU WILL NEED TO START MAKING THE SOUP AT LEAST A DAY IN ADVANCE.

SERVES SIX

INGREDIENTS
  150g/5oz/⅔ cup haricot (navy) beans,
    soaked overnight in cold water
    and drained
  1kg/2¼lb smoked gammon (cured
    or smoked ham) hock
  3 potatoes, quartered
  3 small turnips, sliced in rounds
  150g/5oz purple sprouting broccoli
  salt and ground black pepper

1 Put the drained beans and gammon
into a flameproof casserole and cover
with 2 litres/3½ pints/8 cups water.
Slowly bring to the boil, skim off any
scum, then turn down the heat and
cook gently, covered, for about 1¼ hours.

2 Drain, reserving the broth. Return the
broth to the casserole and add the
potatoes, turnips and drained beans.

3 Meanwhile, strip all the gammon off
the bone and return the bone to the
broth. Discard the rind, fat and gristle
and chop half the meat coarsely. Reserve
the remaining meat for another recipe.

4 Add the chopped meat to the
casserole. Discard the hard stalks from
the broccoli and add the leaves and florets
to the broth. Simmer for 10 minutes.
Season generously with pepper, then
remove the bone and leave the soup to
stand for at least half a day.

5 To serve, reheat the soup, add a little
more seasoning if necessary, and ladle
into soup bowls.

COOK'S TIP
The leftover gammon can be chopped
into bitesize pieces and added to rice or
vegetable dishes, or tortillas.

Energy 242kcal/1020kJ; Protein 22.6g; Carbohydrate 23.4g, of which sugars 3g; Fat 7.1g, of which saturates 2.3g; Cholesterol 19mg; Calcium 61mg; Fibre 5.8g; Sodium 751mg.

MISO SOUP

A BOWL OF MISO SOUP IS AS ESSENTIAL TO A JAPANESE MEAL AS A BOWL OF STICKY RICE. SLITHERS OF FRESH TOFU AND STRIPS OF WAKAME SEAWEED ARE ALSO A MUST.

SERVES FOUR

INGREDIENTS

5g/¹/₈oz dried wakame
½ × 225–285g/8–10¹/₄oz packet
  fresh soft tofu or long-life silken
  tofu
400ml/14fl oz/1²/₃ cups second
  dashi stock or the same amount of
  water and 5ml/1 tsp dashi-no-moto
45ml/3 tbsp miso
2 spring onions (scallions),
  finely chopped
shichimi togarashi or sansho
  (optional), to serve
ground black pepper

1 Soak the wakame in a large bowl of cold water for 15 minutes. Drain and chop into stamp-size pieces.

2 Cut the tofu into 1cm/½in strips, then cut horizontally through the strips. Cut the thin strips into squares.

3 Bring the dashi stock to the boil. Put the miso in a small cup and mix with 60ml/4 tbsp hot stock from the pan. Reduce the heat to low and pour two-thirds of the miso into the pan of stock.

4 Taste the soup and add more miso if required. Add the wakame and the tofu and increase the heat. Just before the soup comes to the boil again, add the spring onions and remove from the heat. Do not boil. Serve sprinkled with shichimi togarashi or sansho, if liked.

COOK'S TIPS

• To make first dashi stock, put a 10cm/4in square piece of dried kombu into a pan. Pour in 600ml/1 pint/2¹/₂ cups water and soak for an hour. Heat to near boiling point, then remove from the heat. Remove and reserve the kombu for the second dashi. Add 20g/³/₄oz kezuri-bushi to the pan and heat on low. Do not stir. Just before it reaches boiling point, turn off the heat. Allow the flakes to settle down to the bottom of the pan. Strain and reserve the kezuri-bushi flakes for the second dashi stock.

• To make second dashi stock, put the reserved kombu and kezuri-bushi from the first dashi into a pan with 600ml/1 pint/2¹/₂ cups water. Bring to the boil, then simmer for 15 minutes until the stock is reduced by a third. Add 15g/¹/₂oz kezuri-bushi to the pan. Immediately remove from the heat. Skim any scum from the surface. Leave to stand for 10 minutes, then strain.

Energy 35kcal/146kJ; Protein 3g; Carbohydrate 2.1g, of which sugars 0.8g; Fat 1.7g, of which saturates 0.3g; Cholesterol 1mg; Calcium 154mg; Fibre 0.2g; Sodium 274mg.

SPICY COUSCOUS AND SHELLFISH BROTH

SOME COUSCOUS DISHES INCLUDE A SOUP-LIKE STEW, WHICH IS LADLED OVER THE COOKED COUSCOUS AND MOPPED UP WITH LOTS OF BREAD. IN THIS RECIPE, MUSSELS AND PRAWNS HAVE BEEN USED.

SERVES FOUR TO SIX

INGREDIENTS

500g/1¼lb/3 cups medium couscous
5ml/1 tsp salt
600ml/1 pint/2½ cups warm water
45ml/3 tbsp sunflower oil
5–10ml/1–2 tsp harissa
75g/3oz/6 tbsp butter
500g/1¼lb mussels in their shells,
  scrubbed, with beards removed
500g/1¼lb uncooked prawns
  (shrimp) in their shells
juice of 1 lemon
2 shallots, finely chopped
5ml/1 tsp coriander seeds, roasted
  and ground
5ml/1 tsp cumin seeds, roasted
  and ground
2.5ml/½ tsp ground turmeric
2.5ml/½ tsp cayenne pepper
5–10ml/1–2 tsp plain (all-purpose)
  flour
600ml/1 pint/2½ cups fish stock
120ml/4fl oz/½ cup double
  (heavy) cream
salt and ground black pepper
small bunch of fresh coriander
  (cilantro), finely chopped, to serve

1 Preheat the oven to 180°C/350°F/ Gas 4. Place the couscous in a bowl. Stir the salt into the water, then pour over the couscous, stirring. Set aside for 10 minutes.

2 Stir the sunflower oil into the harissa to make a paste, then, using your fingers, rub it into the couscous and break up any lumps. Tip into an ovenproof dish. Dice 25g/1oz/2 tbsp of the butter and dot it over the couscous. Cover with foil and heat in the oven for about 20 minutes.

COOK'S TIP
Eaten on its own, couscous has a bland flavour, but readily absorbs the flavours of other foods, making it a good filling base for many dishes.

3 Meanwhile, put the mussels and prawns in a pan, add the lemon juice and 50ml/2fl oz/¼ cup water, cover and cook for 3–4 minutes, shaking the pan, until the mussels have opened. Drain the shellfish, reserving the liquor, and shell about two-thirds of the mussels and prawns. Discard any closed mussels.

4 Heat the remaining butter in a large pan. Cook the shallots for 5 minutes, or until softened. Add the spices and fry for 1 minute. Off the heat, stir in the flour, the fish stock and shellfish cooking liquor. Bring to the boil, stirring. Add the cream and simmer, stirring occasionally, for about 10 minutes. Season with salt and pepper, add the shellfish and most of the fresh coriander. Heat through, then sprinkle with the remaining coriander.

5 Fluff up the couscous with a fork or your fingers, working in the melted butter. To serve, pass round the couscous and ladle the broth over the top.

Energy 496kcal/2062kJ; Protein 17.2g; Carbohydrate 45.5g, of which sugars 1.2g; Fat 28.3g, of which saturates 14g; Cholesterol 152mg; Calcium 134mg; Fibre 0.6g; Sodium 636mg

TOFU AND BEANSPROUT SOUP

THE AROMATIC, SPICY BROTH IS SIMMERED TO INTENSIFY THE FLAVOUR OF THE STOCK BEFORE ADDING THE TOFU, BEANSPROUTS AND NOODLES.

SERVES FOUR

INGREDIENTS

200g/7oz firm tofu
150g/5oz/dried thick rice noodles
1 litre/1¾ pints/4 cups
  vegetable stock
1 red chilli, seeded and finely sliced
15ml/1 tbsp light soy sauce
juice of 1 small lime
10ml/2 tsp palm sugar
5ml/1 tsp finely sliced garlic
5ml/1 tsp finely chopped fresh
  root ginger
90g/3½oz beansprouts
30ml/2 tbsp chopped fresh mint
15ml/1 tbsp chopped fresh
  coriander (cilantro)
15ml/1 tbsp chopped fresh
  sweet basil
50g/2oz roasted peanuts,
  roughly chopped
spring onion (scallion) slivers and red
  (bell) pepper slivers to garnish

1 Cut the tofu into cubes and set aside.

2 Place the noodles in a bowl and pour over enough boiling water to cover. Soak for 10–15 minutes, until soft. Drain, rinse and set aside.

3 Meanwhile, place the stock, red chilli, soy sauce, lime juice, palm sugar, garlic and ginger in a wok over a high heat. Bring to the boil, cover, reduce to a low heat and simmer gently for 10–12 minutes.

4 Add the drained noodles, tofu and beansprouts and cook gently for 2–3 minutes. Remove from the heat and stir in the chopped herbs.

5 Ladle the soup into bowls and scatter over the peanuts. Garnish with spring onion and red pepper slivers if liked.

COOK'S TIP
Use firm tofu in this soup as the softer variety will disintegrate during cooking.

Energy 266kcal/1110kJ; Protein 10.4g; Carbohydrate 37g, of which sugars 4.3g; Fat 8.1g, of which saturates 1.4g; Cholesterol 0mg; Calcium 300mg; Fibre 1.1g; Sodium 277mg.

UDON NOODLE SOUP

THIS INVIGORATING JAPANESE-STYLE SOUP IS FLAVOURED WITH JUST A HINT OF CHILLI AND SOYA BEAN PASTE. UDON ARE ROUND NOODLES MADE FROM WHEAT FLOUR AND WATER.

SERVES FOUR

INGREDIENTS
1 litre/1¾ pints/4 cups water
45ml/3 tbsp mugi miso (bean paste)
200g/7oz/2 scant cups udon noodles
   or soba noodles
30ml/2 tbsp sake or dry sherry
15ml/1 tbsp rice or wine vinegar
45ml/3 tbsp Japanese soy sauce
115g/4oz asparagus tips or
   mangetouts (snowpeas), thinly
   sliced diagonally
50g/2oz/scant 1 cup shiitake
   mushrooms, stalks removed and
   thinly sliced
1 carrot, sliced into julienne strips
3 spring onions (scallions), thinly
   sliced diagonally
5ml/1 tsp dried chilli flakes, to serve
salt and ground black pepper

1 Bring the water to the boil in a pan. Pour 150ml/¼ pint/⅔ cup of the boiling water over the miso and stir until dissolved, then set aside.

2 Meanwhile, bring another large pan of lightly salted water to the boil, add the noodles and cook according to the packet instructions until just tender.

3 Drain the noodles in a colander. Rinse under cold running water, then drain again.

COOK'S TIP
Miso is a thick paste made from soya beans combined with barley, rice or wheat. It ranges in colour and depth of flavour, from light and sweet to strong, and dark.

4 Add the sake or sherry, rice or wine vinegar and soy sauce to the pan of boiling water. Boil gently for 3 minutes or until the alcohol has evaporated, then reduce the heat and stir in the miso mixture. Add the asparagus or mangetouts, mushrooms, carrot and spring onions, and simmer for 2 minutes until the vegetables are just tender. Season to taste.

Energy 254kcal/1076kJ; Protein 10.2g; Carbohydrate 48.1g, of which sugars 4.9g; Fat 3.6g, of which saturates 0.1g; Cholesterol 0mg; Calcium 37mg; Fibre 3.4g; Sodium 814mg.

SALADS

What is striking about this chapter is the sheer range of salads that can be made using pulses and grains. Look for a Thai-style Beansprout and Daikon Salad, North African inspired Tofu and Wild Rice Salad or Bean Salad with Tuna and Red Onion, which has a French twist. Pulses and grains add both substance and nutritional value to salads, transforming them from side dishes to complete main meals.

WHITE BEAN SALAD WITH
RED PEPPER DRESSING

THE SPECKLED HERB AND RED PEPPER DRESSING ADDS A WONDERFUL COLOUR CONTRAST TO THIS SALAD, WHICH IS BEST SERVED WARM. CANNED BEANS ARE USED FOR CONVENIENCE.

SERVES FOUR

INGREDIENTS

1 large red (bell) pepper
60ml/4 tbsp olive oil
1 large garlic clove, crushed
25g/1oz/1 cup fresh oregano leaves
  or flat leaf parsley
15ml/1 tbsp balsamic vinegar
2 x 400g/14oz cans flageolet beans,
  drained and rinsed
400g/14oz can cannellini beans,
  drained and rinsed
salt and ground black pepper

1 Preheat the oven to 200°C/400°F/ Gas 6. Place the red pepper on a baking sheet, brush with oil and roast for 30 minutes or until the skin wrinkles and the flesh is soft.

2 Remove the pepper from the oven and place in a plastic bag. Seal and leave to cool. (This makes the skin easier to remove.)

3 When the pepper is cool enough to handle, remove it from the bag and peel off the skin. Rinse under cold running water. Slice the pepper in half, remove the seeds and dice. Set aside.

4 Heat the remaining oil in a pan and cook the garlic for 1 minute until softened. Remove from the heat, then add the oregano or parsley, the red pepper and any juices, and the balsamic vinegar.

5 Put the beans in a large bowl and pour over the dressing. Season to taste, then stir gently until combined. Serve warm.

Energy 267kcal/1117kJ; Protein 11.1g; Carbohydrate 29.8g, of which sugars 8.3g; Fat 12.2g, of which saturates 1.8g; Cholesterol 0mg; Calcium 133mg; Fibre 10.6g; Sodium 591mg.

BEAN SALAD WITH TUNA AND RED ONION

THIS TASTY SALAD MAKES A GREAT LIGHT MAIN MEAL IF SERVED WITH A GREEN SALAD, SOME GARLIC MAYONNAISE AND PLENTY OF WARM, CRUSTY BREAD.

SERVES FOUR

INGREDIENTS
- 250g/9oz/1⅓ cups dried haricot (navy) or cannellini beans, soaked overnight in cold water
- 1 bay leaf
- 200–250g/7–9oz fine French (green) beans, trimmed
- 1 large red onion, very thinly sliced
- 45ml/3 tbsp chopped fresh flat leaf parsley
- 200g/7oz can good-quality tuna in olive oil, drained
- 200g/7oz cherry tomatoes, halved
- salt and ground black pepper
- a few onion rings, to garnish

For the dressing
- 90ml/6 tbsp extra virgin olive oil
- 15ml/1 tbsp tarragon vinegar
- 5ml/1 tsp tarragon mustard
- 1 garlic clove, finely chopped
- 5ml/1 tsp grated lemon rind
- a little lemon juice
- pinch of caster (superfine) sugar

1 Drain the beans and bring them to the boil in fresh water with the bay leaf added. Boil rapidly for 10 minutes, then reduce the heat and boil steadily for 1–1½ hours, until tender. Drain well. Discard the bay leaf.

3 Blanch the French beans in plenty of boiling water for 3–4 minutes. Drain, refresh under cold water and drain thoroughly again.

5 Flake the tuna into large chunks with a knife and toss it into the beans with the tomato halves.

6 Arrange the salad on four individual plates. Drizzle the remaining dressing over the salad and scatter the remaining chopped parsley on top. Garnish with a few onion rings and serve immediately, at room temperature.

2 Meanwhile, place all the dressing ingredients apart from the lemon juice and sugar in a jug and whisk until mixed. Season and add the lemon juice and a pinch of caster sugar, if liked.

4 Place both types of beans in a bowl. Add half the dressing and toss to mix. Stir in the onion and half the chopped parsley, then season to taste with salt and pepper.

Energy 434kcal/1817kJ; Protein 29g; Carbohydrate 31g, of which sugars 4.5g; Fat 22.4g, of which saturates 3.3g; Cholesterol 25mg; Calcium 113mg; Fibre 12g; Sodium 165mg.

BROWN BEAN SALAD

BROWN BEANS, SOMETIMES CALLED FUL MEDAMES, ARE AVAILABLE FROM HEALTH-FOOD SHOPS AND MIDDLE EASTERN GROCERY STORES. DRIED BROAD BEANS OR BLACK OR RED KIDNEY BEANS MAKE A GOOD SUBSTITUTE. THIS IS A FILLING, HEALTHY AND NUTRITIOUS LUNCH TIME SALAD.

SERVES SIX

INGREDIENTS

350g/12oz/1½ cups dried
  brown beans
3 fresh thyme sprigs
2 bay leaves
1 onion, halved
4 garlic cloves, crushed
7.5ml/1½ tsp crushed cumin seeds
3 spring onions (scallions), chopped
90ml/6 tbsp chopped fresh parsley
20ml/4 tsp lemon juice
90ml/6 tbsp olive oil
3 hard-boiled eggs, roughly chopped
1 gherkin, roughly chopped
salt and ground black pepper

COOK'S TIP
The cooking time for the brown beans may vary depending on the age of the beans – the older they are, the longer they take.

1 Put the beans in a bowl with plenty of cold water and leave to soak overnight. Drain, transfer to a pan and cover with fresh water. Bring to the boil and boil rapidly for 10 minutes.

2 Reduce the heat and add the thyme, bay leaves and onion. Simmer very gently for about 1 hour, until tender. Drain and discard the herbs and onion.

3 Place the beans in a large bowl. Mix together the garlic, cumin seeds, spring onions, parsley, lemon juice and oil in a small bowl, and add a little salt and pepper. Pour over the beans and toss the ingredients lightly together.

4 Gently stir in the eggs and gherkin. Transfer the salad to a serving dish and serve at once.

Energy 355kcal/1488kJ; Protein 19.5g; Carbohydrate 32g, of which sugars 2.6g; Fat 17.6g, of which saturates 3g; Cholesterol 114mg; Calcium 92mg; Fibre 11.2g; Sodium 55mg.

COUSCOUS SALAD

THERE ARE MANY WAYS OF SERVING COUSCOUS, EITHER AS AN ACCOMPANIMENT OR AS A DISH IN ITS OWN RIGHT AS IN THIS SALAD RECIPE. THIS DELICATE SALAD HAS A NORTH AFRICAN FLAVOUR THAT IS EXCELLENT WITH GRILLED CHICKEN OR KEBABS.

SERVES FOUR

INGREDIENTS
275g/10oz/1²/₃ cups couscous
550ml/18fl oz/2¹/₂ cups boiling
  vegetable stock
16–20 black olives
2 small courgettes (zucchini)
25g/1oz/¹/₄ cup flaked (sliced)
  almonds, toasted
60ml/4 tbsp olive oil
15ml/1 tbsp lemon juice
15ml/1 tbsp chopped fresh
  coriander (cilantro)
15ml/1 tbsp chopped fresh parsley
good pinch of ground cumin
good pinch of cayenne pepper
salt

1 Place the couscous in a bowl and pour over the boiling stock. Stir with a fork and then set aside for 10 minutes for the stock to be absorbed. Fluff up with a fork.

2 Halve the olives, discarding the stones (pits). Top and tail the courgettes and cut them into small julienne strips.

3 Carefully mix the courgettes, olives and toasted almonds into the couscous.

4 Mix together the olive oil, lemon juice, herbs, spices and a pinch of salt in a small bowl. Stir into the salad.

Energy 310kcal/1289kJ; Protein 5.7g; Carbohydrate 36g, of which sugars 0.6g; Fat 16.7g, of which saturates 2.1g; Cholesterol 0mg; Calcium 61mg; Fibre 1.5g; Sodium 286mg.

QUINOA SALAD WITH MANGO

SINCE QUINOA HAS A MILD, SLIGHTLY BITTER TASTE, IT IS BEST COMBINED WITH INGREDIENTS THAT HAVE A MORE ROBUST FLAVOUR, SUCH AS FRESH HERBS, CHILLI, FRUIT AND NUTS, AS IN THIS SUPER-HEALTHY SALAD. YOU COULD SERVE THIS SALAD WITH SLICES OF GRIDDLED HALLOUMI CHEESE.

SERVES FOUR

INGREDIENTS
130g/4 1/2 oz quinoa
1 mango
60ml/4 tbsp pine nuts
large handful fresh basil,
    roughly chopped
large handful fresh flat leaf parsley,
    roughly chopped
large handful fresh mint,
    roughly chopped
1 mild long fresh red chilli, seeded
    and chopped
For the dressing
1 tbsp lemon juice
1 tbsp extra virgin olive oil
salt and ground black pepper

1 Put the quinoa in a pan and cover with cold water. Season with salt and bring to the boil. Reduce the heat, cover the pan with a lid and simmer for 12 minutes or until the quinoa is tender. Drain well.

2 Meanwhile, prepare the mango. Cut vertically down each side of the stone (pit). Taking the two large slices, cut the flesh into a criss-cross pattern down to (but not through) the skin.

3 Press each half inside out, then cut the mango cubes away from the skin.

4 Toast the pine nuts for a few minutes in a dry frying pan until golden, then remove from the heat.

5 Mix together the ingredients for the dressing and season well.

6 Put the cooked quinoa into a bowl and add the herbs and chilli. Pour the dressing into the bowl and fork lightly until combined. Season to taste and transfer to a bowl or four shallow dishes. Arrange the mango on top of the herby quinoa and sprinkle with the pine nuts.

Energy 206kcal/857kJ; Protein 4.5g; Carbohydrate 23.1g, of which sugars 6.2g; Fat 11.2g, of which saturates 1g; Cholesterol 0mg; Calcium 62mg; Fibre 2.5g; Sodium 9mg.

THAI-STYLE SEITAN SALAD

SEITAN IS MADE FROM WHEAT GLUTEN AND IS USUALLY USED AS A MEAT REPLACEMENT. LIKE TOFU, IT HAS A MILD FLAVOUR THAT BENEFITS FROM BEING MARINATED BEFORE COOKING. THIS IS A HEALTHY AND FILLING SALAD WITH A CITRUS TWIST.

SERVES FOUR

INGREDIENTS
  30ml/2 tbsp light soy sauce
  15ml/1 tbsp runny honey
  30ml/2 tbsp olive oil
  250g/9oz seitan, cut into
    2cm/¾in strips
  2 handfuls baby spinach leaves,
    tough stalks removed and
    leaves shredded
  2 handfuls rocket (arugula) leaves
  12 cherry tomatoes, halved
  1 fresh red chilli, seeded and cut
    into fine strips
  30ml/2 tbsp chopped fresh coriander
    (cilantro)
  1 handful fresh basil, leaves torn
For the dressing:
  45ml/3 tbsp lime juice
  30ml/2 tbsp olive oil
  10ml/2 tsp sesame oil
  15ml/1 tbsp light soy sauce
  15ml/1 tbsp grated fresh root ginger
  1 small garlic clove, finely chopped
  1 green chilli, seeded and
    finely chopped
  2.5ml/½ tsp palm sugar or soft light
    brown sugar

1 Mix together the ingredients for the dressing and set aside until step 5.

2 Mix together the soy sauce, honey and half the oil in a shallow dish.

3 Add the seitan and leave to marinate for at least 1 hour.

4 Remove the seitan from the marinade using tongs. Discard the marinade. Heat a wok until hot. Pour in the remaining olive oil and stir-fry the seitan for a few minutes until beginning to turn crisp.

5 Arrange the spinach, rocket leaves and tomatoes on a serving platter, then add the seitan. Spoon the dressing over and garnish with the chilli, coriander and basil.

Energy 132kcal/547kJ; Protein 7g; Carbohydrate 3g, of which sugars 2.7g; Fat 10.3g, of which saturates 1.4g; Cholesterol 0mg; Calcium 431mg; Fibre 1.9g; Sodium 79mg.

TOFU AND CUCUMBER SALAD

A NUTRITIOUS AND REFRESHING SALAD WITH A CHILLI-SPIKED, SWEET-AND-SOUR DRESSING, WHICH GOES PARTICULARLY WELL WITH THE MILD TASTING TOFU AND CRISP VEGETABLES.

SERVES FOUR TO SIX

INGREDIENTS
1 small cucumber
115g/4oz tofu
oil, for frying
115g/4oz/½ cup beansprouts
salt
celery leaves, to garnish
For the dressing
1 small onion, grated
2 garlic cloves, crushed
5–7.5ml/1–1½ tsp chilli sauce
30–45ml/2–3 tbsp dark soy sauce
15–30ml/1–2 tbsp rice vinegar
10ml/2 tsp dark brown sugar

1 Cut the cucumber into neat cubes. Sprinkle with salt to extract excess liquid. Set aside, while preparing the remaining ingredients.

2 Cut the tofu into cubes. Heat a little oil in a pan and fry on both sides until golden brown. Drain on kitchen paper.

3 To make the dressing, shake together the onion, garlic and chilli sauce in a screw-top jar. Add the soy sauce, vinegar, sugar and salt to taste.

4 Just before serving, rinse the cucumber under cold running water. Drain and dry thoroughly. Toss the cucumber, tofu and beansprouts together in a serving bowl and pour over the dressing. Garnish with the celery leaves and serve the salad at once.

Energy 30kcal/125kJ; Protein 2.7g; Carbohydrate 2.8g, of which sugars 2.1g; Fat 1g, of which saturates 0.1g; Cholesterol 0mg; Calcium 111mg; Fibre 0.6g; Sodium 537mg.

PUY LENTIL AND CABBAGE SALAD

THIS WARM, CRUNCHY SALAD MAKES A SATISFYING AND NUTRITIOUS MEAL IF SERVED WITH
CRUSTY FRENCH BREAD OR WHOLEMEAL ROLLS.

SERVES FOUR TO SIX

INGREDIENTS

225g/8oz/1 cup puy lentils
1.5 litres/2½ pints/6¼ cups water
3 garlic cloves
1 bay leaf
1 small onion, peeled and studded
  with 2 cloves
15ml/1 tbsp olive oil
1 red onion, finely sliced
15ml/1 tbsp fresh thyme leaves
350g/12oz cabbage, finely shredded
finely grated rind and juice of
  1 lemon
15ml/1 tbsp raspberry vinegar
salt and ground black pepper

1 Rinse the lentils in cold water and place in a large pan with the water, one of the garlic cloves, the bay leaf and clove-studded onion. Bring to the boil and cook for 10 minutes. Reduce the heat, cover and simmer gently for 15–20 minutes. Drain and discard the onion, garlic and bay leaf.

2 Crush the remaining garlic cloves. Heat the oil in a large pan. Add the red onion, crushed garlic and thyme and cook for 5 minutes, until softened.

3 Add the cabbage and cook for 3–5 minutes, until just cooked but still crunchy.

4 Stir in the cooked lentils, lemon rind and juice and the raspberry vinegar. Season to taste and serve warm.

Energy 147kcal/623kJ; Protein 10.1g; Carbohydrate 22g, of which sugars 3.9g; Fat 2.7g, of which saturates 0.3g; Cholesterol 0mg; Calcium 58mg; Fibre 4.7g; Sodium 9mg.

FRUITY BROWN RICE SALAD

THE BROWN RICE GIVES THIS SALAD A PLEASANT NUTTY FLAVOUR AND TEXTURE THAT SUITS THE ORIENTAL-STYLE DRESSING, WHILE THE PINEAPPLE PIECES ADD SWEETNESS AND A DISTINCT FLAVOUR.

SERVES FOUR TO SIX

INGREDIENTS

115g/4oz/²/₃ cup brown rice
1 small red (bell) pepper, seeded
  and diced
200g/7oz can corn drained
45ml/3 tbsp sultanas (golden raisins)
225g/8oz can pineapple pieces
  in fruit juice
15ml/1 tbsp light soy sauce
15ml/1 tbsp sunflower oil
15ml/1 tbsp hazelnut oil
1 garlic clove, crushed
5ml/1 tsp finely chopped fresh
  root ginger
salt and ground black pepper
4 spring onions (scallions), sliced,
  to garnish

1 Cook the brown rice in a large pan of lightly salted boiling water for about 30 minutes, or until it is tender. Drain thoroughly and cool. Meanwhile, prepare the garnish. Slice the spring onions at an angle, as shown, then set aside.

2 Tip the rice into a large serving bowl and add the red pepper, corn and sultanas. Drain the pineapple pieces, reserving the juice, then add them to the rice mixture and toss lightly.

3 Pour the reserved pineapple juice into a clean screw-top jar. Add the soy sauce, sunflower and hazelnut oils, garlic and root ginger. Season with salt and pepper. Close the jar tightly and shake well to combine.

4 Pour the dressing over the salad and toss well. Scatter the spring onions over the top and serve.

COOK'S TIP
Hazelnut oil gives a wonderfully distinctive flavour to any salad dressing. Like olive oil, it contains mainly mono-unsaturated fats.

Energy 191kcal/806kJ; Protein 2.9g; Carbohydrate 36.3g, of which sugars 15.2g; Fat 4.8g, of which saturates 0.7g; Cholesterol 0mg; Calcium 14mg; Fibre 1.6g; Sodium 272mg.

PEPPERY BEAN SALAD

*THIS VIBRANT SALAD USES CANNED BEANS FOR SPEED AND CONVENIENCE. TRY VARYING THE
SELECTION OF BEANS ACCORDING TO WHAT YOU HAVE TO HAND OR PERSONAL PREFERENCE.*

SERVES FOUR TO SIX

INGREDIENTS
  425g/15oz can red kidney beans
  425g/15oz can black-eyed beans (peas)
  425g/15oz can chickpeas
  1/4 red (bell) pepper
  1/4 green (bell) pepper
  6 radishes
  15ml/1 tbsp sliced spring onion
    (scallion), to garnish
  salt
For the dressing
  5ml/1 tsp ground cumin
  15ml/1 tbsp tomato ketchup
  30ml/2 tbsp olive oil
  15ml/1 tbsp white wine vinegar
  1 garlic clove, crushed
  2.5ml/1/2 tsp hot pepper sauce

1 Rinse and drain the red kidney beans, black-eyed beans and chickpeas. Turn them into a large bowl.

2 Core, seed and chop the red and green peppers. Trim the radishes and slice thinly. Add the peppers, radishes and spring onion to the beans.

3 Mix together the cumin, ketchup, oil, vinegar and garlic in a small bowl. Add a little salt and hot pepper sauce to taste and stir again thoroughly.

4 Pour the dressing over the salad and mix. Chill the salad for at least 1 hour before serving, garnished with the sliced spring onion.

Energy 243kcal/1025kJ; Protein 14.1g; Carbohydrate 37.6g, of which sugars 9.1g; Fat 5g, of which saturates 0.8g; Cholesterol 0mg; Calcium 146mg; Fibre 12.8g; Sodium 823mg.

Egg and Fennel Tabbouleh with Nuts

Tabbouleh is a well-known and popular Middle Eastern salad of bulgur wheat, flavoured with lots of parsley, mint, lemon juice and garlic. This variation of the classic has the same basic ingredients but with a few additions.

SERVES FOUR

INGREDIENTS
250g/9oz/1¼ cups bulgur wheat
4 small eggs
1 fennel bulb
1 bunch of spring onions (scallions),
  chopped
25g/1oz/½ cup drained sun-dried
  tomatoes in oil, sliced
45ml/3 tbsp chopped fresh parsley
30ml/2 tbsp chopped fresh mint
75g/3oz/½ cup black olives
60ml/4 tbsp olive oil
30ml/2 tbsp garlic oil
30ml/2 tbsp lemon juice
50g/2oz/½ cup chopped
  hazelnuts, toasted
pitta bread, warmed, to serve
salt and ground black pepper

1 Place the bulgur wheat in a bowl; pour in boiling water to cover and leave to soak for about 15 minutes.

2 Drain the bulgur wheat in a metal sieve, and place the sieve over a pan of boiling water. Cover the pan and sieve with a lid and steam for about 10 minutes. Fluff up the grains with a fork and spread out on a metal tray. Set aside to cool.

3 Hard-boil the eggs for 8 minutes. Cool under running water, peel and quarter, or, using an egg slicer, slice not quite all the way through.

4 Halve and finely slice the fennel. Boil in salted water for 6 minutes, drain and cool under running water.

5 Combine the eggs, fennel, spring onions, sun-dried tomatoes, parsley, mint and olives with the bulgur wheat. Dress with olive oil, garlic oil and lemon juice and sprinkle with hazelnuts. Season well and serve with pitta bread.

COOK'S TIP
If you are short of time, soak the bulgur wheat in boiling water for about 20 minutes until the grains are tender. Drain and rinse under cold water to cool, then drain thoroughly.

Energy 512kcal/2129kJ; Protein 15.7g; Carbohydrate 50.9g, of which sugars 2.8g; Fat 28g, of which saturates 4.1g; Cholesterol 190mg; Calcium 135mg; Fibre 3.9g; Sodium 509mg.

LENTIL SALAD WITH RED ONIONS AND GARLIC

THIS DELICIOUS, GARLICKY LENTIL SALAD CAN BE SERVED WARM OR COLD AS AN ACCOMPANIMENT TO CHICKEN, MEAT, FISH OR VEGETABLE DISHES, AS AN APPETIZER OR A SALAD IN ITS OWN RIGHT. SERVE THE SALAD WITH A GENEROUS SPOONFUL OF PLAIN YOGURT.

SERVES FOUR

INGREDIENTS

45ml/3 tbsp olive oil
2 red onions, chopped
2 tomatoes, peeled, seeded
  and chopped
10ml/2 tsp ground turmeric
10ml/2 tsp ground cumin
175g/6oz/¾ cup brown or green
  lentils, picked over and rinsed
900ml/1½ pints/3¾ cups vegetable
  stock or water
4 garlic cloves, crushed
small bunch of fresh coriander
  (cilantro), finely chopped
salt and ground black pepper
1 lemon, cut into wedges, to serve

1 Heat 30ml/2 tbsp of the oil in a large pan or flameproof casserole and fry the onions until soft. Add the tomatoes, turmeric and cumin, then stir in the lentils.

2 Pour in the stock or water and bring to the boil, then reduce the heat and simmer until the lentils are tender and almost all the liquid has been absorbed.

3 In a separate pan, fry the garlic in the remaining oil until golden brown. Toss the garlic into the lentils with the fresh coriander and season to taste. Serve warm or at room temperature, with wedges of lemon for squeezing juice over to taste.

VARIATION
If you prefer, you can replace the lentils with mung beans – they work just as well.

Energy 244kcal/1025kJ; Protein 12.3g; Carbohydrate 29.2g, of which sugars 6.6g; Fat 9.5g, of which saturates 1.3g; Cholesterol 0mg; Calcium 78mg; Fibre 6.1g; Sodium 16mg.

POTATO AND CELLOPHANE NOODLE SALAD

GLASS NOODLES, BEAN THREAD VERMICELLI OR MUNG BEAN VERMICELLI ARE ALL NAMES FOR CELLOPHANE NOODLES. THEY SIMPLY REQUIRE SOAKING IN HOT WATER BEFORE USE.

SERVES FOUR

INGREDIENTS
  2 potatoes, peeled and cut into
    eighths
  175g/6oz cellophane noodles
  60ml/4 tbsp vegetable oil
  1 onion, finely sliced
  5ml/1 tsp ground turmeric
  60ml/4 tbsp gram (chickpea) flour
  5ml/1 tsp grated lemon rind
  60–75ml/4–5 tbsp lemon juice
  45ml/3 tbsp fish sauce
  4 spring onions (scallions), finely
    sliced
  salt and ground black pepper

1 Place the potatoes in a pan. Add water to cover, bring to the boil and cook for about 15 minutes until tender but firm. Drain the potatoes and set them aside to cool.

2 Meanwhile, soak the noodles in a pan of boiling water for 3 minutes. Drain and rinse under cold running water. Drain well.

COOK'S TIP
Instead of cellophane noodles you could use ultra-thin rice sticks, available from Asian stores.

3 Heat the oil in a frying pan. Add the onion and turmeric and fry for about 5 minutes until golden brown. Drain the onion, reserving the oil.

4 Heat a small frying pan. Add the gram flour and stir constantly for about 4 minutes until it turns light golden brown in colour.

5 Mix the potatoes, noodles and fried onion in a large bowl. Add the reserved oil and the toasted gram flour with the lemon rind and juice, fish sauce and spring onions. Mix together well and adjust the seasoning to taste if necessary. Serve at once.

Energy 379kcal/1585kJ; Protein 8.2g; Carbohydrate 60g, of which sugars 3.2g; Fat 11.6g, of which saturates 1.7g; Cholesterol 0mg; Calcium 43mg; Fibre 1.4g; Sodium 558mg.

NOODLE, TOFU AND SPROUTED BEAN SALAD

THIS FRAGRANT AND REFRESHING SALAD IS QUICK TO MAKE AND IS BURSTING WITH THE GOODNESS OF TOFU, SPROUTED BEANS AND FRESH VEGETABLES.

SERVES FOUR

INGREDIENTS
25g/1oz bean thread noodles
500g/1¼lb mixed sprouted beans
and pulses (such as aduki,
chickpea, mung, lentil)
4 spring onions (scallions), finely
shredded
115g/4oz firm tofu, diced
1 ripe plum tomato, seeded and
diced
½ cucumber, peeled, seeded
and diced
60ml/4 tbsp chopped fresh coriander
(cilantro)
45ml/3 tbsp chopped fresh mint
60ml/4 tbsp rice vinegar
10ml/2 tsp caster (superfine) sugar
10ml/2 tsp sesame oil
5ml/1 tsp chilli oil
salt and ground black pepper

1 Place the bean thread noodles in a bowl and pour over enough boiling water to cover. Leave to soak for 3–4 minutes and then drain and refresh under cold, running water and drain again; alternatively follow the packet instructions. Using a pair of scissors, cut the noodles into roughly 7.5cm/3in lengths and put into a bowl.

2 Fill a wok one-third full of boiling water and place over a high heat. Add the beans and pulses and blanch for 1 minute. Drain, transfer to the noodle bowl, and add the spring onions, tofu, tomato, cucumber and herbs.

3 Combine the rice vinegar, sugar, sesame and chilli oils, and toss into the noodle mixture. Transfer to a serving dish and chill for 30 minutes before serving.

COOK'S TIP
Fresh sprouted beans are available from most supermarkets, but you can easily sprout them yourself at home.

Energy 121kcal/509kJ; Protein 6.8g; Carbohydrate 14.4g, of which sugars 6.9g; Fat 4.2g, of which saturates 0.6g; Cholesterol 0mg; Calcium 184mg; Fibre 2.4g; Sodium 12mg.

GOAT'S CHEESE, FIG AND COUSCOUS SALAD

Fresh figs and walnuts are perfect partners for couscous and toasted buckwheat. The olive and nut oil dressing contains no vinegar, depending instead on the acidity of the goat's cheese. This salad is substantial enough to make a complete meal.

SERVES FOUR

INGREDIENTS
175g/6oz/1 cup couscous
30ml/2 tbsp toasted buckwheat
1 egg, hard-boiled
30ml/2 tbsp chopped fresh parsley
60ml/4 tbsp olive oil
45ml/3 tbsp walnut oil
115g/4oz rocket (arugula) leaves
½ frisée lettuce
175g/6oz crumbly white
  goat's cheese
50g/2oz/½ cup broken
  walnuts, toasted
4 ripe figs, trimmed and almost cut
  into four (leave the pieces joined at
  the base)

1 Place the couscous and toasted buckwheat in a bowl, cover with boiling water and leave to soak for 15 minutes. Place in a sieve to drain off any remaining water, then spread out on a metal tray and allow to cool.

2 Shell the hard-boiled egg and grate finely.

3 Toss the grated egg, parsley, couscous and buckwheat together in a bowl. Combine the olive and walnut oils and use half to moisten the couscous mixture.

4 Toss the salad leaves in the remaining oil and distribute among four large serving plates.

5 Pile couscous mixture in the centre of each plate and crumble the goat's cheese over the top. Scatter with toasted walnuts, place a fig in the centre of each plate and serve.

Energy 599kcal/2488kJ; Protein 17.3g; Carbohydrate 40.9g, of which sugars 12.6g; Fat 41.7g, of which saturates 11.3g; Cholesterol 88mg; Calcium 173mg; Fibre 2.9g; Sodium 299mg.

TOFU AND WILD RICE SALAD

THE FLAVOURS IN THIS SALAD ARE INFLUENCED BY THE CUISINES OF NORTH AFRICA AND THE EASTERN SEABOARDS OF THE MEDITERRANEAN. IT GOES PARTICULARLY WELL WITH CHARGRILLED VEGETABLES, SUCH AS RED ONIONS, TOMATOES, COURGETTES AND PEPPERS.

SERVES FOUR

INGREDIENTS
  175g/6oz/scant 1 cup basmati rice
  50g/2oz/generous ¼ cup wild rice
  250g/9oz firm tofu, drained
    and cubed
  25g/1oz preserved lemon, finely
    chopped (see Cook's Tip)
  20g/¾oz bunch of parsley, chopped
For the dressing
  1 garlic clove, crushed
  10ml/2 tsp clear honey
  10ml/2 tsp of the preserved
    lemon juice
  15ml/1 tbsp balsamic vinegar
  15ml/1 tbsp olive oil
  1 small fresh red chilli, seeded and
    finely chopped
  5ml/1 tsp harissa paste (optional)
  sea salt and ground black pepper

1 Cook the basmati rice and the wild rice in separate pans until tender. The basmati will take about 10–15 minutes to cook while the wild rice will take about 45–50 minutes. Drain, rinse under cold water and drain again, then place in a large bowl together.

2 Meanwhile whisk together all the dressing ingredients in a small bowl. Add the tofu, stir to coat and leave to marinate while the rice cooks.

COOK'S TIP
Preserved lemons, packed in salt, are available from Middle Eastern delicatessens or from large food halls and some supermarkets.

3 Gently fold the tofu, dressing, preserved lemon and parsley into the rice, check the seasoning and serve.

VARIATION
Look for rose harissa paste, which is available from the special range in some large supermarkets or from delicatessens or food halls. It is exceptionally delicious in this recipe and still fiery hot.

Energy 286kcal/1195kJ; Protein 9.8g; Carbohydrate 48g, of which sugars 2.4g; Fat 5.8g, of which saturates 0.7g; Cholesterol 0mg; Calcium 355mg; Fibre 0.7g; Sodium 7mg.

BEANSPROUT AND DAIKON SALAD

RIBBON-THIN SLICES OF FRESH, CRISP VEGETABLES, EACH WITH THEIR OWN DISTINCT FLAVOUR, MIXED WITH BEANSPROUTS MAKE THE PERFECT FOIL FOR AN UNUSUAL ORIENTAL DRESSING.

SERVES FOUR

INGREDIENTS

225g/8oz/1 cup beansprouts
1 cucumber
2 carrots
1 small daikon radish
1 small red onion, thinly sliced
2.5cm/1in fresh root ginger, peeled
    and cut into thin matchsticks
1 small red chilli, seeded and
    thinly sliced
handful of fresh coriander (cilantro)
    or mint leaves
For the oriental dressing
    15ml/1 tbsp rice vinegar
    15ml/1 tbsp light soy sauce
    15ml/1 tbsp Thai fish sauce
    1 garlic clove, finely chopped
    15ml/1 tbsp sesame oil
    45ml/3 tbsp groundnut oil
    30ml/2 tbsp sesame seeds,
        lightly toasted

1 First make the dressing. Place all the dressing ingredients in a bottle or screw-top jar and shake well. The dressing may be made in advance and will keep well for a couple of days if stored in the refrigerator or a cool place.

COOK'S TIP
Beansprouts have an incredible nutritional value, helping to protect the immune system against fatigue.

2 Wash the beansprouts and drain thoroughly in a colander.

3 Peel the cucumber, cut in half lengthways and scoop out the seeds. Peel the cucumber flesh into long ribbon strips using a potato peeler or mandoline.

4 Peel the carrots and radish into long ribbon strips in the same way as the cucumber.

5 Place the carrots, radish and cucumber in a large, shallow serving dish, add the onion, ginger, chilli and coriander or mint and toss to mix. Pour the dressing over just before serving.

Energy 185kcal/766kJ; Protein 3.9g; Carbohydrate 7.3g, of which sugars 5.7g; Fat 15.8g, of which saturates 2.1g; Cholesterol 0mg; Calcium 79mg; Fibre 2.6g; Sodium 547mg.

BAMBOO SHOOT SALAD

THIS HOT, SHARP-FLAVOURED SALAD ORIGINATED IN NORTH-EASTERN THAILAND. USE CANNED WHOLE
BAMBOO SHOOTS IF YOU CAN FIND THEM — THEY HAVE MORE FLAVOUR THAN SLICED ONES.

SERVES FOUR

INGREDIENTS
    400g/14oz can bamboo shoots,
       in large pieces
    25g/1oz/about 3 tbsp glutinous rice
    30ml/2 tbsp chopped shallots
    15ml/1 tbsp chopped garlic
    45ml/3 tbsp spring onions (scallions)
    30ml/2 tbsp Thai fish sauce
    30ml/2 tbsp fresh lime juice
    5ml/1 tsp sugar
    2.5ml/¹/₂ tsp dried chilli flakes
    20–25 small fresh mint leaves
    15ml/1 tbsp toasted sesame seeds

COOK'S TIP
Glutinous rice does not, in fact, contain
any gluten – it's just sticky.

1 Rinse the bamboo shoots under cold
running water, then drain them and pat
them thoroughly dry with kitchen paper
and set them aside.

2 Dry-roast the rice in a frying pan until
it is golden brown. Leave to cool slightly,
then tip into a mortar and grind to fine
crumbs with a pestle.

3 Transfer the rice to a bowl and add
the shallots, garlic, spring onions, fish
sauce, lime juice, sugar, chilli flakes
and half the mint leaves. Mix well.

4 Add the bamboo shoots to the bowl
and toss to mix. Serve sprinkled with
the toasted sesame seeds and the
remaining mint leaves.

Energy 88kcal/368kJ; Protein 4.5g; Carbohydrate 11.6g, of which sugars 4.4g; Fat 2.8g, of which saturates 0.4g; Cholesterol 0mg; Calcium 55mg; Fibre 2.2g; Sodium 7mg.

SIDE DISHES

Rice, couscous and polenta are classic
accompaniments to a wide variety of main
meals. These grains readily absorb the flavour of
other ingredients, such as herbs and spices, and
provide satisfying and filling side dishes that
complement a whole range of fish, poultry, meat
and vegetarian courses. They are complex
carbohydrates, so offer a filling and nutritious
addition to a meal.

SAFFRON RICE

THIS DELIGHTFULLY FRAGRANT, BUTTERY PILAFF IS WONDERFUL WITH ALL KINDS OF SPICY DISHES, ESPECIALLY THOSE FEATURING SEAFOOD, CHICKEN OR LAMB.

SERVES FOUR

INGREDIENTS

350g/12oz/generous 1½ cups
   basmati rice
good pinch of saffron threads
   (about 15 threads)
25g/1oz/2 tbsp butter
1 onion, finely chopped
6 green cardamom pods, lightly
   crushed
5ml/1 tsp salt
2–3 fresh bay leaves
600ml/1 pint/2½ cups well-flavoured
   chicken or vegetable stock
   or water

1 Put the rice into a sieve and rinse well under cold running water. Tip it into a bowl, add cold water to cover and set aside to soak for 30–40 minutes. Drain in the sieve.

2 Toast the saffron threads in a dry pan over a low heat for 1–2 minutes, then place in a small bowl and add 30ml/ 2 tbsp warm water. Leave to soak for 10–15 minutes.

3 Melt the butter in a heavy pan, then cook the onion with the cardamoms very gently for 8–10 minutes, until soft and buttery yellow.

4 Add the drained rice and stir to coat the grains. Add the salt and bay leaves, followed by the stock and saffron with its liquid. Bring to the boil, stir, then reduce the heat to very low and cover tightly. Cook for 10–12 minutes, until the rice has absorbed all the liquid.

5 Lay a clean, folded dish towel over the pan under the lid and press on the lid to wedge it firmly in place. Leave to stand for 10–15 minutes.

6 Fluff up the grains of rice with a fork. Turn into a warmed serving dish and serve immediately.

COOK'S TIP
After boiling, when all the liquid has been absorbed, basmati rice is set aside to finish cooking in its own heat and become tender. Wedging a folded dish towel under the pan lid ensures the heat is not lost and the steam is absorbed.

Energy 366kcal/1528kJ; Protein 6.7g; Carbohydrate 71.1g, of which sugars 0.9g; Fat 5.6g, of which saturates 3.3g; Cholesterol 13mg; Calcium 22mg; Fibre 0.2g; Sodium 530mg.

MUSHROOM PILAU

THIS DISH IS SIMPLICITY ITSELF: THE BASMATI RICE IS INFUSED WITH A DELICIOUS BLEND OF SPICES.
SERVE WITH ANY INDIAN DISH OR WITH ROAST LAMB OR CHICKEN.

SERVES FOUR

INGREDIENTS
    30ml/2 tbsp vegetable oil
    2 shallots, finely chopped
    1 garlic clove, crushed
    3 green cardamom pods
    25g/1oz/2 tbsp ghee or butter
    175g/6oz/2½ cups button
      mushrooms, sliced
    225g/8oz/generous 1 cup basmati
      rice, soaked
    5ml/1 tsp grated fresh root ginger
    good pinch of garam masala
    450ml/¾ pint/scant 2 cups water
    15ml/1 tbsp chopped fresh coriander
      (cilantro)
    salt

1 Heat the oil in a pan and fry the shallots, garlic and cardamom pods over a medium heat for 3–4 minutes.

2 Add the ghee or butter. When it has melted, add the mushrooms and fry for 2–3 minutes more.

3 Add the rice, ginger and garam masala. Stir-fry over a low heat for 2–3 minutes, then stir in the water and a little salt. Bring to the boil, then cover tightly and simmer over a very low heat for 10 minutes.

4 Remove the casserole from the heat. Leave to stand, covered, for 5 minutes. Add the chopped coriander and fork it through the rice. Spoon into a serving bowl and serve at once.

Energy 309kcal/1286kJ; Protein 5.2g; Carbohydrate 46.3g, of which sugars 1g; Fat 11.2g, of which saturates 4g; Cholesterol 13mg; Calcium 18mg; Fibre 0.7g; Sodium 41mg.

COUSCOUS WITH DRIED FRUIT AND NUTS

THIS DISH OF STEAMED COUSCOUS WITH DRIED FRUIT AND NUTS, TOPPED WITH SUGAR AND CINNAMON, IS DELICIOUS SERVED WITH SPICY TAGINES OR GRILLED OR ROASTED MEAT AND POULTRY DISHES. TRY IT AS A SIDE DISH AT YOUR NEXT BARBECUE.

SERVES SIX

INGREDIENTS

500g/1¼lb medium couscous
600ml/1 pint/2½ cups warm water
5ml/1 tsp salt
pinch of saffron threads
45ml/3 tbsp sunflower oil
30ml/2 tbsp olive oil
a little butter
115g/4oz/½ cup dried apricots, cut
  into slivers
75g/3oz/½ cup dried dates, chopped
75g/3oz/generous ½ cup raisins
115g/4oz/1 cup blanched almonds,
  cut into slivers
75g/3oz/¾ cup pistachio nuts
10ml/2 tsp ground cinnamon
45ml/3 tbsp sugar

1 Preheat the oven to 180°C/350°F/ Gas 4. Put the couscous in a bowl. Mix the water, salt and saffron and pour it over the couscous, stirring. Leave to stand for 10 minutes, or until the grains are plump and tender. Add the sunflower oil and, using your fingers, rub it through the grains.

2 In a heavy pan, heat the olive oil and butter and stir in the apricots, dates, raisins, most of the almonds (reserve some for garnish) and pistachio nuts. Cook until the raisins plump up, then tip the nuts and fruit into the couscous and toss together.

3 Tip the couscous into an ovenproof dish and cover with foil. Place in the oven for about 20 minutes, until heated through.

4 Toast the reserved slivered almonds. Pile the hot couscous in a mound on a large serving dish and sprinkle with the cinnamon and sugar – these are usually sprinkled in stripes down the mound. Scatter the toasted almonds over the top and serve hot.

Energy 592kcal/2471kJ; Protein 12.5g; Carbohydrate 77.1g, of which sugars 33.5g; Fat 27.8g, of which saturates 3g; Cholesterol 0mg; Calcium 105mg; Fibre 4.1g; Sodium 81mg.

VEGETABLE COUSCOUS WITH HARISSA

THIS SPICY DISH MAKES AN EXCELLENT VEGETARIAN MAIN MEAL, OR CAN BE SERVED AS AN ACCOMPANIMENT. COUSCOUS IS ONE OF THE EASIEST GRAINS TO PREPARE AND ONLY TAKES A MATTER OF MINUTES. SINCE IT HAS A RELATIVELY MILD FLAVOUR IT GOES WELL WITH AROMATIC SPICES.

SERVES FOUR

INGREDIENTS
45ml/3 tbsp olive oil
1 onion, chopped
2 garlic cloves, crushed
5ml/1 tsp ground cumin
5ml/1 tsp paprika
400g/14oz can chopped tomatoes
300ml/½ pint/1¼ cups
  vegetable stock
1 cinnamon stick
generous pinch of saffron threads
4 baby aubergines (eggplants),
  quartered
8 baby courgettes (zucchini),
  trimmed
8 baby carrots
225g/8oz/1⅓ cups couscous
425g/15oz can chickpeas, drained
175g/6oz/¾ cup pitted prunes
45ml/3 tbsp chopped fresh parsley
45ml/3 tbsp chopped fresh
  coriander (cilantro)
10–15ml/2–3 tsp harissa
salt

1 Heat the olive oil in a large pan. Add the onion and garlic and cook gently for 5 minutes until soft. Add the cumin and paprika and cook, stirring, for 1 minute.

2 Add the tomatoes, stock, cinnamon stick, saffron, aubergines, courgettes and carrots, and season with salt. Bring to the boil, cover, lower the heat and cook gently for 20 minutes until the vegetables are just tender.

3 Line a steamer or colander with a double thickness of muslin (cheesecloth). Soak the couscous according to the instructions on the packet.

COOK'S TIP
Harissa is a chilli-hot, spicy paste from North Africa. You can buy it ready made from selected supermarkets and specialist shops.

4 Add the chickpeas and prunes to the vegetables, stir and cook for 5 minutes.

5 Spread the couscous in the prepared steamer. place the steamer on top of the vegetables, cover and cook for 5 minutes until the couscous is hot.

6 Stir the herbs into the vegetables. Heap the couscous on to a serving dish. Using a slotted spoon, remove the vegetables from the pan and add to the couscous. Spoon over a little sauce and toss gently. Stir the harissa into the remaining sauce and serve separately.

Energy 452kcal/1897kJ; Protein 14.8g; Carbohydrate 72.9g, of which sugars 27.4g; Fat 13.1g, of which saturates 1.8g; Cholesterol 0mg; Calcium 143mg; Fibre 12.2g; Sodium 259mg.

Split Pea and Shallot Mash

This purée makes an excellent alternative to mashed potatoes, and is particularly good with winter pies and nut roasts. It can also be served with warmed pitta bread.

2 Place the peas in a pan, cover with fresh cold water and bring to the boil. Skim off any foam that rises to the surface, then reduce the heat. Add the bay leaf and sage, and simmer for 30–40 minutes until the peas are tender. Add more water during cooking, if necessary.

3 Meanwhile, heat the oil in a frying pan and cook the shallots, cumin seeds and garlic for 3 minutes or until the shallots soften, stirring occasionally. Add the mixture to the split peas while they are still cooking.

4 Drain the split peas, reserving the cooking water. Remove the bay leaf, then place the split peas in a food processor or blender with the butter and season well.

SERVES FOUR TO SIX

INGREDIENTS
225g/8oz/1 cup yellow split peas
1 bay leaf
8 sage leaves, roughly chopped
15ml/1 tbsp olive oil
3 shallots, finely chopped
heaped 1 tsp cumin seeds
1 large garlic clove, chopped
50g/2oz/4 tbsp butter, softened
salt and ground black pepper

COOK'S TIP
Cannellini beans would make a good alternative to the yellow split peas. Soak overnight then drain and rinse. Cover the beans with fresh water and cook for about 1 hour or until tender.

1 Place the split peas in a bowl and cover with cold water. Leave to soak overnight, then rinse and drain.

5 Add 105ml/7 tbsp of the reserved cooking water and blend until the mixture forms a coarse purée. Add more water if the mash seems to be too dry. Adjust the seasoning and serve warm.

Energy 201kcal/845kJ; Protein 9.1g; Carbohydrate 22g, of which sugars 1.5g; Fat 9.2g, of which saturates 4.7g; Cholesterol 18mg; Calcium 23mg; Fibre 2g; Sodium 64mg.

BASMATI RICE AND NUT PILAFF

VEGETARIANS WILL LOVE THIS SIMPLE PILAFF. ADD WILD OR CULTIVATED MUSHROOMS AND DICED CARROTS OR COURGETTES TO MAKE THE DISH MORE SUBSTANTIAL, IF YOU LIKE.

SERVES FOUR

INGREDIENTS
15–30ml/1–2 tbsp sunflower oil
1 onion, chopped
1 garlic clove, crushed
1 large carrot, coarsely grated
225g/8oz/generous 1 cup basmati
  rice, soaked
5ml/1 tsp cumin seeds
10ml/2 tsp ground coriander
10ml/2 tsp black mustard seeds
  (optional)
4 green cardamom pods
450ml/¾ pint/scant 2 cups vegetable
  stock or water
1 bay leaf
75g/3oz/½ cup shelled walnuts and/or
  unsalted cashew nuts
salt and ground black pepper
fresh parsley or coriander (cilantro)
  sprigs, to garnish

1 Heat the oil in a large frying pan. Add the onion, garlic and carrot and cook for 3–4 minutes, stirring occasionally.

2 Drain the rice and add it to the pan with the cumin seeds, ground coriander, black mustard seeds and the green cardamom pods. Cook for 1 minute, stirring to coat the grains in oil.

COOK'S TIP
Use whichever nuts you prefer in this pilaff – even unsalted peanuts taste good – although almonds, brazil nuts, cashew nuts or pistachio nuts add a slightly more exotic flavour.

3 Pour in the vegetable stock or water, add the bay leaf and season well with salt and pepper. Bring to the boil, then lower the heat, cover and simmer very gently for 10–12 minutes.

4 Remove the frying pan from the heat without lifting the lid. Leave to stand in a warm place for about 5 minutes, then check the rice. If it is cooked, there will be small steam holes on the surface of the rice. Remove the bay leaf and the cardamom pods.

5 Stir the walnuts and/or cashew nuts into the rice mixture. Taste to check the seasoning and add more salt and pepper if necessary. Spoon into warmed individual bowls or on to a large platter, garnish with the sprigs of fresh parsley or coriander and serve immediately.

COOK'S TIP
Basmati rice has an aromatic nut-like flavour that goes well with curries and pilaffs.

Energy 370kcal/1538kJ; Protein 7.3g; Carbohydrate 48.7g, of which sugars 3.2g; Fat 16g, of which saturates 1.4g; Cholesterol 0mg; Calcium 38mg; Fibre 1.5g; Sodium 8mg.

SPICY TAMARIND CHICKPEAS

CHICKPEAS MAKE A GOOD BASE FOR MANY VEGETARIAN DISHES. HERE, THEY ARE TOSSED WITH SOUR TAMARIND AND AROMATIC SPICES TO MAKE A DELICIOUSLY LIGHT MEAT-FREE LUNCH OR SIDE DISH.

SERVES FOUR

INGREDIENTS
225g/8oz/1¼ cups dried chickpeas
900ml/1½ pints/3½ cups
  boiling water
50g/2oz tamarind pulp
45ml/3 tbsp vegetable oil
2.5ml/½ tsp cumin seeds
1 onion, very finely chopped
2 garlic cloves, crushed
2.5cm/1in piece fresh root ginger,
  peeled and grated
5ml/1 tsp ground cumin
5ml/1 tsp ground coriander
1.5ml/¼ tsp ground turmeric
1 fresh green chilli, finely chopped
2.5ml/½ tsp salt
225g/8oz tomatoes, peeled and
  finely chopped
2.5ml/½ tsp garam masala
chopped fresh chillies and chopped
  onion, to garnish

1 Put the chickpeas in a large bowl and pour over cold water to cover. Leave to soak for at least 8 hours, or overnight.

2 Drain the chickpeas and put in a pan with at least double their volume of cold water. (Do not add salt to the water because this will toughen the chickpeas and spoil the final dish.)

3 Bring the water to the boil and boil vigorously for at least 10 minutes. Skim off any scum, then drain the chickpeas and tip into a large pan.

4 Pour 750ml/1¼ pints/3 cups of the boiling water over the chickpeas. Cover with the lid and simmer until just tender.

5 Towards the end of the cooking time, put the tamarind in a bowl and break up with a fork. Pour over the remaining boiling water and leave to soak for about 15 minutes.

6 Tip the tamarind into a sieve (strainer) and discard the water. Rub the pulp through, discarding any stones (pits) and fibre.

7 Heat the oil in a large pan, add the cumin seeds and fry for 2 minutes, until they splutter. Add the onion, garlic and ginger and fry for 5 minutes. Add the cumin, coriander, turmeric, chilli and salt, and fry for 3–4 minutes. Add the tomatoes, garam masala and tamarind pulp, and bring to the boil.

8 Stir the tamarind mixture into the chickpeas, cover and cook for a further 1 hour. Either serve straight from the cooking pot, or spoon into a warmed serving dish. Garnish with chopped chilli and onion.

Energy 269kcal/1131kJ; Protein 12.6g; Carbohydrate 30.8g, of which sugars 4.1g; Fat 11.5g, of which saturates 1.3g; Cholesterol 0mg; Calcium 98mg; Fibre 6.8g; Sodium 273mg.

CORNMEAL BAKED WITH CHEESE

CORNMEAL IS FIRST COOKED TO A PORRIDGE-LIKE CONSISTENCY, THEN BAKED WITH FETA AND A STRONG CHEESE TO GIVE IT A PLENTY OF FLAVOUR.

SERVES FOUR TO SIX

INGREDIENTS

130g/4¹/₂oz/generous 1 cup coarse
  ground cornmeal
1 litre/1³/₄ pints/4 cups water
50g/2oz/4 tbsp unsalted (sweet)
  butter
350g/12oz/1¹/₂ cups feta cheese,
  drained and crumbled
50g/2oz/¹/₂ cup grated strong,
  hard cheese (such as Cheddar),
  for sprinkling
salt and ground black pepper
grilled bacon and spring onions
  (scallions), sliced lengthways,
  to garnish
tomato sauce, to serve

1 Preheat the oven to 190°C/375°F/
Gas 5. Stirring occasionally, dry-fry
the cornmeal in a large pan for
3–4 minutes, or until it changes colour.
Remove from the heat.

2 Slowly pour in the water and add a
little salt. Return the pan to the heat
and stir well until the cornmeal thickens
a little. Cover, reduce the heat and leave
to cook for 25 minutes, stirring often.

COOK'S TIP
Cornmeal has a mild flavour and blends
well with ingredients with a more
powerful taste. You can use other types
of cheese in this recipe.

3 Remove from the heat when thick
enough to hold a wide trail when a
wooden spoon is lifted from the mixture.
Stir in the butter and feta cheese and
season well.

4 Spoon into a 20cm/8in greased
springform tin (pan). Bake for 25–30
minutes or until firm. Leave overnight or
for 2–3 hours. Serve sprinkled with
cheese, bacon and spring onions, with
tomato sauce.

Energy 322kcal/1337kJ; Protein 13.3g; Carbohydrate 16.8g, of which sugars 0.9g; Fat 22.1g, of which saturates 14.1g; Cholesterol 67mg; Calcium 274mg; Fibre 0.5g; Sodium 951mg.

JAMAICAN RICE AND PEAS

THIS TRADITIONAL SIDE DISH IS SERVED THROUGHOUT THE CARIBBEAN BUT NOWHERE IS IT MORE POPULAR THAN IN JAMAICA WHERE IT HAS BECOME ALMOST A NATIONAL DISH. THE "PEAS" ARE ACTUALLY RED KIDNEY BEANS WHICH GIVE COLOUR AND SUBSTANCE TO THE COCONUT RICE. SERVE AS AN ACCOMPANIMENT TO CHICKEN, FISH, MEAT OR VEGETABLES.

SERVES FOUR TO SIX

INGREDIENTS
150g/5oz dried red kidney beans
500ml/17fl oz/2¼ cups water
1 tsp salt
15ml/1 tbsp vegetable oil
15ml/1 large onion, chopped
3 garlic cloves, chopped
2 fresh red chillies, seeded and
  chopped
5ml/1 tsp dried thyme
300g/11oz long grain rice
400g/14oz can coconut milk

1 Soak the kidney beans overnight in plenty of cold water. Drain and rinse, then put them into a pan. Cover with fresh cold water and bring to the boil. Allow to boil vigorously for 10 minutes, then reduce the heat, cover the pan, and simmer for 1 hour or until tender.

2 Drain the beans then return them to the pan and cover with 300ml/½ pint/1¼ cups of the water and add the salt. Bring to the boil, then reduce the heat and simmer, covered, for 15 minutes.

3 Meanwhile, heat the oil in a large pan and fry the onion for 10 minutes until softened. Add the garlic, chillies and thyme. Fry, stirring, for 1 minute, then add the rice. Stir well until the rice is coated in the onion mixture.

4 Pour in the coconut milk, the remaining water and the beans and their cooking water. Bring up to the boil, then reduce the heat, stir well and cover the pan. Simmer over a low heat for 25–30 minutes until the rice is tender and the liquid has been absorbed. Remove from the heat and allow the rice and beans to stand for 5 minutes in the covered pan.

Energy 295kcal/1240kJ; Protein 10g; Carbohydrate 58.2g, of which sugars 6.7g; Fat 2.7g, of which saturates 0.4g; Cholesterol 0mg; Calcium 66mg; Fibre 4.6g; Sodium 79mg.

RICE AND VEGETABLE FRITTERS

BROWN RICE GIVES THESE FRITTERS A DELICIOUS NUTTY FLAVOUR AND TEXTURE AND IT IS ALSO A GOOD SOURCE OF B VITAMINS AND FIBRE. THE FRITTERS ARE A GOOD AND CREATIVE WAY OF USING UP ANY LEFTOVER RICE AND ARE THE TASTY AND FILLING ACCOMPANIMENT TO GRILLED OR ROASTED MEAT, PLAIN-COOKED CHICKEN OR FISH.

MAKES SIXTEEN

INGREDIENTS
    200g/7oz cold cooked brown rice
    4 spring onions (scallions), chopped
    1 red (bell) pepper, diced
    2 garlic cloves, crushed
    60ml/4 tbsp freshly grated Parmesan
    1 large egg, lightly beaten
    60ml/4 tbsp double (heavy) cream
    60ml/4 tbsp plain (all-purpose) flour
    vegetable oil, for frying
    salt and ground black pepper

1 Mix together the cooked rice, spring onions, red pepper, garlic, Parmesan, egg, cream, flour and seasoning in a bowl to make a sloppy batter.

2 Heat enough oil to lightly coat the bottom of a frying pan. Place two heaped dessertspoons of the rice mixture into the hot oil and flatten the top slightly with a spatula.

3 Cook the fritters in batches for 3 minutes each side until golden and set. Drain on kitchen paper and keep warm while you cook the remaining mixture.

Energy 92kcal/385kJ; Protein 2.9g; Carbohydrate 8.7g, of which sugars 0.9g; Fat 5.3g, of which saturates 1.4g; Cholesterol 18mg; Calcium 57mg; Fibre 0.5g; Sodium 47mg.

BUCKWHEAT KASHA

KASHA IS A TYPE OF RUSSIAN PORRIDGE, MADE FROM A VARIETY OF GRAINS INCLUDING WHEAT, BARLEY, MILLET AND OATS. THE MOST POPULAR IS BUCKWHEAT, WHICH HAS A DISTINCTIVE NUTTY FLAVOUR THAT BENEFITS FROM TOASTING BEFORE USE.

SERVES FOUR

INGREDIENTS
175g/6oz/scant 1 cup buckwheat
740ml/1¼ pints/3 cups boiling stock
25g/1oz/2 tbsp butter
pinch of freshly grated nutmeg
115g/4oz rindless smoked streaky
  (fatty) bacon, chopped
salt and ground black pepper

1 Dry-fry the buckwheat in a non-stick frying pan for 2 minutes, or until very lightly toasted. Transfer the buckwheat to a pan and add the stock.

COOK'S TIP
It is possible to buy toasted buckwheat. In this case, simply put the buckwheat in a pan and add the stock.

2 Simmer for 15–20 minutes, stirring occasionally to prevent it from sticking. When almost dry, remove from the heat.

3 Add the butter to the buckwheat, season and add the nutmeg. Cover with a lid and let stand for 5 minutes. Meanwhile, dry-fry the bacon for 5 minutes, until lightly browned and crispy. Sprinkle over the kasha. Serve.

Energy 280kcal/1166kJ; Protein 8.8g; Carbohydrate 33.4g, of which sugars 0g; Fat 12.7g, of which saturates 5.6g; Cholesterol 32mg; Calcium 22mg; Fibre 4.4g; Sodium 402mg.

CARTERS' MILLET

THIS DISH ORIGINATED IN SOUTHERN UKRAINE, WHERE IT WAS ONCE COOKED OVER OPEN FIRES. IT IS IDEAL SERVED WITH MEAT, POULTRY OR VEGETABLES.

SERVES FOUR

INGREDIENTS
225g/8oz/scant 1½ cups millet
600ml/1 pint/2½ cups
  vegetable stock
115g/4oz lardons or rindless smoked
  streaky (fatty) bacon, chopped
15ml/1 tbsp olive oil
1 small onion, thinly sliced
225g/8oz/3 cups small field
  mushrooms, sliced
15ml/1 tbsp chopped fresh mint
salt and ground black pepper

3 Add the oil to the pan and cook the onion and mushrooms for 10 minutes, until beginning to brown.

1 Rinse the millet in a sieve under cold running water. Put in a pan with the stock, bring to the boil and simmer, until the stock has been absorbed.

2 Dry-fry the lardons or bacon in a non-stick pan for 5 minutes, until brown and crisp. Remove and set aside.

4 Add the bacon, and the onion and mushroom mixture to the millet. Stir in the mint and season. Heat gently for 1–2 minutes before serving.

Energy 316kcal/1317kJ; Protein 9g; Carbohydrate 43.8g, of which sugars 1g; Fat 10.8g, of which saturates 2.8g; Cholesterol 19mg; Calcium 31mg; Fibre 0.8g; Sodium 377mg.

COUSCOUS-STUFFED SWEET PEPPERS WITH DRIED APRICOTS AND FETA

THESE BELL PEPPERS ARE SOFTENED IN BOILING WATER TO ENSURE REALLY TENDER RESULTS. CHOOSE RED, ORANGE OR YELLOW BELL PEPPERS FOR THE SWEETEST FLAVOUR.

SERVES FOUR

INGREDIENTS
4 (bell) peppers
75g/3oz//1/2 cup instant couscous
75ml/21/2fl oz/1/3 cup boiling
  vegetable stock
15ml/1 tbsp olive oil
10ml/2 tsp white wine vinegar
50g/2oz dried apricots, finely
  chopped
75g/3oz feta cheese, cut into tiny
  cubes
3 ripe tomatoes, skinned, seeded
  and chopped
45ml/3 tbsp toasted pine nuts
30ml/2 tbsp chopped fresh parsley
salt and ground black pepper
flat leaf parsely, to garnish

1 Halve the peppers lengthways, then remove the core and seeds. Place the peppers in a large heatproof bowl and pour over boiling water to cover. Leave to stand for about 3 minutes, then drain thoroughly and set aside.

2 Meanwhile, put the couscous in a small bowl and pour over the stock. Leave to stand for about 5 minutes until all the stock has been absorbed.

3 Using a fork, fluff up the couscous, then stir in the oil, vinegar, apricots, feta cheese, tomatoes, pine nuts and parsley, and season to taste with salt and ground black pepper.

4 Preheat the oven to 190°C/375°F/ Gas 5.

5 Fill the peppers with couscous mixture, gently packing it down using the back of a spoon.

6 Place the peppers filling side up in a lightly greased ovenproof dish, and bake for 20–25 minutes until golden.

VARIATION
Instead of feta cheese, you could grate any hard cheese on to the surface of the stuffed peppers.

Energy 303kcal/1266kJ; Protein 33.7g; Carbohydrate 33.6g, of which sugars 17g; Fat 15.8g, of which saturates 3.9g; Cholesterol 113mg; Calcium 105mg; Fibre 4.3g; Sodium 285mg

GRAM FLOUR PANCAKES <u>WITH</u> FRESH CHILLI CHUTNEY

GRAM FLOUR IS MADE FROM GROUND DRIED CHICKPEAS AND HAS A CREAMY COLOUR AND DISTINCTIVE FLAVOUR. SERVE THESE PANCAKES AND CHILLI CHUTNEY WITH A CHICKEN OR VEGETABLE CURRY.

MAKES ABOUT SIXTEEN PANCAKES

INGREDIENTS
    450g/1lb gram flour
    5ml/1 tsp bicarbonate of soda
    10ml/2 tsp salt
    800ml/28fl oz/3½ cups water
    vegetable oil, for frying
For the fresh chilli chutney
    3 tomatoes, seeded and diced
    60ml/4 tbsp lime juice
    1 red onion, thinly sliced
    2 fresh green chillies, seeded and
       thinly sliced
    45ml/3 tbsp chopped fresh mint

1 To make the pancakes, sift the flour, bicarbonate of soda and salt into a large mixing bowl.

2 Make a well in the centre and pour in the water. Gradually whisk the flour into the water until you have a smooth batter. Leave to stand for 30 minutes.

3 Meanwhile, thoroughly mix together the ingredients for the fresh chilli chutney and set aside while you cook the pancakes.

4 Pour enough oil into a frying pan to cover the base and heat it over a medium heat. Place 2 tablespoons of the batter into the pan. Fry for about 3 minutes on one side, then, using a metal spatula, turn over and cook the other side until set and golden. Cook several pancakes at once depending on the size of the pan. Drain on kitchen paper and keep warm while you make the remaining pancakes.

5 Serve the pancakes hot, with the fresh chilli chutney.

Energy 108kcal/455kJ; Protein 7.3g; Carbohydrate 12.5g, of which sugars 1.2g; Fat 3.2g, of which saturates 0.4g; Cholesterol 0mg; Calcium 50mg; Fibre 0.2g; Sodium 14mg.

OATMEAL SKIRLIE

OATMEAL IS USED TO MAKE SKIRLIE, A SIMPLE PREPARATION THAT CAN BE USED FOR STUFFINGS OR AS AN ACCOMPANIMENT, AND IT IS ESPECIALLY GOOD WITH ROAST MEATS. IT IS TRADITIONALLY COOKED IN LARD BUT MANY PEOPLE PREFER BUTTER.

SERVES FOUR

INGREDIENTS
50g/2oz/¼ cup butter
1 onion, finely chopped
175g/6oz/scant 2 cups medium
   oatmeal
salt and ground black pepper

VARIATION
To add a lovely rich flavour to the skirlie, grate in a little nutmeg and add a pinch of cinnamon towards the end.

1 Melt the butter in a pan over a medium heat and add the onion. Fry gently until it is softened and very slightly browned.

2 Stir in the oatmeal and season with salt and ground black pepper. Cook gently for 10 minutes. Taste for seasoning and serve immediately.

Per portion Energy 282kcal/1182kJ; Protein 6g; Carbohydrate 34.9g, of which sugars 2.2g; Fat 14.2g, of which saturates 6.5g; Cholesterol 27mg; Calcium 36mg; Fibre 3.5g; Sodium 91mg.

COURGETTES AND TOFU WITH TOMATO SAUCE

THIS MEDITERRANEAN-STYLE DISH IS GREAT HOT OR COLD, AND IMPROVES GIVEN A DAY OR TWO COVERED IN THE REFRIGERATOR. IT MAKES THE PERFECT ACCOMPANIMENT TO A NUT OR MEAT ROAST.

SERVES FOUR

INGREDIENTS
  30ml/2 tbsp olive oil
  2 garlic cloves, finely chopped
  4 large courgettes (zucchini), thinly
    sliced on the diagonal
  250g/9oz firm tofu, drained
    and cubed
  1 lemon
  sea salt and ground black pepper
For the tomato sauce
  10ml/2 tsp balsamic vinegar
  5ml/1 tsp sugar
  300ml/½ pint/1¼ cups passata
    (bottled strained tomatoes)
  small bunch of fresh mint, chopped

3 Add the tofu to the pan and brown for a few minutes. Turn gently, then brown again. Grate the rind from half the lemon and reserve for the garnish. Squeeze the lemon juice over the tofu.

4 Season to taste with sea salt and pepper, then leave to sizzle until all the lemon juice has evaporated. Gently stir the courgettes into the tofu until well combined, then remove the pan from the heat.

5 Transfer the courgettes and tofu to a warm serving dish and pour the tomato sauce over the top. Sprinkle with the grated lemon rind. Taste and season with more salt and pepper, if necessary, and serve immediately.

COOK'S TIP
You could serve this dish with plain cooked meat such as chicken.

1 First, make the tomato sauce, Place all the ingredients in a small pan and heat through gently, stirring occasionally.

2 Meanwhile, heat the olive oil in a large non-stick frying pan until very hot, then add the garlic and stir-fry for 30 seconds, until golden. Add the courgettes and stir-fry over a high heat for about 5–6 minutes, or until the slices are golden around the edges. Remove from the pan.

VARIATIONS
• The courgette slices could be grilled (broiled) and then added to the fried garlic before the tofu cubes are browned.
• Aubergine (eggplant) slices could be used instead of the courgettes, but more olive oil may be needed to fry them in step 2.

Energy 141kcal/585kJ; Protein 8.8g; Carbohydrate 6.8g, of which sugars 6.3g; Fat 8.9g, of which saturates 1.3g; Cholesterol 0mg; Calcium 389mg; Fibre 2.4g; Sodium 181mg.

VEGETARIAN

*Grains and pulses are essential in many
vegetarian dishes, where they frequently provide
the protein and carbohydrate content. These
ingredients are the basis for a wide variety of
classic dishes from around the world, including
Lentil Dhal from India, Moroccan Braised
Chickpeas, Jamaican Black Bean Pot and
Teriyaki Soba Noodles from Japan.*

ONE-CRUST BEAN PIE

This free-form wholemeal pastry pie encases a rich tomato, aubergine and kidney bean filling. If your pastry cracks, just patch it up — it adds to the pie's rustic character. The semolina prevents the base of the pie from becoming soggy.

SERVES FOUR

INGREDIENTS
  500g/1¼lb aubergines (eggplants)
  1 red (bell) pepper
  30ml/2 tbsp olive oil
  1 large onion, finely chopped
  1 courgette (zucchini), sliced
  2 garlic cloves, crushed
  15ml/1 tbsp fresh oregano or 5ml/
    1 tsp dried, plus extra fresh oregano
    to garnish
  400g/14oz can red kidney beans,
    drained and rinsed
  115g/4oz/1 cup pitted black
    olives, rinsed
  375g/13oz/⅔ cup passata (bottled
    strained tomatoes)
  1 egg, beaten, or a little milk
  30ml/2 tbsp semolina
  salt and ground black pepper
For the pastry
  75g/3oz/⅔ cup plain (all-purpose)
    flour
  75g/3oz/⅔ cup wholemeal (whole-
    wheat) flour
  75g/3oz/6 tbsp vegetable margarine
  50g/2oz/⅔ cup freshly grated
    Parmesan cheese

1 Preheat the oven to 220°C/425°F/
Gas 7. To make the pastry, sift the plain
and wholemeal flours into a large bowl.
Rub in the vegetable margarine until the
mixture resembles fine breadcrumbs,
then stir in the grated Parmesan. Mix in
enough cold water to form a firm dough.

2 Turn out the dough on to a lightly
floured work surface and form into a
smooth ball. Wrap the dough in clear
film (plastic wrap) or a plastic bag and
chill for about 30 minutes.

3 To make the filling, cube the
aubergines and place them in a
colander. Sprinkle the aubergines
with salt, then leave for about 30
minutes. Rinse and pat dry with kitchen
paper. Meanwhile, place the pepper on
a baking tray and roast in the oven for
20 minutes. Put the pepper in a plastic
bag and leave until cool enough to
handle. Peel and seed, then dice the
flesh. Set aside.

4 Heat the oil in a large heavy frying
pan. Fry the onion for 5 minutes until
softened, stirring occasionally. Add the
aubergines and fry for 5 minutes until
tender. Add the courgette, garlic and
oregano, and cook for a further
5 minutes, stirring frequently. Add the
kidney beans and olives, stir, then add
the passata and pepper. Cook until
heated through, and set aside to cool.

5 Roll out the pastry on a lightly floured
board or work surface to form a rough
30cm/12in round. Place on a lightly
oiled baking sheet. Brush with beaten
egg or milk, sprinkle over the semolina,
leaving a 4cm/1½in border, then spoon
over the filling.

6 Gather up the edges of the pastry to
cover the filling partially – it should be
open in the middle. Brush with the
remaining egg or milk and bake for
30–35 minutes until golden. Garnish
with oregano.

Energy 554kcal/2318kJ; Protein 17.7g; Carbohydrate 56.6g, of which sugars 15.7g; Fat 30.2g, of which saturates 4.2g; Cholesterol 13mg; Calcium 295mg; Fibre 11.6g; Sodium 1353mg

RED ONION TART WITH A CORNMEAL CRUST

WONDERFULLY MILD AND SWEET WHEN COOKED, RED ONIONS GO WELL WITH FONTINA CHEESE AND THYME IN THIS TART. CORNMEAL GIVES THE PASTRY A CRUMBLY TEXTURE TO CONTRAST WITH THE JUICINESS OF THE ONION FILLING. A TOMATO AND BASIL SALAD IS GOOD WITH THE TART.

SERVES FIVE TO SIX

INGREDIENTS
  60ml/4 tbsp olive oil
  1kg/2¼lb red onions, thinly sliced
  2–3 garlic cloves, thinly sliced
  5ml/1 tsp chopped fresh thyme, plus
    a few whole sprigs
  5ml/1 tsp dark brown sugar
  10ml/2 tsp sherry vinegar
  225g/8oz Fontina cheese,
    thinly sliced
  salt and ground black pepper
For the pastry
  115g/4oz/1 cup plain (all-purpose)
    flour
  75g/3oz/¾ cup fine yellow cornmeal
  5ml/1 tsp dark brown sugar
  5ml/1 tsp chopped fresh thyme
  90g/3½oz/7 tbsp butter
  1 egg yolk
  30–45ml/2–3 tbsp iced water

1 To make the pastry, sift the flour and cornmeal into a bowl with 5ml/1 tsp salt. Add black pepper and stir in the sugar and thyme. Rub in the butter until the mixture looks like breadcrumbs. Beat the egg yolk with 30ml/2 tbsp of the iced water and use to bind the pastry, adding the remaining water if necessary. Gather the dough into a ball, wrap in clear film (plastic wrap) and chill it for 30–40 minutes.

2 Heat 45ml/3 tbsp of the oil in a deep frying pan and add the onions. Cover and cook slowly, stirring occasionally, for 20–30 minutes.

3 Add the garlic and chopped thyme, then cook, stirring occasionally, for another 10 minutes. Increase the heat slightly, then add the sugar and sherry vinegar. Cook, uncovered, for another 5–6 minutes, until the onions start to caramelize slightly. Season to taste with salt and pepper.

4 Preheat the oven to 190°C/375°F/ Gas 5. Roll out the pastry thinly and use to line a 25cm/10in loose-base metal flan tin (pan).

5 Prick the pastry all over with a fork and support the sides with foil. Bake for 12–15 minutes, until lightly coloured.

6 Remove the foil and spread the caramelized onions evenly over the base of the pastry case. Add the slices of Fontina and sprigs of thyme, and season with pepper. Drizzle over the remaining oil, then bake for 15–20 minutes, until the filling is piping hot and the cheese is beginning to bubble. Garnish the tart with thyme and serve immediately.

Energy 494kcal/2051kJ; Protein 13.2g; Carbohydrate 38.9g, of which sugars 11.3g; Fat 31.7g, of which saturates 16g; Cholesterol 100mg; Calcium 172mg; Fibre 3.2g; Sodium 307mg.

BULGUR WHEAT, ASPARAGUS AND BROAD BEAN PILAFF

Nutty-textured bulgur wheat is usually simply soaked in boiling water until it is softened, but it can be cooked like rice to make a pilaff. Here it is combined with broad beans, herbs, and lemon and orange rinds, which add a fresh, springtime flavour.

SERVES FOUR

INGREDIENTS
250g/9oz/1½ cups bulgur wheat
750–900ml/1¼–1½ pints/3–3¾
  cups warm vegetable stock
225g/8oz asparagus spears
225g/8oz/2 cups frozen broad (fava)
  beans, thawed
8 spring onions (scallions), chopped
15ml/1 tbsp grated lemon rind
15ml/1 tbsp grated orange rind
40g/1½oz/3 tbsp butter, cut into
  small pieces
60ml/4 tbsp chopped fresh flat
  leaf parsley
30ml/2 tbsp chopped fresh dill, plus
  extra sprigs to garnish
salt and ground black pepper

2 Cut the asparagus spears into 2.5cm/1in lengths, discarding any hard, woody ends from the stems. Add the asparagus pieces to the dish and gently stir these into the bulgur wheat.

3 Cover the dish tightly and place in an unheated oven. Set the oven to 200°C/400°F/Gas 6 and then cook the bulgur wheat and asparagus for 20 minutes.

4 Meanwhile pop the broad beans out of their skins and stir them into the bulgur pilaff, adding a little more stock at the same time. Re-cover the dish and return it to the oven for about 10 minutes.

5 Stir in the spring onions, grated lemon and orange rind. Add a little more stock, if necessary. Cover and return to the oven for 5 minutes.

6 Dot the pieces of butter over the top of the pilaff and leave to stand, covered, for 5 minutes.

7 Add the parsley and dill to the pilaff and stir with a fork. Add salt and plenty of black pepper. Serve hot, garnished with sprigs of fresh dill.

1 Place the bulgur wheat in a shallow, ovenproof earthenware dish and pour over 600ml/1 pint/2½ cups of the stock. Season with salt and pepper.

VARIATIONS
• Use fresh green beans and either fresh or frozen peas in place of the asparagus and broad beans and, instead of using dill, stir in plenty of chopped fresh mint along with the parsley.
• If you'd like to add a little extra colour to the pilaff, then stir in some finely shredded red (bell) pepper, or some peeled and seeded wedges of tomato.

COOK'S TIP
Leaving the bulgur wheat to stand for 5 minutes after cooking helps to give it a light fluffy texture.

Energy 368kcal/1536kJ; Protein 13.4g; Carbohydrate 56.7g, of which sugars 3g; Fat 10.4g, of which saturates 5.4g; Cholesterol 21mg; Calcium 134mg; Fibre 6.2g; Sodium 79mg.

WILD RICE PILAFF

WILD RICE ISN'T A RICE AT ALL, BUT A TYPE OF WILD GRASS. CALL IT WHAT YOU WILL, IT HAS A WONDERFUL NUTTY FLAVOUR AND COMBINES WELL WITH LONG GRAIN RICE IN THIS FRUITY MIXTURE. TOP WITH SLICES OF HALLOUMI CHEESE FOR A MAIN MEAL VEGETARIAN DISH.

SERVES SIX

INGREDIENTS
200g/7oz/1 cup wild rice
40g/1½oz/3 tbsp butter
½ onion, finely chopped
200g/7oz/1 cup long grain rice
475ml/16fl oz/2 cups vegetable stock
75g/3oz/¾ cup slivered or
  flaked (sliced) almonds
115g/4oz/⅔ cup sultanas (golden
  raisins)
30ml/2 tbsp chopped fresh parsley
salt and ground black pepper

1 Bring a large pan of water to the boil. Add the wild rice and 5ml/1 tsp salt. Lower the heat, cover and simmer gently for 45–60 minutes, until the rice is tender. Drain well.

2 Meanwhile, melt 15g/½oz/1 tbsp of the butter in another pan. Add the onion and cook over a medium heat for about 5 minutes until it is just softened. Stir in the long grain rice and cook for 1 minute more.

3 Stir in the stock and bring to the boil. Cover and simmer gently for 30–40 minutes, until the rice is tender and the liquid has been absorbed.

4 Melt the remaining butter in a small pan. Add the almonds and cook until they are just golden. Set aside.

5 Put the rice mixture in a bowl and add the almonds, sultanas and half the parsley. Stir to mix. Taste and adjust the seasoning if necessary. Transfer to a warmed serving dish, sprinkle with the remaining parsley and serve.

COOK'S TIP
Like all rice dishes, this one must be made with well-flavoured stock. If you haven't time to make your own, use a carton or can of good quality stock.

Energy 424kcal/1769kJ; Protein 8.4g; Carbohydrate 68.3g, of which sugars 14.6g; Fat 13g, of which saturates 4g; Cholesterol 14mg; Calcium 69mg; Fibre 1.7g; Sodium 48mg.

FRESH HERB RISOTTO

DISTINCTIVE, NUTTY-FLAVOURED WILD RICE IS COMBINED WITH ARBORIO RICE TO CREATE THIS CREAMY, COMFORTING RISOTTO. AN AROMATIC BLEND OF FRESH HERBS ADDS A LIGHT SUMMERY FLAVOUR. SPRINKLE WITH FRESHLY GRATED PARMESAN BEFORE SERVING.

SERVES FOUR

INGREDIENTS
90g/3½oz/½ cup wild rice
15ml/1 tbsp butter
15ml/1 tbsp olive oil
1 small onion, finely chopped
450g/1lb/2½ cups arborio rice
300ml/½ pint/1¼ cups dry
  white wine
1.2 litres/2 pints/5 cups
  vegetable stock
45ml/3 tbsp chopped fresh oregano
45ml/3 tbsp chopped fresh chives
60ml/4 tbsp chopped fresh flat
  leaf parsley
60ml/4 tbsp chopped fresh basil
75g/3oz/1 cup freshly grated
  Parmesan cheese
salt and ground black pepper

1 Cook the wild rice in boiling salted water according to the instructions on the packet. Drain and set aside.

2 Heat the butter and oil in a large heavy pan. When the butter has melted, add the onion and cook for 3 minutes, Add the arborio rice and cook for 2 minutes, stirring to coat it in the oil mixture.

COOK'S TIP
Risotto rice is essential to achieve the right creamy texture in this dish. Other types of rice simply will not do. Fresh herbs are also a must, but you can use tarragon, chervil, marjoram or thyme instead of those listed here.

3 Pour in the wine and bring to the boil. Reduce the heat and cook for 10 minutes until the wine has evaporated. Add the stock, a little at a time, and simmer, stirring, for 20–25 minutes until the liquid is absorbed and the rice is creamy. Season well.

4 Add the herbs and wild rice; heat for 2 minutes, stirring frequently. Stir in two-thirds of the Parmesan and cook until melted. Serve sprinkled with the remaining Parmesan.

Energy 632kcal/2637kJ; Protein 18g; Carbohydrate 109.3g, of which sugars 1.2g; Fat 12.8g, of which saturates 6.2g; Cholesterol 27mg; Calcium 280mg; Fibre 0.8g; Sodium 232mg.

SAVOURY LENTIL LOAF

IDEAL AS AN ALTERNATIVE TO THE TRADITIONAL MEAT ROAST, THIS WHOLESOME LENTIL AND NUT LOAF IS PERFECT FOR SPECIAL OCCASIONS. IT IS GOOD SERVED WITH A SPICY FRESH TOMATO SAUCE.

SERVES FOUR

INGREDIENTS

30ml/2 tbsp olive oil, plus extra
   for greasing
1 onion, finely chopped
1 leek, finely chopped
2 celery sticks, finely chopped
225g/8oz/3 cups mushrooms,
   chopped
2 garlic cloves, crushed
425g/15oz can lentils, rinsed and
   drained
115g/4oz/1 cup mixed nuts, such as
   hazelnuts, cashew nuts and
   almonds, finely chopped
50g/2oz/½ cup plain (all-purpose)
   flour
50g/2oz/½ cup grated mature (sharp)
   Cheddar cheese
1 egg, beaten
45–60ml/3–4 tbsp chopped fresh
   mixed herbs
salt and ground black pepper
chives and sprigs of fresh flat leaf
   parsley, to garnish

1 Lightly grease and line with baking parchment the base and sides of a 900g/2lb loaf tin (pan) or terrine.

2 Heat the oil in a large pan, add the onion, leek, celery, mushrooms and garlic, then cook for 10 minutes, until the vegetables have softened. Do not let them brown.

3 Remove from the heat. Stir in the lentils, mixed nuts and flour, cheese, egg and herbs. Season well with salt and black pepper and mix thoroughly.

4 Spoon the mixture into the prepared loaf tin or terrine, pressing it right into the corners. Level the surface with a fork, then cover the tin with a piece of foil. Place the loaf tin inside a large deep-sided baking tray and pour in enough near-boiling water to come just over halfway up the side of the tin.

5 Cover and cook slowly for 1–2 hours, or until the loaf is firm to the touch.

6 Leave to cool in the tin for about 15 minutes, then turn out on to a serving plate. Serve hot or cold, cut into thick slices and garnished with herbs.

Energy 484Kcal/2019kJ; Protein 23.7g; Carbohydrate 34.1g, of which sugars 5.1g; Fat 29g, of which saturates 5.4g; Cholesterol 69mg; Calcium 238mg; Fibre 8.7g; Sodium 128mg.

PARSNIPS AND CHICKPEAS

THIS INDIAN-STYLE VEGETABLE STEW MAKES AN IDEAL MEAL FOR VEGETARIANS. THE CHICKPEAS ADD SUBSTANCE AS WELL AS VALUABLE PROTEIN TO THE DISH. COMPLETE THE MEAL WITH WARM INDIAN BREADS, SUCH AS CHAPATI OR NAAN.

SERVES FOUR

INGREDIENTS

  5 garlic cloves, finely chopped
  1 small onion, chopped
  5cm/2in piece fresh root ginger,
    chopped
  2 green chillies, seeded and finely
    chopped
  75ml/5 tbsp cold water
  60ml/4 tbsp groundnut (peanut) oil
  5ml/1 tsp cumin seeds
  10ml/2 tsp coriander seeds
  5ml/1 tsp ground turmeric
  2.5ml/½ tsp chilli powder or
    mild paprika
  50g/2oz/½ cup cashew nuts, toasted
    and ground
  225g/8oz tomatoes, peeled
    and chopped
  400g/14oz can chickpeas, drained
    and rinsed
  900g/2lb parsnips, cut into
    2cm/¾in chunks
  350ml/12fl oz/1½ cups boiling
    vegetable stock
  juice of 1 lime, to taste
  salt and ground black pepper
  chopped fresh coriander (cilantro),
    toasted cashew nuts and natural
    (plain) yogurt, to serve

1 Preheat the oven to 180°C/250°F/Gas 4.

2 Reserve 10ml/2 tsp of the garlic, then place the remainder in a food processor or blender with the onion, ginger and half the chilli. Add the water and process to make a smooth paste.

3 Heat the oil in a large frying pan, add the cumin seeds and cook for about 30 seconds. Stir in the coriander seeds, turmeric, chilli powder or paprika and the ground cashew nuts. Add the ginger and chilli paste and cook, stirring frequently, until the paste bubbles and the water begins to evaporate.

4 Add the tomatoes to the pan and cook for 1 minute. Transfer the mixture to a casserole dish.

5 Add the chickpeas and parsnips to the pot and stir to coat in the spicy tomato mixture, then stir in the stock and season with salt and pepper. Cover with the lid and cook in the oven for 1 hour, or until the parsnips are tender.

6 Stir half the lime juice, the reserved garlic and green chilli into the stew. Re-cover and cook for 30 minutes more, then taste and add more lime juice if needed. Spoon on to plates and sprinkle with fresh coriander leaves and toasted cashew nuts. Serve immediately with a generous spoonful of natural yogurt.

Energy 453Kcal/1899kJ; Protein 14.8g; Carbohydrate 50.1g, of which sugars 16.6g; Fat 23g, of which saturates 4.3g; Cholesterol 0mg; Calcium 148mg; Fibre 15.8g; Sodium 394mg.

SAVOY CABBAGE WITH MUSHROOM BARLEY

THE FIRM TEXTURE OF SAVOY CABBAGE MAKES A GOOD CONTAINER FOR AN EARTHY, RICH STUFFING OF BARLEY AND MIXED CULTIVATED AND WILD MUSHROOMS.

SERVES FOUR

INGREDIENTS

50g/2oz/4 tbsp unsalted (sweet)
   butter
2 onions, chopped
1 celery stick, sliced
225g/8oz assorted wild and
   cultivated mushrooms
175g/6oz/1¼ cups pearl barley
1 fresh thyme sprig
750ml/1¼ pints/3²/₃ cups water
30ml/2 tbsp almond or cashew
   nut butter
½ vegetable stock cube
1 Savoy cabbage
salt and ground black pepper

1 Melt the butter in a large heavy pan, add the onions and celery and fry for 6–8 minutes until soft. Add the mushrooms and cook until they release their juices, then add the barley, thyme, water and the nut butter. Bring to the boil, cover and simmer for 30 minutes. Add the ½ stock cube and simmer for another 20 minutes. Season to taste.

2 Separate the cabbage leaves and cut away the thick stem. Blanch the leaves in salted boiling water for 3–4 minutes. Drain and refresh under cold running water. Drain again.

3 Place a 46cm/18in square of muslin (cheesecloth) over a steaming basket. Reconstruct the cabbage by lining the muslin with large cabbage leaves. Spread a layer of mushroom barley over the leaves.

4 Cover with a second layer of leaves and filling. Continue until the centre is full. Draw together opposite corners of the muslin and tie firmly. Place the cabbage in a steaming basket, set in a pan containing 2.5cm/1in of simmering water, Cover and steam for 30 minutes. To serve, place on a warmed serving plate, untie the muslin and carefully pull it away from underneath the cabbage.

COOK'S TIPS
• A range of nut butters is available in all leading health food stores.
• If planning ahead, the cabbage can be assembled well in advance before the final cooking.
• To ensure richness and flavour use a good portion of ceps, chicken of the woods and field mushrooms.

Energy 354kcal/1485kJ; Protein 8.7g; Carbohydrate 47.5g, of which sugars 9.6g; Fat 15.6g, of which saturates 7.5g; Cholesterol 27mg; Calcium 103mg; Fibre 4.7g; Sodium 127mg.

GOAT'S CHEESE WITH GRAINS AND WALNUTS

ROBUSTLY FLAVOURED BUCKWHEAT IS OFTEN COMBINED WITH OTHER GRAINS. COUSCOUS ALLOWS THE FLAVOUR OF BUCKWHEAT, GOAT'S CHEESE, DRIED CEPS AND TOASTED WALNUTS TO COME THROUGH.

SERVES FOUR

INGREDIENTS
175g/6oz/1 cup couscous
45ml/3 tbsp buckwheat
½oz/15g/¼ cup dried ceps or
  bay boletus
3 eggs
60ml/4 tbsp chopped fresh parsley
10ml/2 tsp chopped fresh thyme
60ml/4 tbsp olive oil
45ml/3 tbsp walnut oil
175g/6oz/1½ cups crumbly white
  goat's cheese
50g/2oz/½ cup broken walnuts,
  toasted
salt and ground black pepper
salad and rye bread, to serve

1 Place the couscous, buckwheat and ceps in a bowl, cover with boiling water and leave to soak for 15 minutes. Drain off any excess liquid.

2 Place the mixture in a large non-stick frying pan, add the eggs, season well, then scramble with a flat wooden spoon over a moderate heat.

3 Stir in the parsley, thyme, olive oil, walnut oil, goat's cheese and walnuts. Season to taste with salt and pepper.

4 Transfer to a large serving dish and serve hot with rye bread and salad.

Energy 597kcal/2475kJ; Protein 19.7g; Carbohydrate 32.2g, of which sugars 1g; Fat 44g, of which saturates 12g; Cholesterol 183mg; Calcium 127mg; Fibre 1g; Sodium 321mg.

GRILLED POLENTA

SLICES OF GRILLED POLENTA ARE DELICIOUS TOPPED WITH SLOWLY CARAMELIZED ONIONS AND BUBBLING TALEGGIO CHEESE. SERVE WITH RADICCHIO LEAVES.

SERVES FOUR

INGREDIENTS
900ml/1½ pints/3¾ cups water
5ml/1 tsp salt
150g/5oz/generous 1 cup polenta
  or cornmeal
50g/2oz/⅓ cup freshly grated
  Parmesan cheese
5ml/1 tsp chopped fresh thyme
90ml/6 tbsp olive oil
675g/1½lb onions, halved and sliced
2 garlic cloves, chopped
a few fresh thyme sprigs
5ml/1 tsp brown sugar
15–30ml/1–2 tbsp balsamic vinegar
2 heads radicchio, cut into thick
  slices or wedges
225g/8oz Taleggio cheese, sliced
salt and ground black pepper

1 In a large pan, bring the water to the boil and add the salt. Adjust the heat so that it simmers. Stirring all the time, add the polenta in a steady stream, then bring to the boil. Cook over a very low heat, stirring frequently, for 30–40 minutes, until thick and smooth.

2 Beat in the Parmesan and chopped thyme, then turn on to a work surface or tray. Spread evenly, then leave to cool.

3 Heat 30ml/2 tbsp of the oil in a frying pan over a moderate heat. Add the onions and stir to coat in the oil, then cover and cook over a very low heat for 15 minutes, stirring occasionally.

4 Add the garlic and most of the thyme sprigs and cook, uncovered, for another 10 minutes, or until light brown.

5 Add the sugar, 15ml/1 tbsp of the vinegar and salt and pepper. Cook for another 5–10 minutes, until soft and well-browned. Taste and add more vinegar and seasoning as necessary.

6 Preheat the grill (broiler). Cut the polenta into thick slices and brush with a little of the remaining oil, then grill (broil) until crusty and lightly browned.

7 Turn the polenta and add the radicchio to the grill rack or pan. Season the radicchio and brush with a little oil. Grill for about 5 minutes, until the polenta and radicchio are browned. Drizzle a little vinegar over the radicchio.

8 Heap the onions on to the polenta. Scatter the cheese and a few sprigs of thyme over both polenta and radicchio. Grill until the cheese is bubbling. Season with pepper and serve immediately.

Energy 611kcal/2534kJ; Protein 22.7g; Carbohydrate 42.5g, of which sugars 11.2g; Fat 37.8g, of which saturates 15.3g; Cholesterol 65mg; Calcium 365mg; Fibre 4.1g; Sodium 457mg.

LAYERED POLENTA BAKE

THIS IS A FORM OF LASAGNE WITH SLICES OF POLENTA REPLACING THE USUAL SHEETS OF PASTA.
LAYERS OF POLENTA ARE INTERSPERSED WITH A RICH TOMATO SAUCE AND CREAMY GORGONZOLA.

SERVES SIX

INGREDIENTS
5ml/1 tsp salt
375g/13oz/3 cups fine polenta
olive oil, for greasing and brushing
25g/1oz/⅓ cup freshly grated
 Parmesan cheese
salt and ground black pepper
For the tomato sauce
15ml/1 tbsp olive oil
2 garlic cloves, chopped
400g/14oz/3 cups chopped tomatoes
15ml/1 tbsp chopped fresh sage
2.5ml/½ tsp soft brown sugar
400g/14oz can cannellini beans,
 rinsed and drained
For the spinach sauce
250g/9oz spinach, tough stalks
 removed
150ml/¼ pint/⅔ cup single
 (light) cream
115g/4oz/1 cup Gorgonzola
 cheese, cubed
large pinch of ground nutmeg

1 Make the polenta. Bring 2 litres/
3½ pints/8 cups water to the boil
in a large heavy pan and add the
salt. Remove the pan from the heat.
Gradually pour in the polenta,
whisking continuously.

2 Return the pan to the heat and stir
constantly for 15–20 minutes until the
polenta is thick and comes away from
the side of the pan. Remove the pan
from the heat.

3 Season well with pepper, then spoon
the polenta on to a wet work surface or
piece of marble. Using a wet spatula,
spread out the polenta until it is
1cm/½in thick. Leave to cool for about
1 hour.

4 Preheat the oven to 190°C/375°F/
Gas 5. To make the tomato sauce, heat
the oil in a pan, then fry the garlic for
1 minute. Add the tomatoes and sage
and bring to the boil. Reduce the heat,
add the sugar and seasoning, and
simmer for 10 minutes until slightly
reduced, stirring occasionally. Stir in the
beans and cook for a further 2 minutes.

5 Meanwhile, wash the spinach
thoroughly and place in a large pan
with only the water that clings to the
leaves. Cover the pan tightly and cook
over a medium heat for about 3 minutes
or until tender, stirring occasionally.
Tip the spinach into a colander and
drain, then squeeze out as much excess
water as possible with the back of a
wooden spoon.

6 Heat the cream, cheese and nutmeg
in a heavy pan. Bring to the boil, then
reduce the heat. Stir in the spinach and
seasoning, then cook gently until
slightly thickened, stirring frequently.

7 Cut the polenta into triangles, then
place a layer in an oiled deep baking
dish. Spoon over the tomato sauce,
then top with another layer of polenta.
Top with the spinach sauce and cover
with the remaining polenta triangles.
Brush with olive oil, sprinkle with
Parmesan and bake for 35–40 minutes.
Heat the grill (broiler) to high and grill
(broil) until the top is golden. Serve.

Energy 436kcal/1820kJ; Protein 16.2g; Carbohydrate 55.3g, of which sugars 4.9g; Fat 16.3g, of which saturates 8g; Cholesterol 32mg; Calcium 267mg; Fibre 5g; Sodium 481mg.

POLENTA PAN PIZZA WITH RED ONIONS

THIS YEAST-FREE PIZZA IS COOKED IN A FRYING PAN RATHER THAN THE OVEN. THE SLIGHTLY CAKEY TEXTURE OF THE BASE IS COMPLEMENTED BY THE GARLICKY RED ONION AND MUSHROOM TOPPING. SERVE WITH A SIMPLE TOMATO AND BASIL SALAD.

SERVES TWO

INGREDIENTS
30ml/2 tbsp olive oil
1 large red onion, sliced
3 garlic cloves, crushed
115g/4oz/1½ cups brown cap
  mushrooms, sliced
5ml/1 tsp dried oregano
115g/4oz mozzarella cheese, diced
15ml/1 tbsp pine nuts (optional)
For the pizza base
50g/2oz/½ cup plain (all-purpose)
  flour, sifted
2.5ml/½ tsp salt
115g/4oz/1 cup fine polenta
5ml/1 tsp baking powder
1 egg, beaten
150ml/¼ pint/⅔ cup milk
25g/1oz/⅓ cup freshly grated
  Parmesan cheese
2.5ml/½ tsp dried chilli flakes
15ml/1 tbsp olive oil

1 To make the topping, heat half the olive oil in a heavy frying pan, add the onion and fry for 10 minutes until tender, stirring occasionally. Remove the onion from the pan and set aside.

2 Add the remaining oil to the pan and fry the garlic for 1 minute until slightly coloured. Add the sliced mushrooms and oregano and cook for 5 minutes more until the mushrooms are tender.

3 To make the pizza base, mix together the flour, salt, polenta and baking powder in a bowl. Make a well in the centre and add the egg. Gradually add the milk, and mix well with a fork to make into a thick, smooth batter. Stir in the Parmesan and chilli flakes.

4 Heat the olive oil in a 25cm/10in heavy flameproof frying pan until very hot. Spoon in the batter and spread evenly. Cook over a moderate heat for about 3 minutes or until the mixture is set. Remove the pan from the heat and run a knife around the edge of the pizza base.

5 Place a plate over the pan and, holding them tightly together, flip over. Slide the pizza base back into the pan on its uncooked side and cook for 2 minutes until golden.

6 Preheat the grill (broiler) to high. Spoon the onions over the pizza base, then top with the mushroom mixture. Scatter the mozzarella on top, then grill (broil) for about 6 minutes until the mozzarella has melted. Sprinkle over the pine nuts (if using) and grill until golden. Serve cut into wedges.

Energy 782kcal/3262kJ; Protein 31.9g; Carbohydrate 77.1g, of which sugars 12.4g; Fat 39.1g, of which saturates 14.5g; Cholesterol 145mg; Calcium 540mg; Fibre 4.8g; Sodium 439mg.

JAMAICAN BLACK BEAN POT

MOLASSES IMPARTS A RICH TREACLE-LIKE FLAVOUR TO THE SPICY SAUCE, WHICH INCORPORATES A STUNNING MIX OF BLACK BEANS, VIBRANT RED AND YELLOW PEPPERS AND ORANGE BUTTERNUT SQUASH. THIS DISH IS DELICIOUS SERVED WITH CORNBREAD OR PLAIN RICE.

SERVES FOUR

INGREDIENTS

225g/8oz/1¼ cups dried black beans
1 bay leaf
30ml/2 tbsp vegetable oil
1 large onion, chopped
1 garlic clove, chopped
5ml/1 tsp English mustard powder
15ml/1 tbsp molasses
30ml/2 tbsp soft dark brown sugar
5ml/1 tsp dried thyme
2.5ml/½ tsp dried chilli flakes
5ml/1 tsp vegetable bouillon powder
1 red (bell) pepper, seeded and diced
1 yellow (bell) pepper, seeded
   and diced
675g/1½lb butternut squash or
   pumpkin, seeded and cut into
   1cm/½in dice
salt and ground black pepper
thyme sprigs, to garnish

1 Soak the beans overnight in plenty of water, then drain and rinse well. Place in a large pan, cover with fresh water and add the bay leaf. Bring to the boil, then boil rapidly for 10 minutes. Reduce the heat, cover, and simmer for 30 minutes until tender. Drain, reserving the cooking water. Preheat the oven to 180°C/350°F/Gas 4.

VARIATION
Black-eyed beans, pinto or chickpeas can be used instead of the black beans but they do not look quite so dramatic.

2 Heat the oil in the pan and sauté the onion and garlic for about 5 minutes until softened, stirring occasionally. Add the mustard powder, molasses, sugar, thyme and chilli, and cook for 1 minute, stirring. Stir in the black beans and spoon the mixture into a flameproof casserole.

3 Add enough water to the reserved cooking liquid to make 400ml/ 14fl oz/1⅔ cups, then mix in the bouillon powder and pour into the casserole. Bake for 25 minutes.

4 Add the peppers and squash or pumpkin and mix well. Cover, then bake for 45 minutes until the vegetables are tender. Serve garnished with thyme.

Energy 222kcal/932kJ; Protein 6.9g; Carbohydrate 35.6g, of which sugars 24.8g; Fat 6.7g, of which saturates 1.1g; Cholesterol 0mg; Calcium 139mg; Fibre 7.6g; Sodium 232mg.

SPICY-HOT MIXED BEAN CHILLI

INSPIRED BY TRADITIONAL TEXAN COOKING, THIS CHILLI COMBINES TEX-MEX WITH CLASSIC TEXAN CORNBREAD. THE DELICIOUS TOPPING OFFERS THE STARCH COMPONENT OF THE DISH, MAKING IT A FILLING ONE-POT MEAL WITH NO NEED FOR ACCOMPANIMENTS.

SERVES FOUR

INGREDIENTS

115g/4oz/generous ½ cup dried
  red kidney beans
600ml/1 pint/2½ cups of water
115g/4oz/generous ½ cup dried
  black-eyed beans (peas)
1 bay leaf
15ml/1 tbsp vegetable oil
1 large onion, finely chopped
1 garlic clove, crushed
5ml/1 tsp ground cumin
5ml/1 tsp chilli powder
5ml/1 tsp mild paprika
2.5ml/½ tsp dried marjoram
450g/1lb mixed vegetables such
  as potatoes, carrots, aubergines
  (eggplants), parsnips and celery
1 vegetable stock cube
400g/14oz can chopped tomatoes
15ml/1 tbsp tomato purée (paste)
salt and ground black pepper
For the cornbread topping
250g/9oz/2¼ cups fine cornmeal
30ml/2 tbsp wholemeal
  (whole-wheat) flour
7.5ml/1½ tsp baking powder
1 egg, plus 1 egg yolk lightly beaten
300ml/½ pint/1¼ cups milk

1 Preheat the oven to 150°C/300°F/ Gas 2. Put the beans in a bowl and pour over at least twice their volume of cold water. Leave to soak overnight.

2 Drain the beans and rinse well, then place in a pan with the water and the bay leaf. Bring to the boil and boil rapidly for 10 minutes. Turn off the heat, leave to cool for a few minutes. Pour the beans into a large ovenproof dish and put in the oven.

3 Heat the oil in a pan, add the onion and cook for 7–8 minutes. Add the garlic, cumin, chilli powder, paprika and marjoram and cook for 1 minute. Tip into the casserole dish and stir.

4 Prepare the vegetables, peeling or trimming them as necessary, then cut into 2cm/¾in chunks.

5 Add the vegetables to the bean mixture, making sure that those that may discolour, such as potatoes and parsnips, are submerged. It doesn't matter if the other vegetables are not completely covered. Cover with the lid and bake for 3 hours, or until the beans are tender.

6 Add the stock cube and chopped tomatoes to the cooking pot, then stir in the tomato purée and season with salt and ground black pepper. Replace the lid and bake for a further 30 minutes until the mixture is at boiling point.

7 To make the topping, combine the cornmeal, flour, baking powder and a pinch of salt in a bowl. Make a well in the centre and add the egg, egg yolk and milk. Mix, then spoon over the bean mixture. Cover and cook for 1 hour, or until the topping is firm and cooked.

Energy 613Kcal/2595kJ; Protein 29.6g; Carbohydrate 97.4g, of which sugars 15.8g; Fat 14.5g, of which saturates 3.4g; Cholesterol 112mg; Calcium 257mg; Fibre 13.4g; Sodium 413mg.

SWEET-AND-SOUR MIXED BEAN HOTPOT

THIS IMPRESSIVE-LOOKING DISH, TOPPED WITH SLICED POTATOES, IS INCREDIBLY EASY, MAKING THE MOST OF DRIED AND CANNED INGREDIENTS FROM THE KITCHEN CUPBOARD AND COMBINING THEM WITH A DELICIOUSLY RICH AND TANGY TOMATO SAUCE.

SERVES SIX

INGREDIENTS

40g/1½oz/3 tbsp butter
4 shallots, peeled and finely chopped
40g/1½oz/⅓ cup plain (all-purpose)
  or wholemeal (whole-wheat) flour
300ml/½ pint/1¼ cups passata
  (bottled strained tomatoes)
120ml/4fl oz/½ cup unsweetened
  apple juice
60ml/4 tbsp soft light brown sugar
60ml/4 tbsp tomato ketchup
60ml/4 tbsp dry sherry
60ml/4 tbsp cider vinegar
60ml/4 tbsp light soy sauce
400g/14oz can butter (lima) beans
400g/14oz can flageolet (small
  cannellini) beans
400g/14oz can chickpeas
175g/6oz green beans, cut into
  2.5cm/1in lengths
225g/8oz/3 cups mushrooms, sliced
15ml/1 tbsp chopped fresh thyme
15ml/1 tbsp fresh marjoram
450g/1lb unpeeled potatoes
15ml/1 tbsp olive oil
salt and ground black pepper
fresh herbs, to garnish

1 Melt the butter in a pan, add the shallots and fry gently for 5–6 minutes, until softened. Add the flour and cook for 1 minute, stirring all the time, then gradually stir in the passata.

2 Add the apple juice, sugar, tomato ketchup, sherry, vinegar and light soy sauce to the pan and stir in. Bring the mixture to the boil, stirring constantly until it thickens. Season. Preheat the oven to 180°C/350°F/Gas 4.

VARIATIONS
• You can vary the proportions and types of beans used, depending on what you have in the store cupboard (pantry).
• Kidney beans and borlotti beans would work well and can be either interchanged with any of the beans used here, or combined with them.

3 Rinse the beans and chickpeas and drain well. Place them in an ovenproof dish with the green beans and mushrooms and pour over the sauce. Add the thyme and marjoram. Stir well.

4 Thinly slice the potatoes and par-boil them for 5 minutes. Drain well.

5 Arrange the potato slices on top of the beans, overlapping them slightly. Brush with half the olive oil. Cover and cook for 1 hour, or until the potatoes are just tender.

6 Uncover and brush the remaining oil over the potatoes. Cook for a further 30 minutes, to brown the potato topping. Serve garnished with herbs.

Energy 483Kcal/2042kJ; Protein 18.5g; Carbohydrate 73.3g, of which sugars 24.8g; Fat 13.8g, of which saturates 4.5g; Cholesterol 14mg; Calcium 134mg; Fibre 10.9g; Sodium 826mg.

BUTTER BEAN TAGINE

YOU EITHER LOVE OR HATE BUTTER BEANS. THIS HEARTY DISH IS SUBSTANTIAL ENOUGH TO BE SERVED ON ITS OWN OR WITH A LEAFY SALAD AND FRESH, CRUSTY BREAD.

SERVES FOUR

INGREDIENTS

115g/4oz/⅔ cup butter (lima) beans, soaked overnight
30–45ml/2–3 tbsp olive oil
1 onion, chopped
2–3 garlic cloves, crushed
25g/1oz fresh root ginger, peeled and chopped
pinch of saffron threads
16 cherry tomatoes
generous pinch of sugar
handful of fleshy black olives, pitted
5ml/1 tsp ground cinnamon
5ml/1 tsp paprika
small bunch of flat leaf parsley
salt and ground black pepper

1 Rinse the beans and place them in a large pan with plenty of water. Bring to the boil and boil for about 10 minutes, then reduce the heat and simmer gently for 1–1½ hours until tender. Drain the beans and refresh under cold water.

2 Heat the olive oil in a heavy pan. Add the onion, garlic and ginger, and cook for about 10 minutes, or until softened but not browned. Stir in the saffron threads, followed by the cherry tomatoes and a sprinkling of sugar.

3 As the tomatoes begin to soften, stir in the butter beans. When the tomatoes have heated through, stir in the olives, ground cinnamon and paprika. Season to taste and sprinkle over the parsley. Serve immediately.

COOK'S TIP

If you are in a hurry, you could use 2 x 400g/14oz cans of butter beans for this tagine. Make sure you rinse the beans well before adding to the recipe as canned beans tend to be salty.

Energy 117kcal/487kJ; Protein 3.5g; Carbohydrate 8.5g, of which sugars 2.2g; Fat 7.9g, of which saturates 1.2g; Cholesterol 0mg; Calcium 25mg; Fibre 3.3g; Sodium 635mg.

LENTIL FRITTATA

THICK, VEGETABLE-BASED OMELETTES, OTHERWISE KNOWN AS FRITTATA OR TORTILLA, ARE FAMILIAR DISHES IN MANY MEDITERRANEAN COUNTRIES AND ARE DELICIOUS AND TASTY.

SERVES FOUR TO SIX

INGREDIENTS
    75g/3oz/scant ½ cup green lentils
    225g/8oz small broccoli florets
    2 red onions, halved and thickly
        sliced
    30ml/2 tbsp olive oil
    8 eggs
    45ml/3 tbsp milk or water
    45ml/3 tbsp chopped mixed
        herbs, such as oregano, parsley,
        tarragon and chives, plus extra
        sprigs to garnish
    175g/6oz cherry tomatoes, halved
    salt and ground black pepper

1 Place the lentils in a pan, cover with cold water and bring to the boil, reduce the heat and simmer for 25 minutes until tender. Add the broccoli, return to the boil and cook for 1 minute.

2 Meanwhile, place the onion slices and olive oil in a shallow earthenware dish about 23–25cm/9–10in in diameter and place in an unheated oven. Set the oven to 200°C/400°F/Gas 6 and cook for 25 minutes.

3 In a bowl, whisk together the eggs, milk or water, a pinch of salt and plenty of black pepper. Stir in the herbs. Drain the lentils and broccoli and stir into the onions. Add the cherry tomatoes. Stir gently to combine.

4 Pour the egg mixture evenly over the vegetables. Reduce the oven to 190°C/375°F/Gas 5. Return the dish to the oven and cook for 10 minutes. Remove from the oven and push the mixture into the centre of the dish using a spatula, allowing the raw mixture in the centre to flow to the edges.

5 Return the dish to the oven and cook the frittata for a further 15 minutes, or until it is just set. Garnish with sprigs of fresh herbs and serve warm, cut into thick wedges.

Energy 212kcal/886kJ; Protein 14g; Carbohydrate 13.9g, of which sugars 5.5g; Fat 11.8g, of which saturates 2.7g; Cholesterol 254mg; Calcium 84mg; Fibre 2.8g; Sodium 106mg.

SPLIT PEA OR LENTIL FRITTERS

THESE SPICY FRITTERS COME FROM THE INDIAN SUBCONTINENT. THEY ARE COUSINS OF FALAFEL.
SERVE WITH A WEDGE OF LEMON AND A SPOONFUL OF FRAGRANT MINT CHUTNEY.

SERVES FOUR TO SIX

INGREDIENTS

250g/9oz/generous 1 cup yellow split
  peas or red lentils, soaked overnight
3–5 garlic cloves, chopped
30ml/2 tbsp roughly chopped fresh
  root ginger
120ml/4fl oz/½ cup chopped fresh
  coriander (cilantro) leaves
2.5–5ml/½–1 tsp ground cumin
1.5–2.5ml/¼–½ tsp ground turmeric
large pinch of cayenne pepper or
  ½–1 fresh green chilli, chopped
50g/2 oz/½ cup gram flour
5ml/1 tsp baking powder
30ml/2 tbsp couscous
2 large or 3 small onions, chopped
vegetable oil, for deep frying
salt and ground black pepper
lemon wedges, to serve

1 Drain the split peas or lentils,
reserving a little of the soaking water.
Put the chopped garlic and ginger in a
food processor or blender and process
until finely minced (ground). Add the
drained peas or lentils, 15–30ml/
1–2 tbsp of the reserved soaking water
and the chopped coriander, and
process to form a purée.

2 Add the cumin, turmeric, cayenne or
chilli, 2.5ml/½ tsp salt, 2.5ml/½ tsp
pepper, the gram flour, baking powder
and couscous to the mixture and
combine. The mixture should form a
thick batter. If it seems too thick, add
a spoonful of soaking water and if it is
too watery, add a little more flour or
couscous. Mix in the onions.

3 Heat the oil in a wide, deep frying
pan, to a depth of about 5cm/2in, until
it is hot enough to brown a cube of
bread in 30 seconds. Using two spoons,
form the mixture into bitesize balls and
slip each one gently into the hot
oil. Cook until golden brown on the
underside, then turn and cook the
second side until golden brown.

4 Remove the fritters from the hot oil
with a slotted spoon and drain well on
kitchen paper. Transfer the fritters to
a baking sheet and keep warm in the
oven until all the mixture is cooked.
Serve hot or at room temperature with
lemon wedges.

Energy 291kcal/1226kJ; Protein 16.5g; Carbohydrate 38.8g, of which sugars 4.6g; Fat 8.6g, of which saturates 1g; Cholesterol 0mg; Calcium 115mg; Fibre 4g; Sodium 33mg.

LENTIL DHAL

THIS SPICY LENTIL DHAL MAKES A SUSTAINING AND COMFORTING MEAL WHEN SERVED WITH RICE OR INDIAN BREADS AND ANY DRY-SPICED DISH, PARTICULARLY A CAULIFLOWER OR POTATO DISH.

SERVES FOUR TO SIX

INGREDIENTS
40g/1½oz/3 tbsp butter or ghee
1 onion, chopped
2 green chillies, seeded and chopped
15ml/1 tbsp chopped fresh
   root ginger
225g/8oz/1 cup yellow or red lentils
900ml/1½ pints/3¾ cups water
45ml/3 tbsp roasted garlic purée
5ml/1 tsp ground cumin
5ml/1 tsp ground coriander
200g/7oz tomatoes, peeled and diced
a little lemon juice
salt and ground black pepper
30–45ml/3–4 tbsp coriander
   (cilantro) sprigs, and fried onion
   and garlic slices, to garnish
For the whole spice mix
30ml/2 tbsp groundnut (peanut) oil
4–5 shallots, sliced
2 garlic cloves, thinly sliced
15g/½oz/1 tbsp butter or ghee
5ml/1 tsp cumin seeds
5ml/1 tsp mustard seeds
3–4 small dried red chillies
8–10 fresh curry leaves

1 Melt the butter or ghee in a large pan and cook the onion, chillies and ginger for 10 minutes, until golden.

2 Stir in the lentils and water. Bring to the boil, reduce the heat and part-cover the pan. Simmer, stirring occasionally, for 50–60 minutes, until soup-like.

3 Stir in the roasted garlic purée, cumin and ground coriander, then season with salt and pepper to taste. Cook for a further 10–15 minutes, uncovered, stirring frequently.

4 Stir in the tomatoes and then adjust the seasoning, adding a little lemon juice to taste.

5 To make the whole spice mix, heat the oil in a small, heavy pan. Add the shallots and fry over a medium heat, stirring occasionally, until crisp and browned. Add the garlic and cook, stirring frequently, until the garlic colours slightly. Use a draining spoon to remove the shallot mixture from the pan and set aside.

6 Melt the butter or ghee in the same pan. Add the cumin and mustard seeds and fry until the mustard seeds pop. Stir in the chillies, curry leaves and shallot mixture, then swirl the mixture into the cooked dhal. Garnish with coriander, onions and garlic, and serve.

Energy 262kcal/1095kJ; Protein 10.3g; Carbohydrate 26.9g, of which sugars 4.6g; Fat 13.3g, of which saturates 6.2g; Cholesterol 23mg; Calcium 36mg; Fibre 3.1g; Sodium 84mg.

CREAMY LEMON PUY LENTILS

TINY, GREEN PUY LENTILS HAVE A GOOD NUTTY FLAVOUR AND, COMBINED WITH LEMON JUICE AND CRÈME FRAÎCHE, MAKE A DELICIOUS, SLIGHTLY TANGY BASE FOR POACHED EGGS.

SERVES FOUR

INGREDIENTS
250g/9oz/generous 1 cup Puy lentils
1 bay leaf
30ml/2 tbsp olive oil
4 spring onions (scallions), sliced
2 large garlic cloves, chopped
15ml/1 tbsp Dijon mustard
finely grated rind and juice of
    1 large lemon
4 plum tomatoes, seeded and diced
4 eggs
60ml/4 tbsp crème fraîche
salt and ground black pepper
30ml/2 tbsp chopped fresh flat leaf
    parsley, to garnish

1 Put the lentils and bay leaf in a pan, cover with cold water, and bring to the boil. Reduce the heat and simmer, partially covered, for 25 minutes or until the lentils are tender. Stir the lentils occasionally and add more water, if necessary. Drain.

2 Heat the oil and fry the spring onions and garlic over a medium heat for 1 minute or until softened.

3 Add the Dijon mustard, lemon rind and juice, and mix well. Stir in the tomatoes and seasoning, then cook gently for 1–2 minutes until the tomatoes are heated through but still retain their shape. Add a little water if the mixture becomes too dry.

4 Meanwhile, poach the eggs in a pan of barely simmering salted water. Add the lentils and crème fraîche to the tomato mixture, remove the bay leaf, and heat through for 1 minute. Top each portion with a poached egg, and sprinkle with parsley.

VARIATION
Green lentils can be used instead of the Puy lentils used in this recipe. The canned variety speed up the cooking time and just need heating through.

Energy 398kcal/1671kJ; Protein 22.4g; Carbohydrate 39g, of which sugars 5.2g; Fat 18.2g, of which saturates 6.6g; Cholesterol 207mg; Calcium 80mg; Fibre 4.2g; Sodium 106mg.

BUCKWHEAT WITH PASTA

THIS COMBINATION OF BUCKWHEAT, MUSHROOMS AND BOW-SHAPED PASTA IS A CLASSIC DISH CALLED KASHA. TO PEOPLE WHO HAVE NOT BEEN RAISED ON BUCKWHEAT IT MAY TASTE GRAINY.

SERVES FOUR TO SIX

INGREDIENTS

25g/1oz dried well-flavoured mushrooms, such as ceps
500ml/17fl oz/2¼ cups boiling stock or water
45ml/3 tbsp vegetable oil or 40g/1½oz/3 tbsp butter
3–4 onions, thinly sliced
250g/9oz mushrooms, sliced
300g/11oz/1½ cups whole, coarse, medium or fine buckwheat
200g/7oz pasta bows
salt and ground black pepper

3 In a large, heavy frying pan, toast the buckwheat over a high heat for 2–3 minutes, stirring. Reduce the heat.

4 Stir the remaining boiling stock or water and the reserved mushroom soaking liquid into the buckwheat, cover the pan, and cook for about 10 minutes until the buckwheat is just tender and the liquid has been absorbed.

5 Meanwhile, cook the pasta in a large pan of salted boiling water as directed on the packet, or until just tender, then drain.

6 When the kasha is cooked, toss in the onions and mushrooms, and the pasta. Season and serve hot.

1 Put the dried mushrooms in a bowl, pour over half the boiling stock or water and leave to stand for 20–30 minutes, until reconstituted. Remove the mushrooms from the liquid, then strain and reserve the liquid.

2 Heat the oil or butter in a frying pan, add the onions and fry for 5–10 minutes until softened and beginning to brown. Remove the onions to a plate, then add the sliced mushrooms to the pan and fry briefly. Add the soaked mushrooms and cook for 2–3 minutes. Return the onions to the pan and set aside.

VARIATION
To cook kasha without mushrooms, omit both kinds and simply add all of the boiling stock in step 4.

Energy 364kcal/1529kJ; Protein 10.3g; Carbohydrate 67g, of which sugars 4g; Fat 7.3g, of which saturates 3.6g; Cholesterol 14mg; Calcium 47mg; Fibre 2.2g; Sodium 48mg.

ADUKI BEAN STUFFED MUSHROOMS

FIELD MUSHROOMS HAVE A RICH FLAVOUR THAT GOES WELL WITH THIS ADUKI BEAN AND LEMON STUFFING. THE GARLICKY PINE NUT ACCOMPANIMENT HAS A SMOOTH, CREAMY CONSISTENCY.

SERVES FOUR TO SIX

INGREDIENTS

- 200g/7oz/1 cup dried or 400g/14oz/ 2 cups drained, canned aduki beans
- 45ml/3 tbsp olive oil, plus extra for brushing
- 1 onion, finely chopped
- 2 garlic cloves, crushed
- 30ml/2 tbsp chopped fresh thyme or 5ml/1 tsp dried thyme
- 8 large field (portabello) mushrooms, stalks finely chopped
- 50g/2oz/1 cup fresh wholemeal (whole-wheat) breadcrumbs
- juice of 1 lemon
- 185g/6½oz/¾ cup goat's cheese, crumbled
- salt and ground black pepper

For the pine nut tarator

- 50g/2oz/½ cup pine nuts, toasted
- 50g/2oz/1 cup cubed white bread
- 2 garlic cloves, chopped
- 200ml/7fl oz/1 cup semi-skimmed (low-fat) milk
- 45ml/3 tbsp olive oil
- 15ml/1 tbsp chopped fresh parsley, to garnish (optional)

1 If using dried beans, soak them overnight, then drain and rinse well. Place in a pan, add enough water to cover and bring to the boil. Boil rapidly for 10 minutes, then reduce the heat, cook for 30 minutes until tender, then drain. If using canned beans, rinse, drain well, then set aside.

2 Preheat the oven to 200°C/400°F/ Gas 6. Heat the oil in a large heavy frying pan, add the onion and garlic and sauté for 5 minutes until softened. Add the thyme and the mushroom stalks and cook for a further 3 minutes, stirring occasionally, until tender.

3 Stir in the beans, breadcrumbs and lemon juice, season well, then cook for 2 minutes until heated through. Mash two-thirds of the beans with a fork or potato masher, leaving the remaining beans whole.

4 Brush a baking dish and the base and sides of the mushrooms with oil, then top each one with a spoonful of the bean mixture. Place the mushrooms in the dish, cover with foil and bake for 20 minutes. Remove the foil. Top each mushroom with some goat's cheese and bake for a further 15 minutes, or until the cheese is melted and bubbly and the mushrooms are tender.

5 To make the pine nut tarator, place all the ingredients in a food processor or blender and blend until smooth and creamy. Add more milk if the mixture appears too thick. Sprinkle with parsley, and serve with the stuffed mushrooms.

COOK'S TIP

When cooked, aduki beans have a slightly sweet flavour and mealy texture that blends well with herbs and strongly flavoured ingredients. They are perfect for stuffings, bean pâtés and as a base for vegetable roasts and bakes.

Energy 406kcal/1694kJ; Protein 17.5g; Carbohydrate 25.9g, of which sugars 5.9g; Fat 26.6g, of which saturates 8g; Cholesterol 31mg; Calcium 159mg; Fibre 6.1g; Sodium 573mg.

MOROCCAN BRAISED CHICKPEAS

THIS SWEET AND SPICY VEGETARIAN DISH IS A REAL TREAT. SERVE IT HOT AS A MAIN COURSE WITH RICE OR COUSCOUS OR SERVE COLD AS A SALAD, DRIZZLED WITH OLIVE OIL AND LEMON JUICE.

SERVES FOUR

INGREDIENTS

250g/9oz/1½ cups dried chickpeas, soaked overnight in cold water
30ml/2 tbsp olive oil
2 onions, cut into wedges
10ml/2 tsp ground cumin
1.5ml/¼ tsp ground turmeric
1.5ml/¼ tsp cayenne pepper
15ml/1 tbsp ground coriander
5ml/1 tsp ground cinnamon
300ml/½ pint/1¼ cups vegetable stock
2 carrots, sliced
115g/4oz/½ cup ready-to-eat dried apricots, halved
50g/2oz/scant ½ cup raisins
25g/1oz/¼ cup flaked (sliced) almonds
30ml/2 tbsp chopped fresh coriander (cilantro)
30ml/2 tbsp chopped fresh flat leaf parsley
salt and ground black pepper

1 Place the chickpeas in a pan with plenty of cold water. Bring to the boil and boil rapidly for 10 minutes, then place the chickpeas in a casserole dish, cover with lukewarm water and cover.

2 Place in an unheated oven and set the temperature to 200°C/400°F/Gas 6. Cook for 1 hour, then reduce the oven temperature to 160°C/325°/Gas 3. Cook for another hour, or until the chickpeas are tender.

3 Meanwhile, place the olive oil and onions in a frying pan and cook for about 6 minutes, or until softened. Add the cumin, turmeric, cayenne, coriander and cinnamon and cook for 2–3 minutes. Stir in the stock, carrots, apricots, raisins and almonds and bring to the boil.

4 Drain the chickpeas, add the spicy vegetable mixture and stir. Cover and return to the oven for 30 minutes.

5 Season with salt and pepper, lightly stir in half the fresh coriander and parsley and serve sprinkled with the remainder.

Energy 380kcal/1601kJ; Protein 16.6g; Carbohydrate 52.9g, of which sugars 23.2g; Fat 12.8g, of which saturates 1.4g; Cholesterol 0mg; Calcium 173mg; Fibre 10.4g; Sodium 47mg.

CHICKPEA RISSOLES

THESE CHICKPEA RISSOLES ARE CHEAP TO MAKE, VERY APPETIZING AND CAN BE SERVED SOLO WITH DRINKS OR THEY CAN FORM PART OF A LARGER MEZE TABLE. RADISHES, ROCKET AND OLIVES ARE TRADITIONAL ACCOMPANIMENTS.

SERVES FOUR

INGREDIENTS

300g/11oz/scant 1½ cups chickpeas, soaked overnight in water to cover
105ml/7 tbsp extra virgin olive oil
2 large onions, chopped
15ml/1 tbsp ground cumin
2 garlic cloves, crushed
3–4 fresh sage leaves, chopped
45ml/3 tbsp chopped flat leaf parsley
1 large (US extra large) egg, lightly beaten
45ml/3 tbsp self-raising (self-rising) flour
50g/2oz/½ cup plain (all-purpose) flour
salt and ground black pepper
radishes, rocket (arugula) and olives, to serve

1 Drain the chickpeas, rinse them under cold water and drain again. Tip them into a large pan, cover with plenty of fresh cold water and bring them to the boil. Skim the froth from the surface of the water with a slotted spoon until the liquid is clear.

2 Cover the pan and cook for 1¼–1½ hours, or until the chickpeas are very soft. Alternatively (and this is the better method) cook them in a pressure cooker under full pressure for 20–25 minutes. Once the chickpeas are soft, set aside a few tablespoons of the liquid from the chickpeas, then strain them, discarding the rest of the liquid. Tip the chickpeas into a food processor, add 30–45ml/2–3 tbsp of the reserved liquid and process to a velvety mash.

3 Heat 45ml/3 tbsp of the olive oil in a large frying pan, add the onions and sauté until they are light golden. Add the cumin and the garlic and stir for a few seconds until their aroma rises. Stir in the chopped sage leaves and the parsley, and set aside.

4 Scrape the chickpea mash into a large bowl and add the egg, the self-raising flour and the fried onion and herb mixture. Add plenty of salt and pepper, and mix well.

5 Take large walnut-size pieces of the mixture and flatten them so that they look like thick, round mini-burgers.Coat the rissoles lightly in the plain flour. Heat the remaining olive oil in a frying pan and fry the rissoles in batches until they are crisp and golden on both sides. Drain on kitchen paper and serve hot with the radishes, rocket and olives.

COOK'S TIP
Wet your hands slightly when shaping the mixture, as this helps to prevent the mixture from sticking to them.

Energy 552kcal/2312kJ; Protein 21.3g; Carbohydrate 63.7g, of which sugars 8.2g; Fat 25.3g, of which saturates 3.6g; Cholesterol 48mg; Calcium 234mg; Fibre 10.8g; Sodium 95mg.

BARLEY RISOTTO <u>WITH</u> ROASTED SQUASH

THIS RISOTTO IS MORE LIKE A PILAFF, MADE WITH SLIGHTLY CHEWY, NUTTY-FLAVOURED PEARL BARLEY, THAN A CLASSIC ITALIAN RISOTTO THAT IS MADE WITH RICE. SWEET LEEKS AND ROASTED SQUASH ARE SUPERB WITH THIS EARTHY GRAIN.

SERVES FOUR TO FIVE

INGREDIENTS
200g/7oz/1 cup pearl barley
1 butternut squash, peeled, seeded
  and cut into chunks
10ml/2 tsp chopped fresh thyme
60ml/4 tbsp olive oil
25g/1oz/2 tbsp butter
4 leeks, cut into fairly thick
  diagonal slices
2 garlic cloves, finely chopped
175g/6oz chestnut mushrooms, sliced
2 carrots, coarsely grated
about 120ml/4fl oz/½ cup
  vegetable stock
30ml/2 tbsp chopped fresh flat
  leaf parsley
50g/2oz Pecorino cheese, grated
  or shaved
45ml/3 tbsp pumpkin seeds, toasted,
  or chopped walnuts
salt and ground black pepper

1 Rinse the barley, then cook it in simmering water, keeping the pan part-covered, for 35–45 minutes, or until tender. Drain. Preheat the oven to 200°C/400°F/Gas 6.

2 Place the squash in a roasting pan with half the thyme. Season with pepper and toss with half the oil. Roast, stirring once, for 30–35 minutes, until tender and beginning to brown.

3 Heat half the butter with the remaining oil in a large pan. Cook the leeks and garlic gently for 5 minutes.

4 Add the mushrooms and remaining thyme, then cook until the liquid from the mushrooms evaporates and they begin to fry.

5 Stir in the carrots and cook for 2 minutes, then add the barley and most of the stock. Season well and part-cover the pan. Cook for a further 5 minutes. Pour in the remaining stock if the mixture seems dry.

6 Stir in the parsley, the remaining butter and half the Pecorino, then stir in the squash. Add seasoning to taste and serve immediately, sprinkled with the toasted pumpkin seeds or walnuts and the remaining Pecorino.

Energy 409kcal/1713kJ; Protein 11.8g; Carbohydrate 43.4g, of which sugars 7.1g; Fat 22.1g, of which saturates 6.6g; Cholesterol 21mg; Calcium 249mg; Fibre 4.9g; Sodium 159mg

EGG AND LENTIL CURRY

EGGS ARE AN EXCELLENT ADDITION TO VEGETARIAN CURRIES AND, COMBINED WITH LENTILS, MAKE A SUBSTANTIAL AND EXTREMELY TASTY DISH. NUTRITIONALLY, EGGS AND LENTILS ARE AN EXCELLENT SOURCE OF PROTEIN AS WELL AS VITAMINS AND MINERALS.

SERVES FOUR

INGREDIENTS

75g/3oz/½ cup green lentils
750ml/1¼ pints/3 cups vegetable
 stock
6 eggs
30ml/2 tbsp oil
3 cloves
1.5ml/¼ tsp black peppercorns
1 onion, finely chopped
2 green chillies, finely chopped
2 garlic cloves, crushed
2.5cm/1in piece of fresh root ginger,
 peeled and chopped
30ml/2 tbsp curry paste
400g/14oz can chopped tomatoes
2.5ml/½ tsp sugar
2.5ml/½ tsp garam masala

1 Wash the lentils thoroughly under cold running water, checking for small stones. Put the lentils in a large, heavy pan with the vegetable stock. Cover and simmer gently for about 15 minutes or until the lentils are soft. Drain and set aside.

2 Cook the eggs in boiling water for 10 minutes. Remove from the boiling water and set aside to cool slightly. When cool enough to handle, peel and cut in half lengthways.

3 Heat the oil in a large frying pan and fry the cloves and peppercorns for about 2 minutes. Add the onion, chillies, garlic and ginger, and fry the mixture for a further 5–6 minutes, stirring frequently.

4 Stir in the curry paste and fry for a further 2 minutes, stirring constantly.

5 Add the chopped tomatoes and sugar and stir in 175ml/6fl oz/¾ cup water. Simmer for about 5 minutes until the sauce thickens, stirring occasionally. Add the boiled eggs, drained lentils and garam masala. Cover and simmer for a further 10 minutes, then serve.

COOK'S TIP
You can substitute red lentils for the green if liked. Red lentils tend to disintegrate more when cooking, which will give a smoother curry.

Energy 258kcal/1081kJ; Protein 15.3g; Carbohydrate 17g, of which sugars 4.9g; Fat 15.1g, of which saturates 3.3g; Cholesterol 285mg; Calcium 103mg; Fibre 3.6g; Sodium 149mg.

PUMPKIN AND PISTACHIO RISOTTO

VEGETARIANS TIRED OF THE STANDARD DINNER PARTY FARE WILL LOVE THIS ELEGANT COMBINATION
OF CREAMY, GOLDEN RICE AND ORANGE PUMPKIN, AND SO WILL EVERYONE ELSE. IT LOOKS
PARTICULARLY IMPRESSIVE SERVED IN THE HOLLOWED-OUT PUMPKIN SHELL.

SERVES FOUR

INGREDIENTS

1.2 litres/2 pints/5 cups vegetable
  stock or water
generous pinch of saffron threads
30ml/2 tbsp olive oil
1 onion, chopped
2 garlic cloves, crushed
900g/2lb pumpkin, peeled, seeded
  and cut into 2cm/¾in cubes (about
  7 cups)
400g/14oz/2 cups risotto rice
200ml/7fl oz/scant 1 cup dry
  white wine
30ml/2 tbsp freshly grated Parmesan
  cheese
50g/2oz/½ cup pistachio nuts,
  coarsely chopped
45ml/3 tbsp chopped fresh marjoram
  or oregano, plus leaves to garnish
salt, freshly grated nutmeg and
  ground black pepper

1 Bring the stock or water to the boil
and reduce to a low simmer. Ladle a
little of it into a small bowl. Add the
saffron threads and leave to infuse.

2 Heat the oil in a large, heavy pan or
deep frying pan. Add the onion and
garlic and cook gently for about
5 minutes until softened. Add the
pumpkin and rice, and stir to coat
everything in oil. Cook for a few more
minutes until the rice looks transparent.

3 Pour in the wine and allow it to
bubble hard. When it has been
absorbed, add a quarter of the hot
stock or water and the saffron liquid.
Stir until all the liquid has been
absorbed. Gradually add the remaining
stock or water, a little at a time, allowing
the rice to absorb the liquid before
adding more, and stirring constantly.
After 20–30 minutes the rice should be
golden yellow, creamy and *al dente*.

4 Stir in the Parmesan cheese, cover
the pan and leave the risotto to stand
for 5 minutes. To finish, stir in the
pistachio nuts and marjoram or
oregano. Season to taste with a little
salt, nutmeg and pepper, scatter
over a few marjoram or oregano leaves
and serve.

Energy 585kcal/2441kJ; Protein 14.4g; Carbohydrate 87.3g, of which sugars 5.7g; Fat 15.9g, of which saturates 3.5g; Cholesterol 8mg; Calcium 196mg; Fibre 3.2g; Sodium 151mg.

TOFU AND GREEN BEAN CURRY

BEANCURD, ALSO KNOWN AS TOFU, IS AVAILABLE FROM SUPERMARKETS. IT HAS A SILKY APPEARANCE,
SOFT TEXTURE AND MILD FLAVOUR THAT BENEFITS FROM BEING COMBINED WITH STRONGER FLAVOURS.

SERVES FOUR TO SIX

INGREDIENTS

600ml/1 pint/2½ cups coconut milk
15ml/1 tbsp red curry paste
45ml/3 tbsp Thai fish sauce
10ml/2 tsp palm sugar (jaggery) or
  soft light brown sugar
225g/8oz button (white) mushrooms
115g/4oz green beans, trimmed
175g/6oz tofu, rinsed and cut into
  2cm/¾in cubes
4 kaffir lime leaves, torn
2 fresh red chillies, sliced
fresh coriander (cilantro) sprigs,
  to garnish

1 Pour about one-third of the coconut milk into a wok or large pan. Cook until an oily sheen appears on the surface.

2 Add the red curry paste, fish sauce and sugar to the coconut milk. Mix together thoroughly.

3 Add the button mushrooms. Stir well and cook over a medium heat for about 1 minute. Stir in the rest of the coconut milk and bring back to the boil.

4 Add the green beans and cubes of tofu and allow to simmer gently for another 4–5 minutes.

5 Stir in the kaffir lime leaves and red chillies. Serve garnished with the fresh coriander sprigs.

Energy 63kcal/265kJ; Protein 3.9g; Carbohydrate 8.2g, of which sugars 7.8g; Fat 1.8g, of which saturates 0.4g; Cholesterol 0mg; Calcium 189mg; Fibre 0.8g; Sodium 647mg.

KENYAN MUNG BEAN STEW

THE LOCAL NAME FOR THIS VEGETARIAN STEW IS DENGU. IT IS A GOOD EXAMPLE OF HOW AFRICAN COOKS ADD VARIETY AND NUTRITION TO A DIET THAT DEPENDS LARGELY ON SEASONAL PRODUCE.

SERVES FOUR

INGREDIENTS
225g/8oz/1¼ cups mung beans,
    soaked overnight
25g/1oz/2 tbsp ghee or butter
2 garlic cloves, crushed
1 red onion, chopped
30ml/2 tbsp tomato purée (paste)
½ green (bell) pepper, seeded and
    cut into small cubes
½ red (bell) pepper, seeded and cut
    into small cubes
1 fresh green chilli, seeded and
    finely chopped
300ml/½ pint/1¼ cups water

1 Put the mung beans in a large pan, cover with water, bring to the boil and boil until the beans are very soft and the water has evaporated. Remove the pan from the heat and mash the beans with a fork or potato masher until smooth. Set aside.

2 Heat the ghee or butter in a separate pan, add the garlic and onion and fry for 4–5 minutes, until golden. Add the tomato purée and cook for a further 2–3 minutes, stirring all the time.

3 Stir in the mashed beans, then add the green and red peppers and chilli.

COOK'S TIP
Mung beans can be found in most Asian shops and larger supermarkets. If unavailable, use whole green lentils.

4 Add the water, stirring well to mix all the ingredients together.

5 Pour the mixture into a clean pan and simmer for about 10 minutes, then spoon into a serving dish and serve immediately.

Energy 229kcal/965kJ; Protein 14.5g; Carbohydrate 31.1g, of which sugars 5.5g; Fat 6g, of which saturates 3.5g; Cholesterol 13mg; Calcium 61mg; Fibre 6.8g; Sodium 65mg.

TERIYAKI SOBA NOODLES

TERIYAKI SAUCE IS EASY TO PREPARE AT HOME USING INGREDIENTS THAT ARE EASY TO FIND. JAPANESE SOBA NOODLES ARE MADE FROM BUCKWHEAT FLOUR, WHICH GIVES THEM A UNIQUE TEXTURE AND COLOUR.

3 Meanwhile, heat the groundnut or vegetable oil in a wok or large frying pan until very hot. Add the tofu and fry for 8–10 minutes until golden, turning it occasionally to crisp all sides. Carefully remove from the wok or pan and leave to drain on kitchen paper. Cut the tofu into 1cm/½in slices with a sharp knife.

4 To prepare the teriyaki sauce, mix the soy sauce, sake or dry sherry, mirin and sugar together, then heat the mixture in the wok or frying pan.

5 Toss in the noodles and stir to coat them in the sauce. Heat through for 1–2 minutes, then spoon into warmed individual serving bowls with the tofu and asparagus. Scatter the spring onions and carrot on top and sprinkle with the chilli flakes and sesame seeds. Serve immediately.

SERVES FOUR

INGREDIENTS
350g/12oz soba noodles
30ml/2 tbsp toasted sesame oil
200g/7oz/½ bunch asparagus tips
30ml/2 tbsp groundnut (peanut) or
   vegetable oil
225g/8oz tofu
2 spring onions (scallions), cut into
   thin strips
1 carrot, cut into matchstick strips
2.5ml/½ tsp chilli flakes
15ml/1 tbsp sesame seeds
For the teriyaki sauce
60ml/4 tbsp dark soy sauce
60ml/4 tbsp Japanese sake or
   dry sherry
60ml/4 tbsp mirin
5ml/1 tsp caster (superfine) sugar

1 Cook the noodles according to the instructions on the packet, then drain and rinse well under cold running water. Set aside.

2 Heat the sesame oil in a griddle pan or in a baking tray placed under the grill until very hot. Turn down the heat to medium, then cook the asparagus for 8–10 minutes, turning frequently, until tender and browned. Set aside.

VARIATION
Use rice or cellophane (mung bean) noodles instead of soba noodles, if you wish.

Energy 609kcal/2551kJ; Protein 16.6g; Carbohydrate 71.4g, of which sugars 6.5g; Fat 28.7g, of which saturates 3.5g; Cholesterol 0mg; Calcium 331mg; Fibre 4.1g; Sodium 13mg.

VEGETABLE GADO-GADO

A DELICIOUS COMBINATION OF EGG NOODLES, FRUIT AND VEGETABLES ARE SERVED WITH A SPICY PEANUT SAUCE IN THIS EXOTIC DISH. SERVE ON A BANANA LEAF FOR SPECIAL OCCASIONS.

SERVES SIX

INGREDIENTS
½ cucumber
2 pears (not too ripe) or 175g/6oz
  wedge of yam bean
1–2 eating apples
juice of ½ lemon
mixed salad leaves
6 small tomatoes, cut in wedges
3 slices fresh pineapple, cored and
  cut in wedges
3 eggs, hard boiled and shelled
175g/6oz egg noodles, cooked,
  cooled and chopped
deep-fried onions
For the peanut sauce
2–4 fresh red chillies, seeded
  and ground, or 15ml/1 tbsp
  chilli sambal
300ml/½ pint/1¼ cups
  coconut milk
350g/12oz/1¼ cups crunchy
  peanut butter
15ml/1 tbsp dark soy sauce or dark
  brown sugar
5ml/1 tsp tamarind pulp, soaked in
  45ml/3 tbsp warm water
coarsely crushed peanuts
salt

2 Simmer gently until the sauce thickens, then stir in the soy sauce or sugar. Strain in the juice from the soaked tamarind, add salt to taste and stir well. Spoon into a bowl and sprinkle with a few coarsely crushed peanuts.

VARIATION
Quail's eggs can be used instead of normal eggs and look very attractive in this dish. Hard boil for 3 minutes and halve or leave whole.

3 To make the salad, core the cucumber and peel the pears or yam bean. Cut them into matchsticks. Finely shred the apples and sprinkle them with the lemon juice. Spread a bed of salad leaves on a flat platter, then pile all the fruit and vegetables on top.

4 Add the sliced or quartered hard-boiled eggs, the chopped noodles and the deep-fried onions. Serve at once, with the sauce.

1 Make the peanut sauce. Put the ground chillies or chilli sambal in a pan. Pour in the coconut milk, then stir in the peanut butter. Heat gently, stirring, until well blended.

Energy 577kcal/2411kJ; Protein 21.2g; Carbohydrate 46.3g, of which sugars 21g; Fat 35.5g, of which saturates 8.4g; Cholesterol 95mg; Calcium 88mg; Fibre 6.8g; Sodium 482mg.

VEGETABLE AND EGG NOODLE RIBBONS

SERVE THIS ELEGANT, COLOURFUL NOODLE DISH WITH A TOSSED GREEN SALAD AS A LIGHT LUNCH OR AS A STARTER FOR SIX TO EIGHT PEOPLE.

SERVES FOUR

INGREDIENTS
1 large carrot, peeled
2 courgettes (zucchini)
50g/2oz/4 tbsp butter
15ml/1 tbsp olive oil
6 fresh shiitake mushrooms,
  finely sliced
50g/2oz/½ cup frozen peas, thawed
350g/12oz thick egg noodles
10ml/2 tsp chopped mixed fresh
  herbs such as marjoram, chives
  and basil
salt and ground black pepper
25g/1oz Parmesan cheese, to serve
  (optional)

1 Slice thin strips from the carrot and from the courgettes.

2 Heat the butter with the olive oil in a frying pan. Stir in the carrots and mushrooms; fry for 2 minutes. Add the courgettes and peas and stir-fry until the courgettes are cooked. Season.

3 Meanwhile, cook the noodles in a large pan of boiling water. Drain and tip them into a bowl. Add the vegetables and toss to mix.

4 Sprinkle over the mixed herbs and season to taste. If using the Parmesan cheese, grate it over the top.

Energy 496kcal/2082kJ; Protein 13.5g; Carbohydrate 67.7g, of which sugars 5.2g; Fat 20.9g, of which saturates 9.1g; Cholesterol 53mg; Calcium 56mg; Fibre 4.7g; Sodium 242mg.

BUCKWHEAT NOODLES WITH GOAT'S CHEESE

WHEN YOU DON'T FEEL LIKE DOING A LOT OF COOKING, TRY THIS GOOD FAST SUPPER DISH. THE EARTHY FLAVOUR OF BUCKWHEAT GOES WELL WITH THE NUTTY, PEPPERY TASTE OF ROCKET LEAVES, OFFSET BY THE DELICIOUSLY CREAMY GOAT'S CHEESE.

SERVES FOUR

INGREDIENTS
350g/12oz buckwheat noodles
50g/2oz/4 tbsp butter
2 garlic cloves, finely chopped
4 shallots, sliced
75g/3oz/1½ cups hazelnuts, lightly
  roasted and roughly chopped
large handful rocket (arugula) leaves
175g/6oz goat's cheese
salt and ground black pepper

1 Cook the noodles in a large pan of boiling water until just tender. Drain well.

3 Add the hazelnuts and fry for about 1 minute. Add the rocket leaves and, when they start to wilt, toss in the noodles and heat through.

4 Season with salt and pepper. Crumble in the goat's cheese and serve immediately.

COOK'S TIP
Long pasta, such as spaghetti, linguine or tagliatelle, would also work well in this recipe.

2 Heat the butter in a large frying pan. Add the garlic and shallots and cook for 2–3 minutes, stirring all the time, until the shallots are soft.

Energy 700kcal/2930kJ; Protein 22.4g; Carbohydrate 69.4g, of which sugars 4.2g; Fat 38.9g, of which saturates 15.2g; Cholesterol 67mg; Calcium 111mg; Fibre 4g; Sodium 342mg.

POULTRY
AND MEAT

*Pulses, legumes and grains were traditionally
used to eke out a small quantity of meat or
poultry in a dish, which may have been
expensive or in short supply. Many recipes
in this chapter have become, over the years,
long-standing classic favourites, such as Boston
Baked Beans, French Cassoulet and the
Tex-Mex dish, Chilli Con Carne.*

CHICKEN AND SPLIT PEA KORESH

A TRADITIONAL PERSIAN KORESH — A THICK SAUCY STEW SERVED WITH RICE — IS USUALLY MADE WITH LAMB, BUT HERE CHICKEN IS USED TO CREATE A LIGHTER, LOWER-FAT DISH.

SERVES FOUR

INGREDIENTS
50g/2oz/¼ cup green split peas
45ml/3 tbsp olive oil
1 large onion, finely chopped
450g/1lb boneless chicken thighs
600ml/1 pint/2½ cups boiling
  chicken stock
5ml/1 tsp ground turmeric
2.5ml/½ tsp ground cinnamon
1.5ml/¼ tsp freshly grated nutmeg
30ml/2 tbsp dried mint
2 aubergines (eggplants), diced
8 ripe tomatoes, diced
2 garlic cloves, crushed
salt and ground black pepper
fresh mint, to garnish
plain boiled rice, to serve

1 Put the split peas in a large bowl. Pour in cold water to cover and leave to soak for at least 6 hours or overnight.

2 Tip the split peas into a sieve (strainer) and drain well. Place in a large pan, cover with fresh cold water and bring to the boil. Boil rapidly for 10 minutes, then rinse, drain and set aside.

3 Heat 15ml/1 tbsp of the oil in a large flameproof casserole. Add the onion and cook for about 5 minutes. Add the chicken and cook until golden on all sides. Add the split peas, hot chicken stock, turmeric, cinnamon, nutmeg and mint.

4 Bring to the boil, reduce the heat so that the liquid simmers gently, and cover the casserole. Cook for 40 minutes, until the chicken is cooked and the split peas are tender.

5 Meanwhile, heat the remaining 30ml/2 tbsp of oil in a frying pan, add the diced aubergines and cook for about 5 minutes until lightly browned. Add the tomatoes and garlic and cook for a further 2 minutes, stirring.

6 Add the aubergine mixture to the chicken with some seasoning. Mix lightly and cook for 10 minutes, or until the split peas are tender. Sprinkle with fresh mint leaves to garnish and serve with plain boiled rice.

Energy 313kcal/1313kJ; Protein 29.7g; Carbohydrate 21.4g, of which sugars 12.7g; Fat 12.7g, of which saturates 2.4g; Cholesterol 118mg; Calcium 57mg; Fibre 5.7g; Sodium 128mg.

CHICKEN WITH CHICKPEAS AND ALMONDS

THE ALMONDS IN THIS TASTY MOROCCAN-STYLE RECIPE ARE PRE-COOKED, ADDING AN INTERESTING TEXTURE AND FLAVOUR TO THE CHICKEN.

SERVES FOUR

INGREDIENTS
75g/3oz/½ cup blanched almonds
75g/3oz/½ cup chickpeas, soaked overnight and drained
4 part-boned chicken breast portions, skinned
50g/2oz/4 tbsp butter
2.5ml/½ tsp saffron threads
2 Spanish (Bermuda) onions, sliced
900ml/1½ pints/3¾ cups chicken stock
1 small cinnamon stick
60ml/4 tbsp chopped fresh flat leaf parsley, plus extra to garnish
lemon juice, to taste
salt and ground black pepper

1 Place the blanched almonds and the chickpeas in a large flameproof casserole of water and bring to the boil. Boil for 10 minutes, then reduce the heat. Simmer for 1–1½ hours until the chickpeas are soft. Drain and set aside.

2 Place the skinned chicken pieces in the casserole, together with the butter, half of the saffron, and salt and plenty of black pepper. Heat gently, stirring, until the butter has melted.

3 Add the onions and stock, bring to the boil, then add the reserved cooked almonds, chickpeas and cinnamon stick. Cover with a tightly fitting lid and cook very gently for 45–60 minutes until the chicken is completely tender.

4 Transfer the chicken and chickpea mixture to a serving plate and keep warm. Bring the sauce to the boil and cook over a high heat until it is well reduced, stirring frequently.

5 Add the chopped parsley and remaining saffron to the casserole and cook for a further 2–3 minutes. Sharpen the sauce with a little lemon juice, then pour the sauce over the chicken and serve, garnished with extra fresh parsley.

Energy 431kcal/1803kJ; Protein 44.4g; Carbohydrate 11g, of which sugars 1.6g; Fat 23.6g, of which saturates 7.9g; Cholesterol 132mg; Calcium 110mg; Fibre 4g; Sodium 180mg.

MUSHROOM-PICKER'S CHICKEN PAELLA

A GOOD PAELLA IS BASED ON A FEW WELL CHOSEN INGREDIENTS, PARTICULARLY THE RIGHT TYPE OF RICE. HERE, WILD MUSHROOMS COMBINE WITH CHICKEN AND VEGETABLES.

SERVES FOUR

INGREDIENTS
- 45ml/3 tbsp olive oil
- 1 onion, chopped
- 1 small fennel bulb, sliced
- 225g/8oz assorted wild and cultivated mushrooms
- 1 garlic clove, crushed
- 3 chicken legs, chopped in half through the bone
- 350g/12oz/1⅔ cups paella rice
- 900ml/1½ pints/3¾ cups boiling chicken stock
- 1 pinch saffron threads or 1 sachet saffron powder
- 1 thyme sprig
- 400g/14oz can butter (lima) beans, drained
- 75g/3oz/¾ cup frozen peas

1 Heat the olive oil in a large frying pan or paella pan.

2 Add the onion and fennel, and fry over a gentle heat for 3–4 minutes.

3 Add the mushrooms and garlic, and cook until the juices begin to run, then increase the heat to evaporate the juices. Push the onion and mushrooms to one side. Add the chicken and cook, turning often, until half cooked. If necessary, remove the mushroom mixture and return it to the pan when the chicken is part cooked.

4 Stir in the rice, add the stock, saffron, thyme, butter beans and peas. Bring to a simmer and then cook gently for 15 minutes without stirring.

5 Remove from the heat and cover with a circle of baking parchment and a clean dish towel. Allow the paella to finish cooking in its own heat for about 5 minutes.

Energy 581kcal/2430kJ; Protein 30.9g; Carbohydrate 87.2g, of which sugars 3.2g; Fat 12g, of which saturates 2g; Cholesterol 79mg; Calcium 59mg; Fibre 7.4g; Sodium 496mg.

BALTI CHICKEN <u>WITH</u> SPLIT PEAS

THIS IS RATHER AN UNUSUAL COMBINATION OF FLAVOURS AND TEXTURES BUT IT WORKS NEVERTHELESS. THE MANGO POWDER GIVES A DELICIOUS TANGY FLAVOUR TO THIS SPICY DISH.

SERVES FOUR TO SIX

INGREDIENTS

75g/3oz/½ cup yellow split peas
60ml/4 tbsp corn oil
2 leeks, chopped
6 large dried red chillies
4 curry leaves
5ml/1 tsp mustard seeds
10ml/2 tsp mango powder
2 tomatoes, chopped
2.5ml/½ tsp chilli powder
5ml/1 tsp ground coriander
5ml/1 tsp salt
450g/1lb/3¼ cups skinless, boneless chicken, cubed
1 tbsp chopped fresh coriander (cilantro)

1 Soak the split peas overnight. Drain and wash them. Remove any stones.

2 Put the split peas into a pan with enough water to cover, and boil for about 45 minutes, until they are soft but not mushy. Drain and set to one side in a bowl.

3 Heat the oil in a deep frying pan, balti pan or skillet. Lower the heat slightly and add the leeks, dried red chillies, curry leaves and mustard seeds. Stir-fry gently for a few minutes.

4 Add the mango powder, tomatoes, chilli powder, ground coriander, salt and chicken, and stir-fry for 7–10 minutes.

5 Mix in the cooked split peas and fry for a further 2 minutes, or until you are sure that the chicken is cooked right through.

6 Garnish with fresh coriander.

Energy 196kcal/822kJ; Protein 20.3g; Carbohydrate 9.8g, of which sugars 2.6g; Fat 8.7g, of which saturates 1.2g; Cholesterol 47mg; Calcium 41mg; Fibre 2.5g; Sodium 51mg.

SLOW-COOKER BOSTON BAKED BEANS

THE SLOW COOKER WAS ACTUALLY INVENTED FOR MAKING BAKED BEANS. MOLASSES GIVES THE BEANS A VERY RICH FLAVOUR AND DARK COLOUR, BUT YOU CAN REPLACE IT WITH MAPLE SYRUP IF YOU PREFER.

SERVES EIGHT

INGREDIENTS
450g/1lb/2½ cups dried haricot
   (navy) beans
4 whole cloves
2 onions, peeled
1 bay leaf
90ml/6 tbsp tomato ketchup
30ml/2 tbsp molasses
30ml/2 tbsp dark brown sugar
15ml/1 tbsp Dijon-style mustard
475ml/16fl oz/2 cups unsalted
   vegetable stock
225g/8oz piece of salt pork
salt and ground black pepper

1 Rinse the beans, then place in a large bowl. Cover with cold water and leave to soak for at least 8 hours or overnight.

2 Drain and rinse the beans. Place them in a large pan, cover with plenty of cold water and bring to the boil. Boil gently for about 10 minutes, then drain and tip into the dish for the slow cooker.

3 Stick 2 cloves in each of the onions. Add them to the pot with the bay leaf, burying them in the beans.

4 In a bowl, blend together the ketchup, molasses, sugar, mustard and stock, and pour over the beans. Add more stock, or water, if necessary, so that the beans are almost covered with liquid. Cover with the lid and switch the slow cooker to low. Cook for 2–3 hours.

5 Towards the end of the cooking time, place the salt pork in a pan of boiling water and cook for 3 minutes.

6 Using a sharp knife, score the pork rind in deep 1.5cm/½in cuts. Add the salt pork to the cooking pot, pushing it down just below the surface of the beans, skin side up. Cover the pot with the lid and cook for a further 2–3 hours, until the pork and beans are tender.

7 Remove the pork from the beans and set aside until cool enough to handle, Using a sharp knife, slice off the rind and fat and finely slice the meat.

8 Using a spoon, skim off any fat from the top of the beans, then stir in the pieces of meat. Taste before adding salt and black pepper, and serve hot.

COOK'S TIP
To cook the beans in a conventional oven, place them in a flameproof casserole. Cook at 150°C/300°F/Gas 2 for 1½–2 hours in step 4, until the beans are just tender. In step 6, cook for a further 1½–2 hours, or until both meat and beans are thoroughly cooked.

Energy 235kcal/997kJ; Protein 19.2g; Carbohydrate 37.4g, of which sugars 13g; Fat 2g, of which saturates 0.5g; Cholesterol 18mg; Calcium 92mg; Fibre 9.5g; Sodium 221mg.

PORK WITH CHICKPEAS AND ORANGE

THIS WINTER SPECIALITY IS A FAMILIAR DISH IN CRETE. ALL YOU NEED TO SERVE WITH THIS LOVELY DISH IS FRESH BREAD AND A BOWL OF BLACK OLIVES.

SERVES FOUR

INGREDIENTS

350g/12oz/1¾ cups dried chickpeas,
   soaked overnight in water to cover
75–90ml/5–6 tbsp extra virgin
   olive oil
675g/1½lb boneless leg of pork, cut
   into large cubes
1 large onion, sliced
2 garlic cloves, chopped
400g/14oz can chopped tomatoes
grated rind of 1 orange
1 small dried red chilli
salt and ground black pepper

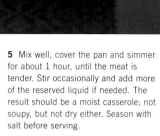

1 Drain the chickpeas, rinse them under cold water and drain them again. Place them in a large, heavy pan. Pour in enough cold water to cover generously, put a lid on the pan and bring to the boil.

2 Skim the surface, replace the lid and cook gently for 1–1½ hours, depending on the age and pedigree of the chickpeas. Alternatively, cook them in a pressure cooker for 20 minutes under full pressure. When the chickpeas are soft, drain them, reserving the cooking liquid, and set them aside.

3 Heat the olive oil in the clean pan and brown the meat cubes in batches. As each cube browns, lift it out with a slotted spoon and put it on a plate. When all the meat cubes have been browned, add the onion to the oil remaining in the pan and sauté the slices until light golden. Stir in the garlic, then as soon as it becomes aromatic, add the tomatoes and orange rind.

VARIATION
Chickpeas are used in this classic Greek dish but you could also use cannellini or haricot (navy) beans.

4 Crumble in the chilli. Return the chickpeas and meat to the pan, and pour in enough of the reserved cooking liquid to cover. Add the black pepper, but not salt at this stage.

5 Mix well, cover the pan and simmer for about 1 hour, until the meat is tender. Stir occasionally and add more of the reserved liquid if needed. The result should be a moist casserole; not soupy, but not dry either. Season with salt before serving.

Energy 645kcal/2706kJ; Protein 56.1g; Carbohydrate 50.5g, of which sugars 8.2g; Fat 25.6g, of which saturates 4.9g; Cholesterol 106mg; Calcium 171mg; Fibre 11.1g; Sodium 163mg.

PORK TENDERLOIN <u>WITH</u> SPINACH AND PUY LENTILS

LEAN PORK TENDERLOIN IS SUCCULENT AND DELICIOUS WRAPPED IN SPINACH AND COOKED ON A BED OF TINY FRENCH PUY LENTILS, FLAVOURED WITH COCONUT.

SERVES FOUR

INGREDIENTS
500–675g/1¼–1½lb pork tenderloin
15ml/1 tbsp sunflower oil
15g/½oz/1 tbsp butter
8–12 large spinach leaves
1 onion, chopped
1 garlic clove, finely chopped
2.5cm/1in piece fresh root ginger,
   finely grated
1 red chilli, finely chopped (optional)
250g/9oz/generous 1 cup Puy lentils
750ml/1¼ pints/3 cups chicken or
   vegetable stock
200ml/7fl oz/scant 1 cup
   coconut cream
salt and ground black pepper

1 Cut the pork tenderloin widthways into two equal pieces. Season well with salt and ground black pepper.

2 Heat the sunflower oil and butter in a heavy frying pan, add the pork tenderloin and cook over a high heat until browned on all sides. Remove the meat from the pan using a metal spatula and set aside.

3 Meanwhile, add the spinach leaves to a large pan of boiling water and cook for 1 minute, or until just wilted. Drain immediately in a colander and refresh under cold running water. Drain well.

4 Arrange the spinach leaves on the work surface, overlapping them to form a rectangle. Put the pork on top, wrap the leaves around the pork to enclose it.

5 Add the onion to the oil in the frying pan and cook for about 5 minutes, stirring occasionally, until softened. Add the chopped garlic, grated ginger and finely chopped chilli, if using, and fry for a further 1 minute.

6 Add the lentils to the onion mixture in the frying pan and then stir in the chicken or vegetable stock. Bring to the boil, then boil rapidly for 10 minutes.

7 Preheat the oven to 190°C/375°F/Gas 5. Remove the pan from the heat and stir in the coconut cream until well blended. Transfer the onion and lentil mixture to an ovenproof casserole and arrange the pork tenderloins on top.

8 Cover the casserole and cook in the oven for 45 minutes, or until the lentils and pork are cooked.

9 To serve, remove the spinach-wrapped pork tenderloins from the casserole using a slotted spoon or tongs and cut the pork into thick slices. Stir the lentils and spoon them, with some of the cooking juices, on to warmed, individual plates and top each portion with a few of the pork slices.

VARIATIONS
• Wrap the pork in slices of prosciutto, instead of the spinach leaves, and tie in place with string or secure with wooden cocktail sticks (toothpicks).
• Use 4 large chicken or duck breast portions in place of the pork tenderloin. Check the chicken or duck after about 30 minutes cooking time. Cut the breast portions into thick, diagonal slices to serve. The chicken would also be good wrapped with prosciutto.

Energy 410kcal/1729kJ; Protein 42.7g; Carbohydrate 34.4g, of which sugars 4.3g; Fat 12.3g, of which saturates 4.3g; Cholesterol 87mg; Calcium 93mg; Fibre 6g; Sodium 191mg.

ITALIAN PORK SAUSAGE STEW

THIS HEARTY CASSEROLE, MADE WITH SPICY SAUSAGES AND HARICOT BEANS, IS FLAVOURED WITH FRAGRANT FRESH HERBS AND DRY ITALIAN WINE. SERVE WITH ITALIAN BREAD FOR MOPPING UP THE DELICIOUS JUICES. REMEMBER TO LEAVE TIME FOR THE BEANS TO SOAK BEFORE COOKING.

3 Meanwhile, heat the oil in a pan and cook the sausages until browned all over. Transfer to the casserole and pour away all but 15ml/1 tbsp of the fat.

4 Preheat the oven to 160°C/325°F/ Gas 3. Add the onion and celery to the pan and cook gently for 5 minutes until softened but not coloured. Add the wine, rosemary and bay leaf and bring to the boil. Pour over the sausages, add the stock. Cover and cook in the oven for about 1½ hours.

SERVES FOUR

INGREDIENTS
    225g/8oz/1½ cups dried haricot
      (navy) beans
    2 sprigs fresh thyme
    30ml/2 tsp olive oil
    450g/1lb fresh Italian pork sausages
    1 onion, finely chopped
    2 sticks celery, finely diced
    300ml/½ pint/1¼ cups dry red or
      white wine, preferably Italian
    1 fresh rosemary sprig
    1 bay leaf
    300ml/½ pint/1¼ cups boiling
      vegetable stock
    200g/7oz can chopped tomatoes
    ¼ head dark green cabbage such as
      cavolo nero or Savoy, finely
      shredded
    salt and ground black pepper
    chopped fresh thyme, to garnish
    crusty Italian bread, to serve

1 Put the haricot beans in a large bowl and cover with cold water. Leave to soak for at least 8 hours, or overnight.

2 Drain the beans and place in a pan with the thyme sprigs and at least twice their volume of cold water. Bring to the boil and boil steadily for 10 minutes, then drain and place in a casserole, discarding the thyme.

5 Stir the tomatoes and cabbage into the stew. Season to taste. Cover and cook for about 30 minutes, or until the cabbage is tender. Divide among warmed plates, garnish with chopped fresh thyme and serve with crusty Italian bread.

COOK'S TIP
The stew can be made in a casserole on the hob. The sausages and onions can be browned in the casserole, then the bean mixture simmered gently for about 1¼ hours, or until tender. Softening the cabbage will take about 20 minutes.

Energy 620Kcal/2593kJ; Protein 28.4g; Carbohydrate 47.4g, of which sugars 9.9g; Fat 30.9g, of which saturates 10.8g; Cholesterol 67.5mg; Calcium 205mg; Fibre 7.6g; Sodium 1139mg.

BLACK BEAN STEW

TOLOSA IN THE BASQUE COUNTRY IS FAMOUS FOR ITS BLACK BEAN STEW MADE SPICY WITH VARIOUS SAUSAGES AND PICKLED PORK. HERE IS A SIMPLIFIED VERSION, WITH EXTRA FRESH VEGETABLES THAT ADD WONDERFULLY TO ITS FLAVOUR.

SERVES FIVE TO SIX

INGREDIENTS
    275g/10oz/1½ cups black
      beans, soaked overnight
      in cold water
    675g/1½lb boneless belly
      pork rashers (strips)
    60ml/4 tbsp olive oil
    350g/12oz baby (pearl) onions
    2 celery sticks, thickly sliced
    150g/5oz chorizo, cut into chunks
    10ml/2 tsp paprika
    600ml/1 pint/2½ cups light chicken
      or vegetable stock
    2 green (bell) peppers, seeded
      and cut into large pieces
    salt and ground black pepper

1 Drain the beans. Place in a pan and cover with fresh water. Bring to the boil and boil rapidly for 10 minutes. Drain the beans and put in an ovenproof dish.

2 Preheat the oven to 160°C/325°F/ Gas 3. Cut away any rind from the pork, then cut it into large chunks.

3 Heat the oil in a large frying pan and fry the onions and celery for 3 minutes. Add the pork and fry for 10 minutes, or until the pork is browned.

4 Add the chorizo and fry for 2 minutes, then sprinkle in the paprika. Tip the mixture into the beans and mix well to combine thoroughly.

5 Add the stock to the pan and bring to the boil, then pour over the meat and beans. Cover and bake for 1 hour.

VARIATION
This is the sort of stew to which you can add a variety of winter vegetables, such as chunks of leek, turnip and celeriac.

6 Stir the green peppers into the stew and return it to the oven for a further 15 minutes. Season and serve hot.

Energy 595kcal/2479kJ; Protein 32.5g; Carbohydrate 30.1g, of which sugars 5.2g; Fat 39g, of which saturates 11.9g; Cholesterol 102mg; Calcium 58mg; Fibre 5g; Sodium 1636mg.

PORK EMPANADA

THIS IS A FLAT, TWO-CRUST GALICIAN PIE MADE USING A CORNMEAL DOUGH. FILLINGS VARY ENORMOUSLY, AND MAY INCLUDE FISH SUCH AS SARDINES, OR SCALLOPS FOR SPECIAL OCCASIONS.

SERVES EIGHT

INGREDIENTS

75ml/5 tbsp olive oil
2 onions, chopped
4 garlic cloves, finely chopped
1kg/2¼lb boneless pork loin, diced
175g/6oz smoked gammon (smoked or cured ham) or raw ham, diced
3 red chorizo or other spicy sausages (about 300g/11oz)
3 (bell) peppers (mixed colours), seeded and chopped
175ml/6fl oz/¾ cup white wine
200g/7oz can tomatoes
pinch of saffron threads
5ml/1 tsp paprika
30ml/2 tbsp chopped fresh parsley
salt and ground black pepper
For the cornmeal dough
250g/9oz/2¼ cups cornmeal
7g/2 tsp easy-blend (rapid-rise) dried yeast
5ml/1 tsp caster (superfine) sugar
250g/9oz/2¼ cups plain (all-purpose) flour, plus extra for dusting
5ml/1 tsp salt
200ml/7fl oz/scant 1 cup warm water
30ml/2 tbsp oil
2 eggs, beaten, plus 1 for the glaze

1 Make the filling. Heat 60ml/4 tbsp oil in a frying pan and fry the onions, adding the garlic when the onions begin to colour. Transfer to a flameproof casserole. Add the pork and gammon or ham to the pan, and fry until coloured, stirring. Transfer to the casserole.

2 Add the remaining oil, the sausage and peppers to the pan and fry. Transfer to the casserole. Deglaze the pan with the wine, allowing it to bubble and reduce. Pour into the casserole.

3 Add the tomatoes, saffron, paprika and parsley and season. Cook gently for 20–30 minutes. Leave to cool.

4 Meanwhile make the dough. Mix the cornmeal, dried yeast, sugar, flour and salt in a food processor. Pulse to mix. Gradually add the water, oil and 2 eggs with the motor running, to make a smooth soft dough.

5 Turn the dough into a clean bowl, cover with a dish towel and leave in a warm place for 40–50 minutes, to rise.

6 Preheat the oven to 200°C/400°F/ Gas 6. Grease a shallow roasting pan or dish 30 × 20cm/12 × 8in. Halve the dough. Roll out one half on a floured surface, a little larger than the pan. Lift this in place, leaving the border hanging over the edge.

7 Spoon in the filling. Roll out the lid and arrange it in place. Fold the outside edge over the lid (trimming as necessary) and press gently all round with a fork, to seal the pie. Prick the surface and brush with beaten egg.

8 Bake the pie for 30–35 minutes. Cut the pie into squares.

Energy 649kcal/2717kJ; Protein 44.8g; Carbohydrate 59.6g, of which sugars 9.7g; Fat 24.9g, of which saturates 5.9g; Cholesterol 182mg; Calcium 92mg; Fibre 4g; Sodium 680mg.

PANCETTA AND BROAD BEAN RISOTTO

THIS DELICIOUS RISOTTO MAKES A HEALTHY AND FILLING MEAL WHEN SERVED WITH A MIXED GREEN SALAD. USE SMOKED BACON INSTEAD OF PANCETTA, IF YOU LIKE.

SERVES FOUR

INGREDIENTS
225g/8oz frozen baby broad
   (fava) beans
15ml/1 tbsp olive oil
1 onion, chopped
2 garlic cloves, finely chopped
175g/6oz smoked pancetta, diced
350g/12oz/1¾ cups risotto rice
1.2 litres/2 pints/5 cups
   simmering chicken stock
30ml/2 tbsp chopped fresh mixed
   herbs, such as parsley, thyme
   and oregano
salt and ground black pepper
coarsely chopped fresh parsley,
   to garnish
shavings of Parmesan cheese,
   to serve (see Cook's Tip)

1 First, cook the broad beans in a large pan of lightly salted boiling water for about 3 minutes until tender. Drain and set aside.

COOK'S TIP
To make thin Parmesan cheese shavings, take a rectangular block or long wedge of Parmesan and firmly scrape a vegetable peeler down the side of the cheese to make shavings. The swivel-bladed type of peeler is best for this job.

2 Heat the olive oil in a flameproof casserole. Add the chopped onion, chopped garlic and diced pancetta, and cook gently for about 5 minutes, stirring occasionally.

3 Add the rice to the casserole and cook for 1 minute, stirring. Add 300ml/ ½ pint/1¼ cups of the stock and simmer, stirring frequently until it has been absorbed.

4 Continue adding the stock, a ladleful at a time, stirring frequently until the rice is just tender and creamy, and almost all of the liquid has been absorbed. This will take 30–35 minutes. It may not be necessary to add all the stock.

5 Stir the beans, mixed herbs and seasoning into the risotto. Heat gently, then serve garnished with the chopped fresh parsley and sprinkled with shavings of Parmesan cheese.

Energy 511Kcal/2132kJ; Protein 18g; Carbohydrate 77.6g, of which sugars 1.6g; Fat 13.9g, of which saturates 4g; Cholesterol 28mg; Calcium 55mg; Fibre 3.9g; Sodium 556mg.

CASSOULET

THERE ARE MANY REGIONAL VARIATIONS OF THIS CLASSIC FRENCH CASSEROLE OF SAUSAGE, BEANS AND ASSORTED MEATS, EACH WIDELY DIFFERENT FROM THE NEXT ACCORDING TO ITS TOWN OF ORIGIN.

SERVES EIGHT

INGREDIENTS

225g/8oz/1¼ cups dried haricot
  (navy) beans, soaked for 24 hours
2 large onions, 1 cut into chunks
  and 1 chopped
1 large carrot, quartered and cut
  into chunks
2 cloves
small handful of parsley stalks
225g/8oz lean gammon (smoked or
  cured ham), in one piece
4 duck leg quarters, split into thighs
  and drumsticks
225g/8oz lean lamb, trimmed and cubed
2 garlic cloves, finely chopped
75ml/5 tbsp dry white wine
175g/6oz cooked Toulouse sausage,
  or garlic sausage, skinned and
  coarsely chopped
400g/14oz can chopped tomatoes
salt and ground black pepper
For the topping
75g/3oz/1½ cups fresh white
  breadcrumbs
30ml/2 tbsp chopped fresh parsley
2 garlic cloves, finely chopped

1 Drain and thoroughly rinse the beans, then place them in a large pan and add the chunks of onion, carrot, cloves and parsley stalks. Pour in enough cold water to cover the beans completely and bring to the boil.

2 Boil the beans for 10 minutes, then reduce the heat, cover and simmer for 1½ hours, or until the beans are tender. Skim off any scum that rises to the surface and top up with boiling water as necessary. Drain the cooked beans, reserving the stock; discard the onion, carrot, cloves and parsley stalks.

3 Meanwhile, put the gammon into a pan and cover with cold water. Bring to the boil, reduce the heat and simmer for 10 minutes. Drain and discard the water, leave until cool enough to handle, then cut the meat into chunks. Preheat the oven to 150°C/300°F/Gas 2.

4 Heat a large, flameproof casserole and cook the duck portions in batches until golden brown on all sides. Use a draining spoon to remove the duck portions from the casserole, set aside. Add, and brown, the trimmed and cubed lamb in batches, removing each batch and setting aside.

5 Pour off the excess fat from the casserole, leaving about 30ml/2 tbsp. Cook the onion and garlic in this fat until softened but not coloured. Stir in the wine and remove from the heat.

6 Spoon a layer of beans into the casserole. Add the duck, then the lamb, gammon, sausage, tomatoes and more beans. Season each layer as you add the ingredients. Pour in enough of the reserved stock to cover the ingredients. Cover, and cook in the oven for 2½ hours. Check occasionally to ensure the beans are covered, add more stock if necessary.

7 Mix together the topping ingredients and sprinkle over the cassoulet. Cook, uncovered, for a further 30 minutes.

Energy 378kcal/1586kJ; Protein 31.1g; Carbohydrate 28.5g, of which sugars 6.7g; Fat 16.5g, of which saturates 5.6g; Cholesterol 93mg; Calcium 92mg; Fibre 6.6g; Sodium 581mg.

CLAY-POT LAMB SHANKS WITH BEANS

A HEARTY WINTER MEAL, THE LAMB SHANKS ARE SLOWLY COOKED IN A CLAY POT UNTIL TENDER ON A BED OF TASTY BEANS AND VEGETABLES.

SERVES FOUR

INGREDIENTS

175g/6oz/1 cup dried cannellini
   beans, soaked overnight in
   cold water
150ml/¼ pint/⅔ cup water
45ml/3 tbsp olive oil
4 large lamb shanks, about
   225g/8oz each
1 large onion, chopped
450g/1lb carrots, cut into
   thick chunks
2 celery sticks, cut into thick chunks
450g/1lb tomatoes, quartered
250ml/8fl oz/1 cup vegetable stock
4 fresh rosemary sprigs
2 bay leaves
salt and ground black pepper

1 Soak a clay pot and its lid in a sink of cold water for 15 minutes. Drain and rinse the cannellini beans and place in a large pan of unsalted boiling water and boil rapidly for 10 minutes, then drain.

2 Place the 150ml/¼ pint/⅔ cup water in the drained clay pot and then add the drained cannellini beans.

3 Heat 30ml/2 tbsp of the olive oil in a large frying pan, add the lamb shanks and cook over a high heat, turning the lamb shanks occasionally until browned on all sides. Remove the lamb shanks with a slotted spoon and set aside.

4 Add the remaining oil to the pan, then add the onion and sauté for 5 minutes, until soft and translucent.

5 Add the carrots and celery to the pan and cook for 2–3 minutes. Stir in the quartered tomatoes and vegetable stock and bring to the boil. Transfer the vegetable mixture to the clay pot and season well with pepper, then add the fresh rosemary and bay leaves and stir again to combine.

6 Place the lamb shanks on top of the beans and vegetables. Cover with the pot lid and place it in an unheated oven. Set the oven to 220°C/425°F/ Gas 7 and cook for about 30 minutes, or until the liquid is bubbling.

7 Reduce the oven temperature to 160°C/325°F/Gas 3 and cook for about 1½ hours, or until tender. Season with salt and serve on warmed plates, placing each lamb shank on a bed of beans and vegetables.

COOK'S TIP
An ordinary casserole, which is not pre-soaked, can be used. When using a standard ovenproof dish, with boiling stock added, there is no need to start cooking at a high temperature; preheat the oven to 160°C/325°F/Gas 3 instead.

VARIATIONS
• Dried butter (lima) beans or the smaller haricot (navy) beans can be used in place of the cannellini beans.
• If you prefer, two 400g/14oz cans cannellini beans can be used in this dish – simply place the drained beans in the casserole with the water and continue from step 3.
• A variety of other root vegetables would work well in this recipe – try chopped swede (rutabaga), sweet potatoes, butternut squash, parsnips or celeriac instead of the carrots. In spring, a mixture of baby turnips and baby carrots would also be good.

Energy 602kcal/2525kJ; Protein 62.5g; Carbohydrate 33g, of which sugars 13.9g; Fat 25.4g, of which saturates 7.8g; Cholesterol 184mg; Calcium 125mg; Fibre 11.1g; Sodium 178mg.

LAMB AND PUMPKIN COUSCOUS

PUMPKIN IS A VERY POPULAR MOROCCAN INGREDIENT AND THIS IS A TRADITIONAL COUSCOUS RECIPE, WITH ECHOES OF THE VERY EARLY VEGETABLE COUSCOUS DISHES MADE BY THE BERBERS.

2 Cut the lamb into bitesize pieces and place in the pan with the sliced onions, and add the saffron, ginger, turmeric, pepper and salt. Pour in the water and stir well, then slowly bring to the boil. Cover the pan and simmer for about 1 hour or until the meat is tender.

3 Peel or scrape the carrots and cut them into large chunks. Cut the pumpkin into 2.5cm/1in cubes, discarding the skin, seeds and pith.

4 Stir the carrots, pumpkin and raisins into the meat mixture with the chickpeas, cover the pan and simmer for 30–35 minutes more, stirring occasionally, until the vegetables and meat are completely tender.

5 Meanwhile, prepare the couscous according to the instructions on the packet, and steam on top of the stew, then fork lightly to fluff up. Spoon the couscous on to a warmed serving plate, add the stew and stir the stew into the couscous. Extra gravy can be served separately. Sprinkle some tiny sprigs of fresh parsley over the top and serve immediately.

SERVES FOUR TO SIX

INGREDIENTS
75g/3oz/½ cup chickpeas, soaked overnight and drained
675g/1½lb lean lamb
2 large onions, sliced
pinch of saffron threads
1.5ml/¼ tsp ground ginger
2.5ml/½ tsp ground turmeric
5ml/1 tsp ground black pepper
1.2 litres/2 pints/5 cups water
450g/1lb carrots
675g/1½lb pumpkin
75g/3oz/⅔ cup raisins
400g/14oz/2¼ cups couscous
salt
sprigs of fresh parsley, to garnish

1 Place the chickpeas in a large pan of boiling water. Boil for 10 minutes, then reduce the heat and cook for 1–1½ hours until tender. Drain and place in cold water. Remove the skins by rubbing with your fingers. Discard the skins and drain.

Energy 725Kcal/3034kJ; Protein 34.8g; Carbohydrate 115.4g, of which sugars 69.5g; Fat 16.6g, of which saturates 6.8g; Cholesterol 86mg; Calcium 282mg; Fibre 21.5g; Sodium 297mg.

LAMB AND CARROT CASSEROLE WITH BARLEY

BARLEY AND CARROTS MAKE NATURAL PARTNERS FOR LAMB AND MUTTON. IN THIS CASSEROLE THE BARLEY ADDS TO THE FLAVOUR AND TEXTURE AS WELL AS THICKENING THE SAUCE.

SERVES SIX

INGREDIENTS

675g/1½lb boneless lamb
15ml/1 tbsp vegetable oil
2 onions
675g/1½lb carrots, thickly sliced
4–6 celery sticks, sliced
45ml/3 tbsp pearl barley, rinsed
600ml/1 pint/2½ cups near-boiling
  lamb or vegetable stock
5ml/1 tsp fresh thyme leaves or
  pinch of dried mixed herbs
salt and ground black pepper
spring cabbage and baked potatoes,
  to serve

3 Sprinkle the pearl barley over the vegetables in the casserole, then arrange the lamb pieces on top.

4 Lightly season with salt and ground black pepper, then scatter with the herbs. Pour the stock over the meat, so that all of the meat is covered.

5 Cover the casserole with the lid and cook in the oven for about 2 hours or until the meat, vegetables and barley are tender.

6 Taste and adjust the seasoning before serving with spring cabbage and baked potatoes.

1 Preheat the oven to 160°C/325°F/ Gas 3. Trim the lamb. Cut the meat into 3cm/1¼in pieces. Heat the oil in a frying pan, add the lamb and fry until browned. Remove with a slotted spoon and set aside.

2 Slice the onions and add to the pan. Fry gently for 5 minutes. Add the carrots and celery and cook for 3–4 minutes. Transfer to a casserole.

Energy 310kcal/1295kJ; Protein 24.2g; Carbohydrate 20.6g, of which sugars 12.2g; Fat 15.1g, of which saturates 6.2g; Cholesterol 86mg; Calcium 64mg; Fibre 3.9g; Sodium 139mg.

LAHORE-STYLE LAMB WITH SPLIT PEAS

NAMED AFTER THE CITY OF LAHORE, THIS HEARTY DISH HAS A WONDERFULLY AROMATIC FLAVOUR IMPARTED BY THE WINTER SPICES SUCH AS CLOVES, BLACK PEPPERCORNS AND CINNAMON. SERVE WITH A HOT PUFFY NAAN IN TRUE NORTH INDIAN STYLE.

SERVES FOUR

INGREDIENTS

60ml/4 tbsp vegetable oil
1 bay leaf
2 cloves
4 black peppercorns
1 onion, sliced
450g/1lb lean lamb, boned
  and cubed
1.5ml/¼ tsp ground turmeric
7.5ml/1½ tsp chilli powder
5ml/1 tsp crushed coriander seeds
2.5cm/1in piece cinnamon stick
5ml/1 tsp crushed garlic
7.5ml/1½ tsp salt
1.5 litres/2½ pints/6¼ cups water
50g/2oz/⅓ cup chana dhal or yellow
  split peas
2 tomatoes, quartered
2 fresh green chillies, chopped
15ml/1 tbsp chopped fresh coriander
  (cilantro)

1 Heat the oil in a wok, karahi or large pan. Lower the heat slightly and add the bay leaf, cloves, peppercorns and onion. Fry for about 5 minutes, or until the onion is golden brown.

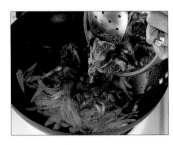

2 Add the cubed lamb, turmeric, chilli powder, coriander seeds, cinnamon stick, garlic and most of the salt, and stir-fry for about 5 minutes over a medium heat.

3 Pour in 900ml/1½ pints/3¾ cups of the water and cover the pan with a lid or foil, making sure the foil does not come into contact with the food. Simmer for 35–40 minutes or until the lamb is tender.

4 Put the chana dhal or split peas into a large pan with the remaining measured water and a good pinch of salt and boil for 45 minutes, or until the water has almost evaporated and the lentils or peas are soft enough to be mashed. If they are too thick, add up to 150ml/¼ pint/⅔ cup water.

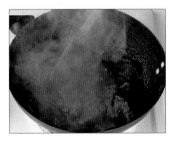

5 When the lamb is tender, remove the lid or foil and stir-fry the mixture using a wooden spoon, until some free oil begins to appear on the sides of the pan.

6 Add the cooked split peas to the lamb and mix together well. Stir in the tomatoes, chillies and chopped fresh coriander and serve.

Energy 331kcal/1379kJ; Protein 26.5g; Carbohydrate 9.7g, of which sugars 1.9g; Fat 20.6g, of which saturates 5.6g; Cholesterol 83mg; Calcium 40mg; Fibre 1.8g; Sodium 99mg.

CHOLENT

THIS IS A LONG-SIMMERED DISH OF BEANS, GRAINS, MEAT AND VEGETABLES. THE ADDITION OF WHOLE BOILED EGGS IS A TRADITIONAL FEATURE. START SOAKING THE BEANS THE DAY BEFORE YOU'RE GOING TO USE THEM; THEY NEED AT LEAST 8 HOURS.

SERVES FOUR

INGREDIENTS

    250g/9oz/1⅓ cups dried haricot
      (navy) beans
    30ml/2 tbsp olive oil
    1 onion, chopped
    4 garlic cloves, finely chopped
    50g/2oz/1¼ cups pearl barley
    15ml/1 tbsp ground paprika
    pinch of cayenne pepper
    1 celery stick, chopped
    400g/14oz can chopped tomatoes
    3 carrots, sliced
    1 small turnip, diced
    2 baking potatoes, peeled and cut
      into chunks
    675g/1½lb mixture of beef brisket,
      stewing beef and smoked beef, cut
      into cubes
    1 litre/1¾ pints/4 cups boiling
      beef stock
    30ml/2 tbsp easy-cook (converted)
      white rice
    4 eggs, at room temperature
    salt and ground black pepper

1 Place the beans in a large bowl. Pour over plenty of cold water to cover and leave to soak for at least 8 hours, or overnight if you like.

2 Drain the beans well, then place them in a large pan, cover with fresh cold water and bring to the boil. Boil them steadily for about 10 minutes, skimming off any froth that rises to the surface, then drain well and set aside.

3 Preheat the oven to 160°C/325°F/Gas 3. Meanwhile, heat the oil in a pan, add the onion and garlic, and cook gently for about 10 minutes, or until soft. Transfer to a large casserole.

4 Add the beans, barley, paprika, cayenne, celery, tomatoes, carrots, turnip and potatoes to the onion. Mix well and place the meats on top.

5 Cover and cook in the oven for 3 hours, or until the meat and vegetables are very tender. Add the rice, stir, and season with salt and pepper.

6 Rinse the eggs in tepid water, then lower them, one at a time, into the casserole. Cover and cook for a further 45 minutes, or until the rice is cooked. Serve hot, making sure each portion contains a whole egg.

Energy 860Kcal/3607kJ; Protein 58.9g; Carbohydrate 74.2g, of which sugars 13.7g; Fat 38.8g, of which saturates 12.7g; Cholesterol 341mg; Calcium 164mg; Fibre 10.9g; Sodium 639mg.

CHILLI CON CARNE

ORIGINALLY MADE WITH FINELY CHOPPED BEEF, CHILLIES AND KIDNEY BEANS BY HUNGRY LABOURERS WORKING ON THE TEXAN RAILROAD, THIS FAMOUS TEX-MEX STEW HAS BECOME AN INTERNATIONAL FAVOURITE. SERVE WITH RICE OR BAKED POTATOES TO COMPLETE THIS HEARTY MEAL.

SERVES EIGHT

INGREDIENTS
 1.2kg/2½lb lean braising steak
 30ml/2 tbsp sunflower oil
 1 large onion, chopped
 2 garlic cloves, finely chopped
 15ml/1 tbsp plain (all-purpose) flour
 300ml/½ pint/1¼ cups red wine
 300ml/½ pint/1¼ cups beef stock
 30ml/2 tbsp tomato purée (paste)
 fresh coriander (cilantro) leaves,
  to garnish
 salt and ground black pepper
For the beans
 30ml/2 tbsp olive oil
 1 onion, chopped
 1 red chilli, seeded and chopped
 2 x 400g/14oz cans red kidney
  beans, drained and rinsed
 400g/14oz can chopped tomatoes
For the topping
 6 tomatoes, peeled and chopped
 1 green chilli, seeded and chopped
 30ml/2 tbsp chopped fresh chives
 30ml/2 tbsp chopped fresh coriander
  (cilantro)
 150ml/¼ pint/⅔ cup sour cream

1 Cut the meat into small cubes. Season the flour and place it on a plate. Toss a batch of meat in it.

2 Meanwhile, heat the oil in a large, flameproof casserole. Add the chopped onion and garlic, and cook until softened but not coloured.

VARIATION
This stew is equally good served with tortillas instead of rice. Wrap the tortillas in foil and warm through in the oven.

3 Use a draining spoon to remove the onion from the pan, then add the floured beef and cook over a high heat until browned on all sides. Remove from the pan and set aside, then flour and brown another batch of meat.

4 When the last batch of meat is browned, return the first batches with the onion to the pan. Stir in the wine, stock and tomato purée. Bring to the boil, reduce the heat and simmer for 45 minutes, or until the beef is tender.

5 Meanwhile, for the beans, heat the olive oil in a frying pan and cook the onion and chilli until softened. Add the kidney beans and tomatoes, and simmer gently for 20–25 minutes, or until thickened and reduced.

6 Mix the tomatoes, chilli, chives and coriander for the topping. Ladle the meat mixture on to warmed plates. Add a layer of bean mixture and tomato topping. Finish with sour cream and garnish with coriander leaves.

Energy 480kcal/2013kJ; Protein 38.6g; Carbohydrate 29.8g, of which sugars 12.4g; Fat 23.6g, of which saturates 8.8g; Cholesterol 114mg; Calcium 127mg; Fibre 9g; Sodium 544mg.

SHREDDED DUCK AND BEAN-THREAD NOODLES

*This refreshing, piquant salad makes a mouthwatering first course or light meal.
The rich flavour of duck is offset by the addition of fresh, raw vegetables and zesty
dressing. If you prefer, you can use shredded chicken in place of the duck.*

SERVES FOUR

INGREDIENTS
  4 duck breast portions
  30ml/2 tbsp Chinese rice wine
  10ml/2 tsp finely grated fresh
    root ginger
  60ml/4 tbsp soy sauce
  15ml/1 tbsp sesame oil
  15ml/1 tbsp clear honey
  10ml/2 tsp Chinese five-spice powder
  toasted sesame seeds, to sprinkle
For the noodles
  150g/5oz bean-thread noodles
  a small handful of fresh mint leaves
  a small handful of coriander
    (cilantro) leaves
  1 red (bell) pepper, seeded and finely
    sliced
  4 spring onions (scallions), finely
    shredded or sliced
  50g/2oz mixed salad leaves
For the dressing
  45ml/3 tbsp light soy sauce
  30ml/2 tbsp mirin
  10ml/2 tsp golden caster (superfine)
    sugar
  1 garlic clove, crushed
  10ml/2 tsp chilli oil

1 Place the duck breast portions in a non-metallic bowl. Mix together the rice wine, ginger, soy sauce, sesame oil, clear honey and five-spice powder. Pour over the duck, toss to coat, cover and marinate in the refrigerator for 3–4 hours.

2 Place a large sheet of double thickness foil on a heatproof plate and place the duck breast portions and marinade on top. Fold the foil to enclose the duck and juices and scrunch the edges to seal.

3 Place a trivet or steamer rack in a large wok and pour in 5cm/2in water. Bring to the boil and carefully lower the plate on to it. Cover tightly, reduce the heat and steam for 50–60 minutes. Remove from the wok and leave to rest for 15 minutes.

4 Meanwhile, place the noodles in a large bowl and pour over enough boiling water to cover. Cover and soak for 5–6 minutes. Drain, refresh under cold water and drain again. Transfer to a large bowl with the herbs, red pepper, spring onions and salad leaves.

5 Mix together all the dressing ingredients. Remove the skin from the duck breasts and roughly shred the flesh using a fork. Divide the noodle salad among four plates and top with the shredded duck. Spoon over the dressing, sprinkle with the sesame seeds and serve immediately.

Energy 348kcal/1457kJ; Protein 23.4g; Carbohydrate 41.5g, of which sugars 10.6g; Fat 11.2g, of which saturates 2g; Cholesterol 110mg; Calcium 58mg; Fibre 1.6g; Sodium 1724mg.

FISH AND SHELLFISH

*From oriental Steamed Fish Skewers on
Herbed Rice Noodles and Smoked Trout
Cannelloni, to Creamy Fish Pilau and Red
Rice Salad Niçoise, the recipes in this chapter
show the true versatility of pulses, legumes and
grains. Every eating occasion is catered for,
whether you're looking for a light summer lunch
or hearty Sunday dinner.*

ROAST COD WITH PANCETTA AND BUTTER BEANS

THICK COD STEAKS WRAPPED IN PANCETTA AND ROASTED MAKE A SUPERB SUPPER DISH WHEN SERVED ON A BED OF BUTTER BEANS, WITH SWEET AND JUICY CHERRY TOMATOES ON THE SIDE.

SERVES FOUR

INGREDIENTS

200g/7oz/1 cup butter (lima) beans,
   soaked overnight in cold water
2 leeks, thinly sliced
2 garlic cloves, chopped
8 fresh sage leaves
90ml/6 tbsp fruity olive oil
8 thin pancetta slices
4 thick cod steaks, skinned
12 cherry tomatoes
salt and ground black pepper

1 Drain the beans, place them in a pan and cover with cold water. Bring to the boil and skim off the foam on the surface. Lower the heat, then stir in the leeks, garlic, 4 sage leaves and 30ml/ 2 tbsp of the olive oil. Simmer for 1–1½ hours until the beans are tender, adding more water if necessary. Drain, return to the pan, season, stir in 30ml/ 2 tbsp olive oil and keep warm.

2 Preheat the oven to 200°C/400°F/ Gas 6. Wrap two slices of pancetta around the edge of each cod steak, tying it on with kitchen string or securing it with wooden cocktail sticks (toothpicks). Insert a sage leaf between the pancetta and the cod. Season.

VARIATION
You can use cannellini beans for this recipe, and streaky (fatty) bacon instead of pancetta. It is also good made with halibut, hake, haddock or salmon.

3 Heat a heavy frying pan, add 15ml/1 tbsp of the remaining oil and seal the cod steaks two at a time for 1 minute on each side. Transfer them to an ovenproof dish and roast in the oven for 5 minutes.

4 Add the tomatoes to the dish and drizzle over the remaining olive oil. Roast for 5 minutes more, until the cod steaks are cooked but still juicy. Serve them on a bed of butter beans with the roasted tomatoes.

Energy 449kcal/1883kJ; Protein 44.5g; Carbohydrate 25.3g, of which sugars 3.9g; Fat 19.5g, of which saturates 3g; Cholesterol 84mg; Calcium 85mg; Fibre 9.8g; Sodium 403mg.

MUSSELS IN BLACK BEAN SAUCE

FERMENTED BLACK BEANS ARE SALTED BLACK SOYA BEANS THAT ARE SOAKED IN HOT WATER BEFORE USE. THEY GIVE AN AUTHENTIC CHINESE FLAVOUR TO SEAFOOD, POULTRY, MEAT AND VEGETABLE DISHES.

SERVES FOUR

INGREDIENTS

2kg/4½lb mussels
30ml/2 tbsp fermented black beans
30ml/2 tbsp vegetable oil
4 garlic cloves, chopped
2.5cm/1in piece fresh root ginger, peeled and finely chopped
5 spring onions (scallions), sliced, green and white parts separated
60ml/4 tbsp Shoaxing wine or dry sherry
30ml/2 tbsp dark soy sauce
5ml/1 tsp caster (superfine) sugar
90ml/6 tbsp water
5ml/1 tsp cornflour (cornstarch), mixed with a little water
sprigs of fresh coriander (cilantro)

1 Scrub, clean and rinse the mussels well under cold running water. Discard any mussels with broken shells or those that remain open when tapped.

2 Put the black beans into a bowl and cover with just boiled water. Leave to soak for 20 minutes.

3 Drain and partially mash the beans.

4 Heat the oil in a large pan and fry the garlic for a few seconds. Add the ginger and white part of the spring onions and fry, stirring, for a minute until the spring onions have softened.

5 Pour in the Shoaxing wine, bring to the boil and continue to boil until the liquor has reduced by a third.

6 Stir in the soy sauce, sugar and water. Toss in the mussels, cover, and simmer over a medium heat for 5 minutes, shaking the pan occasionally, until the mussels have opened.

COOK'S TIP
Store fermented black beans in a cool, dark and dry place and they will keep indefinitely.

7 Remove the mussels using a slotted spoon and transfer to serving bowls. Discard any that have not opened. Stir the cornflour mixture into the pan with the green part of the spring onions and bring to the boil, stirring. Cook over a low heat until the sauce has thickened slightly. Spoon over the mussels. Garnish with coriander.

Energy 218kcal/921kJ; Protein 27.2g; Carbohydrate 5.1g, of which sugars 2.5g; Fat 8.6g, of which saturates 1.2g; Cholesterol 60mg; Calcium 305mg; Fibre 0.5g; Sodium 852mg

BUCKWHEAT NOODLES <u>WITH</u> SMOKED TROUT

THE LIGHT, CRISP TEXTURE OF THE PAK CHOI BALANCES THE STRONG, EARTHY FLAVOURS OF THE MUSHROOMS AND BUCKWHEAT NOODLES AND THE SMOKINESS OF THE TROUT.

SERVES FOUR

INGREDIENTS
    350g/12oz buckwheat noodles
    30ml/2 tbsp vegetable oil
    115g/4oz/1½ cup fresh shiitake
    mushrooms, stems trimmed
    and quartered
    2 garlic cloves, finely chopped
    15ml/1 tbsp grated fresh root
    ginger
    225g/8oz pak choi (bok choy)
    1 spring onion (scallion), finely
    sliced diagonally
    15ml/1 tbsp dark sesame oil
    30ml/2 tbsp mirin or sweet sherry
    30ml/2 tbsp soy sauce
    2 smoked trout, skinned and boned
    salt and ground black pepper
    30ml/2 tbsp coriander (cilantro)
    leaves and 10ml/2 tsp sesame
    seeds, toasted, to garnish

1 Cook the buckwheat noodles in a pan of boiling water for 7–10 minutes, or until just tender, following the instructions on the packet.

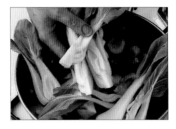

2 Meanwhile, heat the vegetable oil in a large frying pan. Add the shiitake mushrooms and sauté over a medium heat for 3 minutes. Add the garlic, ginger and pak choi, and continue to sauté for 2 minutes.

3 Drain the noodles and add them to the vegetables in the frying pan with the spring onion, sesame oil, mirin or sherry and soy sauce. Toss the mixture thoroughly and season with salt and black pepper to taste.

4 Break the trout into bitesize pieces. Arrange the noodle mixture on individual serving plates. Place the smoked trout on top of the noodles. Garnish with coriander leaves and sesame seeds, and serve immediately.

COOK'S TIP
Mirin is sweet, cooking sake, available from Japanese food stores.

Energy 547kcal/2305kJ; Protein 32g; Carbohydrate 68.3g, of which sugars 3.6g; Fat 18.1g, of which saturates 1.1g; Cholesterol 0mg; Calcium 129mg; Fibre 4.1g; Sodium 672mg.

BUCKWHEAT NOODLES <u>WITH</u> SMOKED SALMON

JAPANESE SOBA OR BUCKWHEAT NOODLES ARE BROWNISH IN COLOUR AND ARE OFTEN A MIXTURE OF BUCKWHEAT AND WHEAT FLOURS. THEY HAVE A DELICIOUS, SLIGHTLY EARTHY FLAVOUR.

SERVES FOUR

INGREDIENTS

225g/8oz buckwheat or soba noodles
15ml/1 tbsp oyster sauce
juice of ½ lemon
30–45ml/2–3 tbsp light olive oil
115g/4oz smoked salmon, cut into
    fine strips
115g/4oz young pea sprouts
2 ripe tomatoes, peeled, seeded and
    cut into strips
15ml/1 tbsp chopped chives
ground black pepper

COOK'S TIP
Young pea sprouts are available for only
a short time. Use rocket (arugula)
instead if you cannot find them.

1 Cook the buckwheat or soba noodles in a large pan of boiling water until tender, following the directions on the packet. Drain, then rinse under cold running water and drain well.

2 Place the noodles in a large bowl. Add the oyster sauce and lemon juice, and season with pepper to taste. Moisten the noodles with the olive oil.

3 Add the smoked salmon, pea sprouts, tomatoes and chives. Mix well and serve at once.

Energy 343kcal/1443kJ; Protein 16.3g; Carbohydrate 47.9g, of which sugars 3.8g; Fat 10.9g, of which saturates 1.2g; Cholesterol 10mg; Calcium 29mg; Fibre 3.5g; Sodium 814mg.

RED RICE SALAD NIÇOISE

WITH ITS SWEET NUTTINESS, RED RICE GOES WELL IN THIS CLASSIC SALAD. THE TUNA OR SWORDFISH COULD BE BARBECUED OR PAN-FRIED BUT TAKE CARE NOT TO OVERCOOK IT.

SERVES SIX

INGREDIENTS

about 675g/1½lb fresh tuna or
  swordfish, sliced into 2cm/¾in
  thick steaks
350g/12oz/1¾ cups Camargue
  red rice
fish or vegetable stock or water
450g/1lb green beans
450g/1lb broad (fava) beans, shelled
1 Romaine lettuce
450g/1lb cherry tomatoes, halved
  unless tiny
30ml/2 tbsp coarsely chopped fresh
  coriander (cilantro)
3 hard-boiled eggs
175g/6oz/1½ cups pitted
  black olives
olive oil, for brushing
For the marinade
1 red onion, roughly chopped
2 garlic cloves
½ bunch fresh parsley
½ bunch fresh coriander (cilantro)
10ml/2 tsp paprika
45ml/3 tbsp olive oil
45ml/3 tbsp water
30ml/2 tbsp white wine vinegar
15ml/1 tbsp fresh lime or
  lemon juice
salt and ground black pepper
For the dressing
30ml/2 tbsp fresh lime or
  lemon juice
3ml/1 tsp Dijon mustard
½ garlic clove, crushed (optional)
60ml/4 tbsp olive oil
60ml/4 tbsp sunflower oil

COOK'S TIP
A good salad niçoise is a feast for the
eyes as well as the palate. Arrange the
ingredients with care, either on a large
serving dish or individual salad plates.

1 Make the marinade by mixing all the
ingredients in a food processor and
processing them for 30–40 seconds
until the vegetables and herbs are
finely chopped.

2 Prick the tuna or swordfish steaks all
over with a fork, arrange them in a
shallow dish and pour on the marinade,
turning the fish to coat each piece.
Cover with clear film (plastic wrap) and
leave in a cool place for 2–4 hours.

3 Cook the rice in stock or water,
following the instructions on the
packet, then drain, tip into a bowl and
set aside.

4 Make the dressing. Mix the citrus
juice, mustard and garlic (if using) in a
bowl. Whisk in the oils, then add salt
and freshly ground black pepper to
taste. Stir 60ml/4 tbsp of the dressing
into the rice, then spoon the rice into
the centre of a large serving dish.

5 Cook the green beans and broad
beans in boiling salted water until
tender. Drain, refresh under cold water
and drain again. Remove the outer shell
from the broad beans and add them to
the rice.

6 Discard the outer leaves from the
lettuce and tear the inner leaves into
pieces. Add to the salad with the
tomatoes and coriander. Shell the
hard-boiled eggs and cut them into
sixths. Preheat the grill (broiler).

7 Arrange the tuna or swordfish steaks
on a grill pan. Brush with the marinade
and a little extra olive oil. Grill (broil) for
3–4 minutes on each side, until the fish
is tender and flakes easily when tested
with the tip of a sharp knife. Brush with
marinade and more olive oil when
turning the fish over.

8 Allow the fish to cool a little, then
break the steaks into large pieces. Toss
into the salad with the olives and the
remaining dressing. Decorate with
the eggs and serve.

Energy 685kcal/2874kJ; Protein 41.8g; Carbohydrate 61g, of which sugars 6g; Fat 32.2g, of which saturates 5.7g; Cholesterol 127mg; Calcium 134mg; Fibre 9.2g; Sodium 760mg.

HADDOCK <u>WITH</u> SPICY PUY LENTILS

DARK BROWN-GREY PUY LENTILS HAVE A DELICATE TASTE AND TEXTURE AND HOLD THEIR SHAPE DURING COOKING. RED CHILLI PEPPER AND GROUND CUMIN ADD A HINT OF HEAT AND SPICE.

2 Meanwhile, preheat the oven to 180°C/350°F/Gas 4. Heat the oil in a frying pan, add the onion and cook gently for 8 minutes. Stir in the celery, chilli and cumin, and cook for a further 5 minutes, or until soft but not coloured.

3 Turn the lentils and the remaining liquid into an ovenproof dish and stir in the onion mixture, Rinse the haddock pieces and pat dry on kitchen paper. Sprinkle them with the lemon juice and place on top of the lentils.

4 In a clean bowl, beat together the butter, lemon rind, salt and a generous amount of ground black pepper. Dot the lemon butter over the fish. Cover and cook for about 30 minutes, or until the fish flakes easily, the lentils are tender and most of the stock has been absorbed. Serve immediately, garnished with the lemon wedges.

SERVES FOUR

INGREDIENTS
175g/6oz/¾ cup Puy lentils
600ml/1 pint/2½ cups vegetable
   stock
30ml/2 tbsp olive oil
1 onion, finely chopped
2 celery sticks, finely chopped
1 red chilli, halved, seeded and
   finely chopped
2.5ml/½ tsp ground cumin
4 x 150g/5oz pieces thick haddock
   fillet or steak
10ml/2 tsp lemon juice
25g/1oz/2 tbsp butter, softened
5ml/1 tsp finely grated lemon rind
salt and ground black pepper
lemon wedges, to garnish

1 Put the lentils in a sieve (strainer) and rinse under cold running water. Drain well and place in a pan. Add the stock, bring to the boil and reduce the heat. Simmer for 30 minutes, until the lentils are almost cooked.

COOK'S TIP
Any firm white fish can be cooked in this way. Both cod and swordfish give particularly good results.

Energy 354kcal/1492kJ; Protein 39.4g; Carbohydrate 22.7g, of which sugars 1.6g; Fat 12.4g, of which saturates 4.3g; Cholesterol 67mg; Calcium 63mg; Fibre 4.3g; Sodium 153mg.

CREAMY FISH PILAU

THIS SALMON DISH IS FUSION FOOD AT ITS MOST EXCITING – THE METHOD COMES FROM INDIA AND USES THE INDIGENOUS BASMATI RICE, BUT THE WINE AND CREAM SAUCE IS FRENCH IN FLAVOUR.

SERVES FOUR TO SIX

INGREDIENTS

450g/1lb fresh mussels, scrubbed
350ml/12fl oz/1½ cups white wine
fresh flat leaf parsley sprig
about 675g/1½lb salmon
225g/8oz scallops
about 15ml/1 tbsp olive oil
40g/1½oz/3 tbsp butter
2 shallots, finely chopped
225g/8oz/3 cups button (white)
  mushrooms
275g/10oz/1½ cups basmati rice,
  soaked in cold water for 30 minutes
300ml/½ pint/1¼ cups fish stock
150ml/¼ pint/⅔ cup double
  (heavy) cream
15ml/1 tbsp chopped fresh parsley
225g/8oz large cooked prawns
  (shrimp), peeled and deveined
salt and ground black pepper
fresh flat leaf parsley sprigs,
  to garnish

3 Heat half the oil and all the butter and fry the shallots and mushrooms for 3–4 minutes. Transfer to a bowl. Heat the remaining oil and fry the rice for 2–3 minutes. Spoon into a casserole.

4 Pour the stock, remaining wine and reserved mussel liquid into a frying pan, and bring to the boil. Off the heat, stir in the cream and parsley. Season lightly. Pour over the rice, then add the salmon and the scallop flesh, together with the mushroom mixture. Stir carefully to mix.

5 Cover the casserole tightly. Bake for 30–35 minutes, then add the scallop corals, replace the cover and cook for 4 minutes more. Add the mussels and prawns, cover and cook for 3–4 minutes until the seafood is heated through and the rice is tender. Serve garnished with the parsley sprigs.

1 Preheat the oven to 160°C/325°F/ Gas 3. Place the mussels in a pan with 90ml/6 tbsp of the wine and the parsley. Cover and cook for 4–5 minutes until the mussels have opened. Drain, reserving the cooking liquid. Remove the mussels from their shells, discarding any that have not opened.

2 Cut the salmon into bitesize pieces. Detach the corals from the scallops and cut the white scallop flesh into thick pieces of equal width.

Energy 428kcal/1787kJ; Protein 24.2g; Carbohydrate 39g, of which sugars 1.1g; Fat 15.2g, of which saturates 8.7g; Cholesterol 134mg; Calcium 130mg; Fibre 0.8g; Sodium 200mg.

TROUT WITH BLACK RICE

*PINK TROUT FILLETS COOKED WITH GINGER, GARLIC AND CHILLI MAKE A STUNNING CONTRAST TO
THE NUTTY BLACK RICE — A HEALTHY MEALTIME CHOICE.*

3 While the rice is cooking, preheat the oven to 200°C/400°F/Gas 6. In a small bowl mix together the grated ginger, garlic, chilli and soy sauce.

4 Place the fish, skin-side up, in a lightly oiled shallow baking dish. Using a sharp knife, make several slits in the skin of the fish, then spread the ginger paste all over the fillets.

SERVES TWO

INGREDIENTS
  2.5cm/1in piece fresh root ginger,
    peeled and grated
  1 garlic clove, crushed
  1 fresh red chilli, seeded and
    finely chopped
  30ml/2 tbsp soy sauce
  2 trout fillets, each about 200g/7oz
  oil, for greasing
For the rice
  15ml/1 tbsp sesame oil
  50g/2oz/¾ cup fresh shiitake
    mushrooms, sliced
  8 spring onions (scallions),
    finely chopped
  150g/5oz/¾ cup black rice
  4 slices fresh root ginger
  900ml/1½ pints/3¾ cups
    boiling water

1 Make the rice. Heat the sesame oil in a pan and fry the mushrooms with half the spring onions for 2–3 minutes.

2 Add the rice and sliced ginger to the pan and stir well. Cover with the boiling water and bring to the boil. Reduce the heat, cover and simmer for 25–30 minutes or until the rice is tender. Drain well and cover to keep warm.

5 Cover the dish tightly with foil and cook in the oven for 20–25 minutes or until the trout fillets are cooked through.

6 Divide the rice between two warmed serving plates. Remove the ginger. Lay the fish on top and sprinkle over the reserved spring onions, to garnish.

Energy 560kcal/2362kJ; Protein 45.6g; Carbohydrate 63.5g, of which sugars 3.3g; Fat 15.5g, of which saturates 1.4g; Cholesterol 0mg; Calcium 46mg; Fibre 2.3g; Sodium 1187mg.

SEAFOOD PAELLA

THERE ARE AS MANY VERSIONS OF PAELLA AS THERE ARE REGIONS OF SPAIN. THOSE FROM THE COAST CONTAIN SEAFOOD, WHILE INLAND VERSIONS ADD CHICKEN OR PORK. HERE CHORIZO IS ADDED.

SERVES FOUR

INGREDIENTS

45ml/3 tbsp olive oil
1 Spanish (Bermuda) onion, chopped
2 fat garlic cloves, chopped
150g/5oz chorizo sausage, sliced
300g/11oz small squid, cleaned
1 red (bell) pepper, cut into strips
4 tomatoes, peeled, seeded and
    diced, or 200g/7oz can tomatoes
500ml/17fl oz/generous 2 cups
    chicken stock
105ml/7 tbsp dry white wine
200g/7oz/1 cup short grain Spanish
    paella rice
a large pinch of saffron threads
150g/5oz/1 cup fresh or frozen peas
12 large cooked prawns (shrimp), in
    the shell, or 8 langoustines
450g/1lb fresh mussels, scrubbed
450g/1lb medium clams, scrubbed
salt and ground black pepper

1 Heat the olive oil in a paella pan or wok, add the onion and garlic and fry until translucent. Add the chorizo and fry until lightly golden.

2 If the squid are very small, leave them whole, otherwise cut the bodies into rings and the tentacles into pieces. Add the squid to the pan and sauté over a high heat for 2 minutes.

3 Stir in the pepper strips and tomatoes, and simmer gently for 5 minutes, until the pepper strips are tender. Pour in the stock and wine, stir well and bring to the boil.

4 Stir in the rice and saffron threads and season well with salt and pepper. Spread the contents of the pan evenly. Bring the liquid back to the boil, then lower the heat and simmer gently for about 10 minutes.

5 Add the peas, prawns or langoustines, mussels and clams, stirring them gently into the rice.

6 Cook the paella gently for a further 15–20 minutes, until the rice is tender and all the mussels and clams have opened. If any remain closed, discard them. If the paella seems dry, add a little more hot chicken stock. Gently stir everything together and serve piping hot.

Energy 593kcal/2481kJ; Protein 43.1g; Carbohydrate 60.7g, of which sugars 11.2g; Fat 18.3g, of which saturates 3.9g; Cholesterol 308mg; Calcium 192mg; Fibre 4.6g; Sodium 1115mg.

STIR-FRIED JASMINE RICE WITH PRAWNS

THAI JASMINE RICE IS A LONG-GRAINED FRAGRANT RICE WITH A SLIGHTLY STICKY TEXTURE. MAKE SURE IT IS COLD BEFORE USING IN THIS FRAGRANT STIR-FRY.

SERVES FOUR TO SIX

INGREDIENTS

- 45ml/3 tbsp vegetable oil
- 1 egg, beaten
- 1 onion, chopped
- 15ml/1 tbsp chopped garlic
- 15ml/1 tbsp shrimp paste
- 1kg/2¼lb/4 cups cooked jasmine rice
- 350g/12oz cooked shelled prawns (shrimp)
- 50g/2oz/1½ cups thawed frozen peas
- oyster sauce, to taste
- 2 spring onions (scallions), chopped
- 15–20 Thai basil leaves, roughly chopped, plus an extra sprig, to garnish

1 Heat 15ml/1 tbsp of the oil in a wok or frying pan. Add the beaten egg and swirl it around to set like a thin omelette.

2 Cook the omelette (on one side only) over a gentle heat until golden. Slide the omelette on to a board, roll up and cut into thin strips. Set aside.

3 Heat the remaining oil in the wok or pan, add the onion and garlic and stir-fry for 2–3 minutes. Stir in the shrimp paste and mix well until thoroughly combined.

4 Add the rice, prawns and peas, and toss and stir together, until everything is heated through.

5 Season with oyster sauce to taste, taking great care as the shrimp paste is salty. Mix in the spring onions and basil leaves. Transfer to a serving dish and top with the strips of omelette. Serve, garnished with a sprig of basil.

Energy 354kcal/1494kJ; Protein 17.8g; Carbohydrate 53.4g, of which sugars 0.9g; Fat 9.2g, of which saturates 1.5g; Cholesterol 158mg; Calcium 117mg; Fibre 0.8g; Sodium 233mg.

MASOOR DHAL WITH SPICED PRAWNS

SPLIT RED LENTILS GIVE THIS RICHLY SPICED DHAL A VIBRANT COLOUR AND SOOTHING TEXTURE.
TOPPED WITH SPICED PRAWNS, YOU COULD SERVE THIS DISH WITH THE GRAM FLOUR PANCAKES.

SERVES FOUR

INGREDIENTS
30ml/2 tbsp vegetable oil
1 large onion, finely chopped
3 cloves garlic, chopped
2.5cm/1in piece fresh ginger, peeled
  and finely chopped
10ml/2 tsp cumin seeds
10ml/2 tsp ground coriander
5ml/1 tsp hot chilli powder
5ml/1 tsp turmeric
7 curry leaves
1 carrot, chopped
6 fine green beans, cut into thirds
150g/5oz/1¼ cups split red lentils,
  rinsed
850ml/1½/3½ cups pints
  vegetable stock
salt and ground black pepper
For the prawns
5ml/1 tsp ground cumin
5ml/1 tsp ground coriander
5ml/1 tsp hot chilli powder
30ml/2 tbsp groundnut (peanut) oil
20 raw tiger prawns (jumbo shrimp),
  peeled and tail left on, sliced down
  the back and deveined
chopped fresh coriander (cilantro),
  to garnish

2 Heat the oil in a large heavy pan and fry the onion for 8 minutes until softened and beginning to turn golden. Add the garlic, ginger and spices and cook for 1 minute.

3 Next, stir in the curry leaves, carrot, beans and lentils. Cook for 1 minute until coated in the spice mixture then pour in the stock. Bring to the boil then reduce the heat and simmer, half-covered, for 20–25 minutes, stirring occasionally, until the lentils are very tender. Season to taste.

COOK'S TIP
Split red lentils become soft and pulpy when cooked, adding a smooth texture to dishes.

4 Heat a large wok. Add the prawns and their spices and stir-fry for a few minutes until they are pink and just cooked.

5 Divide the dhal among four bowls, top with the prawns and garnish with the coriander.

1 First prepare the prawns. Mix together the ground cumin, ground coriander, chilli powder and oil in a bowl. Pat dry the prawns using kitchen paper and add to the spices, season with salt, and stir well until the prawns are coated in the spice mixture. Set aside to marinate while you cook the dhal.

Energy 298kcal/1250kJ; Protein 19.3g; Carbohydrate 28.6g, of which sugars 5.4g; Fat 12.7g, of which saturates 1.5g; Cholesterol 98mg; Calcium 120mg; Fibre 4.7g; Sodium 143mg.

KARAHI PRAWNS AND BLACK-EYED BEANS

THIS SUBSTANTIAL DRY CURRY CONTAINS A PROTEIN-RICH MIX OF BLACK-EYED BEANS,
PRAWNS AND PANEER. BLACK-EYED BEANS ARE SO NAMED BECAUSE OF THE SMALL BLACK DOT
ON THE SIDE OF THE BEANS.

SERVES FOUR TO SIX

INGREDIENTS
    60ml/4 tbsp corn oil
    2 medium onions, sliced
    2 medium tomatoes, sliced
    7.5ml/1½ tsp garlic pulp
    5ml/1 tsp chilli powder
    5ml/1 tsp ginger pulp
    5ml/1 tsp ground cumin
    5ml/1 tsp ground coriander
    5ml/1 tsp salt
    150g/5oz paneer, cubed
    5ml/1 tsp ground fenugreek
    1 bunch fresh fenugreek leaves
    115g/4oz cooked prawns (shrimp)
    2 fresh red chillies, sliced
    30ml/2 tbsp chopped fresh coriander
        (cilantro)
    50g/2oz/⅓ cup canned black-eyed
        beans (peas), drained
    15ml/1 tbsp lemon juice

1 Heat the oil in a deep frying pan or skillet. Lower the heat slightly and add the onions and tomatoes. Fry for about 3 minutes.

2 Add the garlic, chilli powder, ginger, ground cumin, ground coriander, salt, paneer and the ground and fresh fenugreek. Lower the heat and stir-fry for about 2 minutes.

VARIATION
Substitute canned chickpeas for the black-eyed beans in this recipe.

3 Add the prawns, red chillies, fresh coriander and the black-eyed beans and mix well. Cook for a further 3–5 minutes, stirring occasionally, or until the prawns are heated through.

4 Finally, sprinkle on the lemon juice and serve.

COOK'S TIPS
• When preparing fresh fenugreek, use the leaves whole, but discard the stalks which would add a bitter flavour to the dish.
• Paneer is an Indian semi-soft cheese that can be found in some supermarkets and Indian grocers.

Energy 151kcal/629kJ; Protein 8.5g; Carbohydrate 10.1g, of which sugars 6.6g; Fat 8.7g, of which saturates 1.7g; Cholesterol 41mg; Calcium 72mg; Fibre 1.8g; Sodium 445mg.

BASMATI RICE LAYERED WITH PRAWNS

THIS BIRYANI-STYLE RICE DISH MAKES A MEAL IN ITSELF, REQUIRING ONLY PICKLES OR RAITA AS AN ACCOMPANIMENT. IF SERVING FOR A LARGE GROUP, COMPLETE YOUR TABLE WITH A MIXED VEGETABLE CURRY AND A POTATO CURRY.

SERVES FOUR TO SIX

INGREDIENTS
2 large onions, finely sliced and deep-fried
300ml/½ pint/1¼ cups natural (plain) yogurt
30ml/2 tbsp tomato purée (paste)
60ml/4 tbsp green masala paste
30ml/2 tbsp lemon juice
5ml/1 tsp black cumin seeds
1 piece cinnamon stick, 5cm/2in long, or 2.5ml/ ¼ tsp ground cinnamon
4 green cardamom pods
450g/1lb fresh king prawns (jumbo shrimp), peeled and deveined
225g/8oz/2⅔ cups small whole button (white) mushrooms
225g/8oz/1⅓ cups frozen peas, thawed and drained
450g/llb/2¼ cups basmati rice, soaked for 5 minutes in boiled water and drained
300ml/½ pint/1¼ cups water
1 sachet saffron powder mixed with 90ml/6 tbsp milk
30ml/2 tbsp ghee or unsalted (sweet) butter
salt

1 Mix the first 8 ingredients together in a large bowl. Add salt to taste. Fold the prawns, mushrooms and peas into the marinade and set aside in a cool place for about 2 hours.

2 Grease the base of a heavy pan and add the prawns, vegetables and any marinade juices. Cover with the drained rice and smooth the surface gently until you have an even layer.

3 Pour the water all over the surface of the rice. Make random holes through the rice with the handle of a spoon and pour a little saffron milk into each hole.

4 Place a few knobs of ghee or butter on the surface and place a circular piece of foil directly on top of the rice. Cover and cook over a low heat for 45–50 minutes. Gently toss the rice, prawns and vegetables together and serve hot.

Energy 433kcal/1808kJ; Protein 23.5g; Carbohydrate 70.6g, of which sugars 5.8g; Fat 6.1g, of which saturates 3g; Cholesterol 158mg; Calcium 123mg; Fibre 3.2g; Sodium 189mg

SALMON TERIYAKI WITH BEANSPROUTS

THIS CRISP BEANSPROUT SALAD IS THE PERFECT PARTNER TO THE JAPANESE DISH, SALMON TERIYAKI.
THE TERIYAKI SAUCE GIVES A SWEET A GLOSSY GLAZE TO THE FISH.

SERVES FOUR

INGREDIENTS

4 small salmon fillets with skin on,
    each weighing about 150g/5oz
50g/2oz/1 cup beansprouts, washed
50g/2oz mangetouts (snow peas)
20g/³/₄oz carrot, cut into thin strips
salt
For the teriyaki sauce
    45ml/3 tbsp shoyu (Japanese soy sauce)
    45ml/3 tbsp sake
    45ml/3 tbsp mirin or sweet sherry
    15ml/1 tbsp plus 10ml/2 tsp caster
    (superfine) sugar

1 Make the teriyaki sauce. Mix the
shoyu, sake, mirin and 15ml/1 tbsp
caster sugar in a pan. Heat, stirring,
to dissolve the sugar. Cool for 1 hour.

2 Place the salmon fillets, skin-side
down, in a shallow glass or china dish.
Pour over the teriyaki sauce. Leave to
marinate for 30 minutes.

3 Meanwhile, bring a pan of lightly
salted water to the boil. Add the
beansprouts, then after 1 minute, the
mangetouts. Leave for 1 minute then
add the thin carrot strips. Remove the
pan from the heat after 1 minute, then
drain the vegetables and keep warm.

4 Preheat the grill (broiler) to medium.
Take the salmon fillet out of the sauce
and pat dry with kitchen paper. Reserve
the sauce. Lightly oil a grilling (broiling)
tray. Grill (broil) the salmon for about
6 minutes, turning once, until golden.

5 Meanwhile, pour the remaining
teriyaki sauce into a small pan, add the
remaining sugar and heat until dissolved.
Brush the salmon with the sauce.

6 Continue to grill the salmon until the
surface of the fish bubbles. Turn over
and repeat on the other side.

7 Heap the vegetables on to serving
plates. Place the salmon on top and
spoon over the rest of the sauce.

COOK'S TIP
To save time, you could use ready-made
teriyaki sauce for the marinade. This
useful ingredient comes in bottles and
is handy for marinating chicken before
cooking it on a barbecue. Add a splash
of sake, if you have some.

Energy 321kcal/1337kJ; Protein 31.6g; Carbohydrate 5.3g, of which sugars 4.8g; Fat 16.6g, of which saturates 2.9g; Cholesterol 75mg; Calcium 46mg; Fibre 0.6g; Sodium 873mg.

STIR-FRIED NOODLES WITH SOY SALMON

TERIYAKI SAUCE FORMS THE MARINADE FOR THE SALMON IN THIS RECIPE. SERVED WITH SOFT-FRIED NOODLES, IT MAKES AN IMPRESSIVE DISH.

SERVES FOUR

INGREDIENTS

350g/12oz salmon fillet,
  skinned
30ml/2 tbsp shoyu (Japanese
  soy sauce)
30ml/2 tbsp sake
60ml/4 tbsp mirin or sweet sherry
5ml/1 tsp soft light brown sugar
10ml/2 tsp grated fresh root ginger
3 garlic cloves, 1 crushed, and
  2 sliced into rounds
30ml/2 tbsp groundnut
  (peanut) oil
225g/8oz dried egg noodles, cooked
  and drained
50g/2oz/1 cup alfalfa sprouts
30ml/2 tbsp sesame seeds,
  lightly toasted

3 Preheat the grill (broiler). Drain the salmon, reserving the marinade. Place the salmon in a layer on a baking sheet. Cook under the grill for 2–3 minutes.

4 Meanwhile, heat a wok until hot, add the oil and swirl it around. Add the garlic rounds and cook until golden brown. Remove the garlic and discard.

5 Add the cooked noodles and reserved marinade to the wok and stir-fry for 3–4 minutes until the marinade has reduced to a syrupy glaze and coats the noodles.

6 Toss in the alfalfa sprouts. Transfer immediately to warmed serving plates and top with the salmon. Sprinkle over the toasted sesame seeds. Serve at once.

1 Using a sharp cook's knife, slice the salmon thinly. Spread out the slices in a large, shallow dish, keeping them in a single layer if possible.

2 In a bowl, mix together the shoyu, sake, mirin or sherry, sugar, ginger and crushed garlic. Pour over the salmon, cover and leave for 30 minutes.

Energy 514kcal/2150kJ; Protein 24.9g; Carbohydrate 42g, of which sugars 2.5g; Fat 27.3g, of which saturates 4.8g; Cholesterol 61mg; Calcium 38mg; Fibre 1.8g; Sodium 142mg.

SMOKED TROUT CANNELLONI

ONE OF THE MOST POPULAR PASTA DISHES, CANNELLONI USUALLY HAS A MEAT AND TOMATO FILLING, OR ONE BASED ON SPINACH AND RICOTTA CHEESE. SMOKED TROUT MAKES A DELICIOUS CHANGE.

SERVES FOUR TO SIX

INGREDIENTS
1 large onion, finely chopped
1 garlic clove, crushed
60ml/4 tbsp vegetable stock
2 x 400g/14oz cans chopped
   tomatoes
2.5ml/½ tsp dried mixed herbs
1 smoked trout, about 400g/14oz,
   or 225g/8oz fillets
75g/3oz/½ cup frozen peas, thawed
75g/3oz/1½ cups fresh breadcrumbs
16 no pre-cook cannelloni tubes
salt and ground black pepper
For the sauce
25g/1oz/2 tbsp butter
25g/1oz/¼ cup plain (all-purpose)
   flour
350ml/12fl oz/1½ cups skimmed
   (very low fat) milk
freshly grated nutmeg
25ml/1½ tbsp freshly grated
   Parmesan cheese

1 Put the onion, garlic clove and stock in a large pan. Cover and simmer for 3 minutes. Remove the lid and cook until the stock has reduced entirely.

2 Stir in the tomatoes and dried herbs. Simmer uncovered for 10 minutes, or until the mixture is very thick.

3 Skin the trout with a sharp knife. Flake the flesh, discarding any bones. Put the fish in a bowl and add the tomato mixture, peas and breadcrumbs. Mix well, then season with salt and pepper.

4 Spoon the filling generously into the cannelloni tubes and arrange them in an ovenproof dish. Preheat the oven to 190°C/375°F/Gas 5.

5 Make the sauce. Put the butter, flour and milk into a pan and cook over a medium heat, whisking constantly, until the sauce boils and thickens. Simmer for 2–3 minutes, stirring all the time. Season to taste with salt, freshly ground black pepper and grated nutmeg.

6 Pour the sauce over the stuffed cannelloni and sprinkle with the grated Parmesan cheese. Bake for 30–45 minutes, or until the top is golden and bubbling. Serve immediately.

COOK'S TIP
Smoked trout can be bought as fillets or as whole fish. Look for them in the chiller cabinet of the supermarket.

Energy 367kcal/1548kJ; Protein 24.8g; Carbohydrate 49.7g, of which sugars 11.3g; Fat 9.1g, of which saturates 3.4g; Cholesterol 15mg; Calcium 183mg; Fibre 4g; Sodium 244mg.

SALMON AND BLACK-EYED BEAN STEW

THE ADDITION OF FRESH SALMON TO THIS STEW HELPS TO MAKE IT AN EXTREMELY NOURISHING DISH, AS WELL AS A DELICIOUS WINTER WARMER. THE CANNED BEANS GIVE AN ADDED ENERGY BOOST.

<u>SERVES TWO</u>

INGREDIENTS
150g/5oz salmon fillet, skinned and
  any bones removed
400g/14oz canned black-eyed beans
  (peas) in brine
50g/2oz fresh shiitake mushrooms,
  stalks removed
1 small carrot, peeled
½ mooli (daikon), peeled
5g/⅛oz dashi-kombu (dried kelp
  seaweed), about 10cm/4in square
60ml/4 tbsp water
15ml/1 tbsp shoyu (Japanese
  soy sauce)
7.5ml/1½ tsp mirin or dry sherry
sea salt
2.5cm/1in fresh root ginger, peeled,
  to garnish

COOK'S TIP
In place of the black-eyed beans you
could use cannellini or flageolet beans.

1 Slice the salmon into 1cm/½in-thick strips. Place in a colander, sprinkle with sea salt and leave for 1 hour.

2 Wash away the salt and cut the salmon strips into 1cm/½in cubes. Par-boil in a pan of rapidly boiling water for 30 seconds, then drain. Gently rinse under cold running water to prevent the cubes from cooking further.

3 Slice the ginger for the garnish thinly lengthways, then stack the slices and cut them into thin threads. Soak in cold water for about 30 minutes, then drain well.

4 Drain the can of black-eyed beans into a medium pan. Reserve the beans.

5 Chop all the fresh vegetables into 1cm/½in cubes. Wipe the dashi-kombu with kitchen paper, then snip with scissors. Cut everything as close to the same size as possible.

6 Put the par-boiled salmon, dashi-kombu and vegetables into the pan containing the liquid from the can of beans. Pour the beans on top and add the water and 1.5ml/¼ tsp salt. Bring to the boil. Reduce the heat to low and cook for 6 minutes or until the carrot is cooked.

7 Add the shoyu and cook for a further 4 minutes. Add the mirin or sherry and remove the pan from the heat. Mix well. Leave to rest for 1 hour. Serve warm or cold, with the ginger threads.

Energy 387kcal/1633kJ; Protein 33.7g; Carbohydrate 43.5g, of which sugars 5.6g; Fat 9.9g, of which saturates 1.9g; Cholesterol 38mg; Calcium 70mg; Fibre 8.2g; Sodium 589mg.

MACKEREL <u>WITH</u> SHIITAKE MUSHROOMS <u>AND</u> BLACK BEANS

EARTHY SHIITAKE MUSHROOMS, ZESTY GINGER AND PUNGENT SALTED BLACK BEANS ARE THE PERFECT PARTNERS FOR ROBUSTLY FLAVOURED MACKEREL FILLETS. SERVE WITH BASMATI RICE.

SERVES FOUR

INGREDIENTS

8 x 115g/4oz mackerel fillets
20 dried shiitake mushrooms
15ml/1 tbsp finely julienned fresh
   root ginger
3 star anise
45ml/3 tbsp dark soy sauce
15ml/1 tbsp Chinese rice wine
15ml/1 tbsp salted black beans
6 spring onions (scallions),
   finely shredded
30ml/2 tbsp sunflower oil
5ml/1 tsp sesame oil
4 garlic cloves, very thinly sliced
sliced cucumber, to serve

1 Divide the mackerel fillets between two lightly oiled heatproof plates, with the skin-side up. Using a small, sharp knife, make 3–4 diagonal slits in each one, then set aside.

2 Place the shiitake mushrooms in a bowl and cover with boiling water. Leave to soak for 20–25 minutes. Drain, reserving the liquid, discard the stems and slice the caps thinly.

3 Place a trivet or a steamer rack in a large wok and pour in 5cm/2in of the mushroom liquid (top up with water if necessary). Add half the ginger and the star anise.

4 Push the remaining ginger strips into the slits in the fish and scatter over the sliced mushrooms. Bring the liquid in the wok to a boil and lower one of the prepared plates on to the trivet. Cover, reduce the heat and steam for 10–12 minutes, or until cooked through. Remove from the wok and repeat with the second plate of fish, replenishing the liquid in the wok if necessary.

5 Transfer the steamed fish to a large serving platter. Ladle 105ml/7 tbsp of the steaming liquid into a clean wok with the soy sauce, wine and black beans, place over a gentle heat and bring to a simmer. Spoon over the fish and sprinkle over the spring onions.

6 Wipe out the wok and place it over a medium heat. Add the oils and garlic and stir-fry for a few minutes until lightly golden. Pour over the fish and serve immediately with sliced cucumber and steamed basmati rice.

Energy 693kcal/2872kJ; Protein 45.5g; Carbohydrate 1.9g, of which sugars 0.5g; Fat 55.9g, of which saturates 10.4g; Cholesterol 128mg; Calcium 35mg; Fibre 0.6g; Sodium 152mg.

STEAMED FISH SKEWERS ᴼᴺ HERBED RICE NOODLES

FRESH SUCCULENT FILLETS OF TROUT ARE MARINATED IN A TANGY CITRUS SPICE BLEND, THEN SKEWERED AND STEAMED BEFORE SERVING ON A BED OF FRAGRANT HERB NOODLES.

SERVES FOUR

INGREDIENTS
  4 trout fillets, skinned
  2.5ml/½ tsp turmeric
  15ml/1 tbsp mild curry paste
  juice of 2 lemons
  15ml/1 tbsp sunflower oil
  45ml/3 tbsp chilli-roasted peanuts,
    roughly chopped
  salt and ground black pepper
  chopped fresh mint, to garnish
For the noodles
  300g/11oz rice noodles
  15ml/1 tbsp sunflower oil
  1 red chilli, seeded and finely sliced
  4 spring onions (scallions),
    cut into slivers
  60ml/4 tbsp roughly chopped
    fresh mint
  60ml/4 tbsp roughly chopped fresh
    sweet basil

1 Trim each trout fillet and place in a large bowl. Mix together the turmeric, curry paste, lemon juice and oil, and spoon the mixture over the fish. Season with salt and black pepper, and toss to mix well.

2 For the noodles, place the rice noodles in a bowl and pour over enough boiling water to cover. Leave to soak for 3–4 minutes and then drain. Refresh in cold water, drain and set aside.

3 Thread two bamboo skewers through each trout fillet and arrange in two tiers of a bamboo steamer lined with baking parchment.

4 Cover the steamer and place over a wok of simmering water (making sure the water doesn't touch the bottom of the steamer). Steam the fish skewers for 5–6 minutes, or until the fish is just cooked through.

5 Meanwhile, in a clean wok, heat the oil for the noodles. Add the chilli, spring onions and drained noodles and stir-fry for about 2 minutes and then stir in the chopped herbs. Season with salt and ground black pepper and divide among four bowls or plates.

6 Top each bowl of noodles with a steamed fish skewer and scatter over the chilli-roasted peanuts. Garnish with chopped mint and serve immediately.

COOK'S TIP
Soak the bamboo skewers in water for at least 30 minutes to prevent them from burning during cooking.

Energy 504kcal/2101kJ; Protein 26.5g; Carbohydrate 62.9g, of which sugars 1g; Fat 15.2g, of which saturates 1.7g; Cholesterol 0mg; Calcium 48mg; Fibre 1.4g; Sodium 158mg.

BREADS, BAKES AND DESSERTS

Here is an amazing collection of baked recipes
and tempting desserts all made with grains and
beans, from cooling, creamy cinnamon-spiced
Date and Tofu Ice to warming winter desserts,
such as Caramelized Plums with Coconut Rice.
Grains are milled into the flours used to make
the many varieties of breads, cookies and
savoury biscuits, including Scottish Oatcakes,
Polish Rye Bread and Luxury
Muesli Cookies.

WHOLEMEAL SUNFLOWER BREAD

SUNFLOWER SEEDS GIVE A NUTTY CRUNCHINESS TO THIS WHOLEMEAL LOAF. EAT FRESHLY BAKED AND SERVE WITH A CHUNK OF CHEESE AND RICH TOMATO CHUTNEY.

MAKES ONE LOAF

INGREDIENTS

450g/1lb/4 cups strong wholemeal (whole-wheat) flour
2.5ml/½ tsp easy-blend (rapid-rise) dried yeast
2.5ml/½ tsp salt
50g/2oz/½ cup sunflower seeds, plus extra for sprinkling
300ml/½ pint/1¼ cups warm water

COOK'S TIPS
• Spelt flour, an ancient form of wheat flour, can be substituted for the wholemeal flour to make this loaf.
• Add sesame seeds to the topping.

1 Grease and lightly flour a 450g/1lb loaf tin (pan).

2 Mix together the flour, yeast, salt and sunflower seeds in a large bowl. Make a well in the centre and gradually stir in the warm water. Mix vigorously with a wooden spoon to form a soft, sticky dough. The dough should be quite wet and sticky, so don't be tempted to add any extra flour.

3 Cover the bowl with a damp dish towel and leave the dough to rise in a warm place for 45–50 minutes or until doubled in bulk.

4 Preheat the oven to 200°C/400°F/ Gas 6. Turn out the dough on to a floured work surface and knead for 10 minutes – the dough will still be sticky.

5 Form the dough into a rectangle and place in the loaf tin. Sprinkle the top with sunflower seeds. Cover with a damp dish towel and leave to rise again for a further 15 minutes.

6 Bake for 40–45 minutes until golden – the loaf should sound hollow when tapped underneath. Leave for 5 minutes, then turn out of the tin and leave to cool on a wire rack.

COOK'S TIP
Wholemeal (whole-wheat) flour has a higher fibre content than plain flour because it contains all of the wheat grain, including the bran and germ.

Energy 1686kcal/7136kJ; Protein 67g; Carbohydrate 296.9g, of which sugars 10.3g; Fat 33.6g, of which saturates 3.6g; Cholesterol 0mg; Calcium 226mg; Fibre 43.5g; Sodium 15mg.

POLENTA AND PEPPER BREAD

FULL OF MEDITERRANEAN FLAVOUR, THIS SATISFYING, SUNSHINE-COLOURED BREAD IS BEST EATEN WHILE STILL WARM, DRIZZLED WITH A LITTLE OLIVE OIL AND SERVED WITH SOUP.

MAKES TWO LOAVES

INGREDIENTS

175g/6oz/1½ cups polenta
5ml/1 tsp salt
350g/12oz/3 cups strong white bread flour, plus extra for dusting
5ml/1 tsp sugar
7g/¼oz sachet easy-blend (rapid-rise) dried yeast
1 red (bell) pepper, roasted, peeled and diced
300ml/½ pint/1¼ cups warm water
15ml/1 tbsp olive oil

1 Mix together the polenta, salt, flour, sugar and yeast in a large bowl. Stir in the diced red pepper until it is evenly distributed, then make a well in the centre of the mixture. Grease two loaf tins (pans).

2 Add the water and oil and mix to a soft dough. Knead for 10 minutes until smooth and elastic. Place in an oiled bowl, cover with oiled clear film (plastic wrap) and leave to rise in a warm place for 1 hour until doubled in bulk.

3 Knock back (punch down) the dough, knead lightly, then divide in two. Shape each piece into an oblong and place in the tins. Cover with oiled clear film and leave to rise for 45 minutes. Preheat the oven to 220°C/425°F/Gas 7.

4 Bake for 30 minutes until golden – the loaves should sound hollow when tapped underneath. Leave to cool in the tins for 5 minutes, then transfer to a wire rack to cool.

Energy 985kcal/4164kJ; Protein 24.7g; Carbohydrate 204g, of which sugars 9.7g; Fat 10.9g, of which saturates 1.2g; Cholesterol 0mg; Calcium 623mg; Fibre 8.8g; Sodium 634mg.

SPICY MILLET BREAD

*THIS IS A DELICIOUS SPICY BREAD WITH A GOLDEN CRUST. CUT IT INTO WEDGES, AS YOU WOULD A
CAKE, AND SERVE IT WARM WITH A THICK VEGETABLE SOUP.*

MAKES ONE LOAF

INGREDIENTS
550ml/18fl oz/2½ cups warm water
90g/3½oz/½ cup millet
550g/1lb 6oz/5½ cups strong white
  bread flour
10ml/2 tsp salt
5ml/1 tsp sugar
5ml/1 tsp dried chilli flakes
  (optional)
7g/¼oz sachet easy-blend (rapid-rise)
  dried yeast
25g/1oz/2 tbsp unsalted (sweet) butter
1 onion, roughly chopped
15ml/1 tbsp cumin seeds
5ml/1 tsp ground turmeric

1 In a heavy pan bring 200ml/7fl oz/
scant 1 cup of the water to the boil.
Add the millet, cover and simmer gently
for 20 minutes, until the water is
absorbed. Remove from the heat and
leave to cool until just warm.

2 Mix together the flour, salt, sugar,
chilli flakes, if using, and yeast in a
large bowl. Stir in the millet, then
gradually add the remaining warm water
and mix to form a soft dough.

3 Turn out the dough on to a lightly
floured work surface and knead for
10 minutes. If the dough seems a little
dry, knead well until it becomes smooth
and elastic.

4 Place the dough in an oiled bowl
and cover with oiled clear film (plastic
wrap) or a damp dish towel. Leave to
rise in a warm place for 1 hour until
doubled in bulk.

5 Meanwhile, melt the butter in a
heavy frying pan, add the onion and fry
for 10 minutes until softened, stirring
occasionally. Add the cumin seeds and
turmeric, and fry for a further 5–8
minutes, stirring constantly, until the
cumin seeds begin to pop. Set aside.

COOK'S TIP
To test if a dough has risen properly,
make a small indentation in the top with
your index finger. If the indentation does
not spring back entirely, then rising is
complete; if it springs back at once, the
dough is not ready and should be left for
another 15 minutes before retesting.

6 Knock back (punch down) the dough
by pressing with your knuckles, then
shape into a round. Place the onion
mixture in the middle of the dough and
bring the sides over the filling to make a
parcel, then seal well.

7 Place the loaf on an oiled baking
sheet, seam-side down, cover with oiled
clear film and leave in a warm place for
45 minutes until doubled in bulk.

8 Preheat the oven to 220°C/425°F/
Gas 7. Bake the bread for 30 minutes
until golden. It should sound hollow
when tapped underneath. Cool.

Energy 2460kcal/10425kJ; Protein 63.8g; Carbohydrate 501.9g, of which sugars 15.9g; Fat 35.6g, of which saturates 14.1g; Cholesterol 53mg; Calcium 842mg; Fibre 24g; Sodium 4130mg.

POLISH RYE BREAD

THIS RYE BREAD IS MADE WITH HALF WHITE FLOUR WHICH GIVES IT A LIGHTER, MORE OPEN TEXTURE THAN A TRADITIONAL RYE LOAF. SERVE THINLY SLICED, WITH COLD MEATS AND FISH.

MAKES ONE LOAF

INGREDIENTS
225g/8oz/2 cups rye flour
225g/8oz/2 cups strong white
  bread flour
10ml/2 tsp caraway seeds
10ml/2 tsp salt
20g/¾oz fresh yeast
140ml/scant ¼ pint/scant ⅔ cup
  lukewarm milk
5ml/1 tsp clear honey
140ml/scant ¼ pint/scant ⅔ cup
  lukewarm water
wholemeal (whole-wheat) flour, for
  dusting

1 Lightly grease a baking sheet. Mix the flours, caraway seeds and salt in a large bowl and make a well in the centre.

2 In a bowl or measuring jug (cup), cream the yeast with the milk and honey. Pour into the centre of the flour, add the water and gradually incorporate the surrounding flour and caraway mixture until a dough forms.

3 Turn out the dough on to a lightly floured surface and knead for 8–10 minutes until smooth, elastic and firm. Place in a large, lightly oiled bowl, cover with lightly oiled clear film (plastic wrap) and leave to rise, in a warm place, for about 3 hours, or until doubled in bulk.

4 Turn out the dough on to a lightly floured surface and knock back (punch down). Shape into an oval loaf and place on the prepared baking sheet.

5 Dust the top of the loaf with wholemeal flour, cover with lightly oiled clear film and leave to rise, in a warm place, for 1–1½ hours, or until doubled in size.

6 Preheat the oven to 220°C/425°F/ Gas 7. Using a sharp knife, slash the loaf with two long cuts about 2.5cm/1in apart. Bake the bread for 30–35 minutes, or until the loaf sounds hollow when tapped on the base. Transfer the loaf to a wire rack and set aside to cool.

Energy 1667kcal/7088kJ; Protein 46.4g; Carbohydrate 360.2g, of which sugars 16.2g; Fat 14.6g, of which saturates 3.1g; Cholesterol 8mg; Calcium 567mg; Fibre 33.9g; Sodium 4000mg.

ANADAMA CORNMEAL BREAD

A TRADITIONAL BREAD FROM MASSACHUSETTS, USA, IT IS MADE WITH MOLASSES, CORNMEAL, WHOLEMEAL AND WHITE FLOUR. IT HAS A DENSE AND CHEWY TEXTURE.

MAKES TWO LOAVES

INGREDIENTS
40g/1½ oz/3 tbsp butter
120ml/4fl oz/½ cup molasses
560ml/scant 1 pint/scant
2½ cups plus 30ml/2 tbsp
lukewarm water
50g/2oz/½ cup cornmeal
10ml/2 tsp salt
25g/1oz fresh yeast
275g/10oz/2½ cups wholemeal
(whole-wheat) bread flour
450g/1lb/4 cups strong white
bread flour

1 Grease two 1.5 litre/2½ pint/6 cup loaf tins (pans). Heat the butter, molasses and larger quantity of water in a pan until the butter has melted. Stir in the cornmeal and salt and stir over a low heat until boiling. Cool until lukewarm.

2 In a small bowl, cream the yeast with the lukewarm water, then set aside for 5 minutes.

3 Mix the cornmeal mixture and yeast mixture together in a large bowl. Fold in the wholemeal flour and then the strong white flour to form a sticky dough. Turn out on to a lightly floured surface and knead for 10–15 minutes until the dough is smooth and elastic. Add a little more flour if needed.

4 Place in a lightly oiled bowl, cover with lightly oiled clear film (plastic wrap) and leave to rise, in a warm place, for about 1 hour, or until doubled in bulk.

5 Knead the dough lightly on a well floured surface to knock it back (punch down). Then shape it into two loaves and place them in the prepared tins. Cover with lightly oiled clear film and leave to rise, in a warm place, for about 35–45 minutes, or until doubled in size and the dough reaches the top of the tins.

6 Preheat the oven to 200°C/400°F/ Gas 6. Using a sharp knife, slash the tops of the loaves 3–4 times. Bake the loaves for 15 minutes, then reduce the oven temperature to 180°C/350°F/Gas 4 and bake for a further 35–40 minutes, or until they sound hollow when tapped on the base. Turn out on to a wire rack to cool slightly. Serve warm.

VARIATION
Use a 7g/¼oz sachet easy-blend (rapid-rise) dried yeast instead of fresh. Mix it with the wholemeal (whole-wheat) flour. Add to the cooled, cooked cornmeal mixture, then add the lukewarm water, which would conventionally be blended with the fresh yeast.

Energy 1589kcal/6729kJ; Protein 41.8g; Carbohydrate 321.4g, of which sugars 46.5g; Fat 23.2g, of which saturates 11.3g; Cholesterol 43mg; Calcium 702mg; Fibre 19.9g; Sodium 240mg.

WHEAT TORTILLAS

TORTILLAS ARE THE STAPLE FLAT BREAD IN MEXICO, WHERE THEY ARE OFTEN MADE FROM MASA HARINA, A FLOUR MILLED FROM CORN. THESE SOFT WHEAT TORTILLAS ARE ALSO POPULAR IN THE SOUTH-WESTERN STATES OF THE USA.

MAKES TWELVE TORTILLAS

INGREDIENTS
225g/8oz/2 cups plain (all-purpose)
  flour
5ml/1 tsp salt
4ml/³⁄₄ tsp baking powder
40g/1¹⁄₂oz/3 tbsp lard or white
  cooking fat
150ml/¹⁄₄ pint/²⁄₃ cup warm water

COOK'S TIP
Tortillas are delicious either as an accompaniment or filled with roast chicken or cooked minced meat, refried beans and/or salad.

1 Mix the flour, salt and baking powder in a bowl.

2 Rub in the fat, stir in the water and knead lightly to a soft dough. Cover with clear film (plastic wrap) and leave to rest for 15 minutes. Divide into 12 equal pieces and shape into balls. Roll out on a lightly floured surface into 15–18cm/6–7in rounds. Cover.

3 Heat a frying pan or griddle, add one tortilla and cook for 1¹⁄₂–2 minutes, turning over as soon as the surface starts to bubble. It should stay flexible. Remove from the pan and wrap in a dish towel to keep warm while cooking the remaining tortillas in the same way.

Energy 94kcal/394kJ; Protein 1.8g; Carbohydrate 14.6g, of which sugars 0.3g; Fat 3.5g, of which saturates 1.4g; Cholesterol 3mg; Calcium 26mg; Fibre 0.6g; Sodium 164mg.

DOUBLE CORN BREAD

IN THE AMERICAN SOUTH, CORN BREAD IS MADE WITH WHITE CORNMEAL AND IS FAIRLY FLAT, WHILE IN THE NORTH IT IS THICKER AND MADE WITH YELLOW CORNMEAL. THIS RECIPE COMBINES YELLOW CORNMEAL WITH CORN. IT IS MARVELLOUS SERVED WARM, CUT INTO WEDGES AND BUTTERED.

MAKES ONE LARGE LOAF

INGREDIENTS
75g/3oz/³⁄₄ cup strong white
  bread flour
150g/6oz/1¹⁄₂ cups yellow cornmeal
5ml/1 tsp salt
25ml/1¹⁄₂ tbsp baking powder
15ml/1 tbsp caster (superfine) sugar
50g/2oz/4 tbsp butter, melted
250ml/8fl oz/1 cup milk
3 eggs
200g/7oz/scant 1¹⁄₄ cups canned
  corn, drained

VARIATION
Bake this corn bread in a 20cm/8in square cake tin (pan) instead of a round one if you wish to cut it into squares or rectangles.

1 Preheat the oven to 200°C/400°F/ Gas 6. Grease and base line a 22cm/ 8¹⁄₂in round cake tin (pan). Sift the flour, cornmeal, salt and baking powder together into a large bowl. Stir in the sugar and make a well in the centre.

2 Mix the melted butter, milk and eggs together. Add to the centre of the flour mixture and beat until just combined.

3 Using a wooden spoon, stir the corn quickly into the mixture. Pour into the prepared tin and bake for 20–25 minutes, or until a metal skewer inserted into the centre comes out clean.

4 Invert the bread on to a wire rack and lift off the lining paper. Cool slightly. Serve warm, cut into wedges.

Energy 1818kcal/7623kJ; Protein 54.6g; Carbohydrate 248.9g, of which sugars 48g; Fat 70.3g, of which saturates 33.9g; Cholesterol 692mg; Calcium 520mg; Fibre 8.4g; Sodium 1164mg.

OATMEAL BISCUITS

THESE HOME-MADE OATMEAL BISCUITS MAKE UP IN FLAVOUR ANYTHING THEY MIGHT LOSE IN PRESENTATION — AND THEY MAKE THE IDEAL PARTNER FOR FARMHOUSE CHEESES.

MAKES ABOUT EIGHTEEN

INGREDIENTS
75g/3oz/⅔ cup plain (all-purpose) flour
2.5ml/½ tsp salt
1.5ml/¼ tsp baking powder
115g/4oz/1 cup fine pinhead oatmeal
65g/2½ oz/generous ¼ cup white vegetable fat (shortening)

1 Preheat the oven to 200°C/400°F/Gas 6 and grease a baking sheet.

2 Sieve the flour, salt and baking powder into a mixing bowl. Add the oatmeal and mix well. Rub in the fat to make a crumbly mixture.

3 Gradually add water to the dry ingredients, mixing in just enough to make a stiff dough.

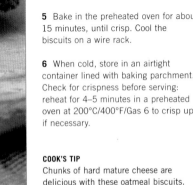

4 Turn out the dough on to a worktop sprinkled with fine oatmeal and knead until smooth and manageable. Roll out to about 3mm/⅛in thick and cut into rounds, squares or triangles. Place on the baking sheets.

5 Bake in the preheated oven for about 15 minutes, until crisp. Cool the biscuits on a wire rack.

6 When cold, store in an airtight container lined with baking parchment. Check for crispness before serving: reheat for 4–5 minutes in a preheated oven at 200°C/400°F/Gas 6 to crisp up if necessary.

COOK'S TIP
Chunks of hard mature cheese are delicious with these oatmeal biscuits. Slices of pear or apple add the finishing touch.

Energy 67kcal/279kJ; Protein 1.2g; Carbohydrate 7.9g, of which sugars 0.1g; Fat 3.6g, of which saturates 1.3g; Cholesterol 1mg; Calcium 10mg; Fibre 0.6g; Sodium 31mg.

MALTED WHEAT AND MIXED SEED CRACKERS

*THESE GRANARY CRACKERS HAVE PLENTY OF CRUNCH AND FLAVOUR PROVIDED BY THE MALTED FLOUR
AND SEEDS THAT ARE USED. THEY TASTE FABULOUS WITH ROBUST FARMHOUSE CHEESES.*

MAKES TWELVE TO FOURTEEN

INGREDIENTS

250g/9oz/2¼ cups Granary (whole-
    wheat) or malted wheat flour
2.5ml/½ tsp salt
2.5ml/½ tsp baking powder
115g/4oz/½ cup butter, chilled
    and diced
1 egg, beaten
30ml/2 tbsp milk, plus extra for
    brushing
15ml/1 tbsp pumpkin seeds
15ml/1 tbsp sunflower seeds
15ml/1 tbsp sesame seeds
2.5ml/½ tsp celery salt

1 Preheat the oven to 180°C/350°F/
Gas 4. Put the flour, salt, baking powder
and butter in a bowl. Rub together until
well combined.

2 Add the egg and milk and mix to a
stiff dough. Roll out on a floured
surface to about 5mm/¼in thick.

3 Using a pastry brush, brush a little
milk over the rolled dough. Sprinkle
all the pumpkin, sunflower and
sesame seeds over the top in an even
layer, then sprinkle the celery salt over
the top.

4 Very gently, roll the rolling pin back
and forth over the seeds to press them
into the dough.

5 Stamp out rounds using a 10cm/4in
plain cookie cutter, and place on a
non-stick baking sheet, spacing them
slightly apart. Alternatively, use a
sharp knife to trim off the rough edges
of the rolled out dough, then cut the
dough into equal-size squares,
rectangles or triangles.

6 Bake the crackers for about
15 minutes, or until just beginning to
brown. Carefully transfer the crackers
to a wire rack to cool completely.

Energy 144kcal/603kJ; Protein 3.4g; Carbohydrate 12.8g, of which sugars 0.5g; Fat 9.2g, of which saturates 4.7g; Cholesterol 31mg; Calcium 39mg; Fibre 1.4g; Sodium 57mg

BARLEY BANNOCK

BANNOCKS ARE FLAT LOAVES ABOUT THE SIZE OF A DINNER PLATE. THEY ARE TRADITIONALLY BAKED ON A GRIDDLE OR GIRDLE. BARLEY FLOUR ADDS A WONDERFULLY EARTHY FLAVOUR TO THE BREAD.

MAKES ONE ROUND LOAF

INGREDIENTS
115g/4oz/1 cup barley flour
50g/2oz/½ cup plain (all-purpose)
    flour or wholemeal (whole-wheat)
    flour
2.5ml/½ tsp salt
2.5ml/½ tsp cream of tartar
25g/1oz/2 tbsp butter or margarine
175ml/6fl oz/¾ cup buttermilk
2.5ml/½ tsp bicarbonate of soda
    (baking soda)

1 Sift the flours, salt and cream of tartar together into a large bowl. Add the butter or margarine and rub into the flour until it resembles fine breadcrumbs.

2 Mix the buttermilk and bicarbonate of soda together. When the mixture starts to bubble add to the flour. Mix together to form a soft dough. Do not over-mix the dough or it will toughen.

3 On a floured surface pat the dough out to form a round about 2cm/¾in thick. Mark the dough into 4 wedges, using a sharp knife.

4 Grease the surface of a griddle with a little vegetable oil. Heat the griddle until hot. Cook the bannock on the griddle for about 8–10 minutes on each side over a gentle heat. Do not cook too quickly or the outside will burn before the centre is cooked. Cool the bannock slightly on a wire rack and eat while still warm.

Energy 759kcal/3202kJ; Protein 23g; Carbohydrate 120.3g, of which sugars 10.7g; Fat 24.1g, of which saturates 13.4g; Cholesterol 60mg; Calcium 346mg; Fibre 18.6g; Sodium 1217mg.

SCOTTISH OATCAKES

THE CRUNCHY TEXTURE OF THESE TEMPTING OATCAKES MAKES THEM DIFFICULT TO RESIST. SERVE WITH BUTTER AND SLICES OF A GOOD MATURE CHEESE.

MAKES EIGHT OATCAKES

INGREDIENTS
115g/4oz/1 cup medium or
    fine oatmeal
1.5ml/¼ tsp salt
pinch of bicarbonate of soda (baking
    soda)
15ml/1 tbsp melted butter, lard or
    white vegetable fat (shortening)
45–60ml/3–4 tbsp hot water

VARIATIONS
• Oatcakes are traditionally cooked on the griddle, but they can also be cooked in the oven at 180°C/350°F/ Gas 4 for about 20 minutes, or until pale golden in colour.
• Small round oatcakes can be stamped out using a 7.5cm/3in plain cutter.

1 Very lightly oil a griddle or heavy frying pan. Mix the oatmeal, salt and soda together in a bowl.

2 Add the melted butter or lard and sufficient hot water to make a dough. Lightly knead on a surface dusted with oatmeal until it is smooth. Cut the dough in half.

3 On an oatmeal-dusted surface roll each piece of dough out as thinly as possible into a round about 15cm/6in across and 5mm/¼ in thick.

4 Cut each round into quarters or farls. Heat the griddle over a medium heat until warm. Transfer the farls, using a metal spatula, to the griddle and cook over a low heat for 4–5 minutes. The edges may start to curl.

5 Using the spatula, carefully turn the farls over and cook for about 1–2 minutes. If you prefer, the second side can be cooked under a preheated grill (broiler) until crisp, but not brown. Transfer to a wire rack to cool. Repeat with the remaining farls.

Energy 72kcal/302kJ; Protein 1.8g; Carbohydrate 10.5g, of which sugars 0g; Fat 2.8g, of which saturates 1g; Cholesterol 4mg; Calcium 8mg; Fibre 1g; Sodium 16mg.

HERBY SEEDED OATCAKES

THE ADDITION OF THYME AND SUNFLOWER SEEDS TO THIS TRADITIONAL RECIPE MAKES THESE OATCAKES AN ESPECIALLY GOOD ACCOMPANIMENT TO PLAIN, MILD OR CREAMY CHEESE.

MAKES THIRTY TWO

INGREDIENTS
175g/6oz/1½ cups plain wholemeal (whole-wheat) flour
175g/6oz/1½ cups fine oatmeal
5ml/1 tsp salt
1.5ml/¼ tsp bicarbonate of soda (baking soda)
75g/3oz/6 tbsp white vegetable fat
15ml/1 tbsp fresh thyme leaves, chopped
90–105ml/6–7 tbsp water
30ml/2 tbsp sunflower seeds
rolled oats, for sprinkling

1 Preheat the oven to 150°C/300°F/Gas 2. Sprinkle two ungreased, non-stick baking sheets with rolled oats.

2 Put the flour, oatmeal, salt and soda in a bowl and rub in the fat until the mixture resembles fine breadcrumbs. Stir in the thyme.

3 Add just enough of the cold water to the dry ingredients to mix them to a stiff, but not sticky, dough.

4 Gently knead the dough on a lightly floured surface until smooth, then cut roughly in half. Press one half of the dough flat and roll out into a 23–25cm/9–10in round. Keep the surface lightly floured to prevent the dough from sticking.

5 Sprinkle sunflower seeds over the dough and press them in with the rolling pin. Cut into triangles and arrange on one of the baking sheets. Repeat with the remaining dough. Bake for 45–60 minutes until crisp but not brown. Cool on wire racks.

Energy 62kcal/259kJ; Protein 1.6g; Carbohydrate 7.7g, of which sugars 0.2g; Fat 3g, of which saturates 0.9g; Cholesterol 0mg; Calcium 6mg; Fibre 0.9g; Sodium 21mg.

APRICOT AND HAZLENUT OAT COOKIES

THESE COOKIE-CUM-FLAPJACKS HAVE A CHEWY, CRUMBLY TEXTURE. THEY ARE SPRINKLED WITH
APRICOTS AND TOASTED HAZELNUTS, BUT ANY COMBINATION OF DRIED FRUIT AND NUTS CAN BE USED.

MAKES NINE

INGREDIENTS

115g/4oz/½ cup unsalted (sweet)
  butter, plus extra for greasing
75g/3oz/scant ½ cup golden caster
  (superfine) sugar
15ml/1 tbsp clear honey
115g/4oz/1 cup self-raising (self-
  rising) flour, sifted
115g/4oz/1 cup rolled oats
75g/3oz/scant ½ cup ready-to-eat
  dried apricots, chopped
For the topping
  25g/1oz/2 tbsp ready-to-eat dried
    apricots, chopped
  25g/1oz/¼ cup hazelnuts, toasted
    and chopped

1 Preheat the oven to 170°C/325°F/
Gas 3. Lightly grease a large baking
sheet. Heat the butter, sugar and honey
in a small heavy pan over a gentle heat,
until the butter melts and the sugar
dissolves, stirring occasionally. Remove
the pan from the heat.

COOK'S TIP
Dried dates, raisins, prunes, apples or
blueberries can be used in place of the
dried apricots.

2 Put the flour, oats and apricots in a
bowl, add the melted mixture and mix
to form a sticky dough. Divide the
dough into nine pieces and place on the
baking sheet. Press into 1cm/½in thick
rounds. Sprinkle the apricots and
hazelnuts over the cookies and press
them into the dough.

3 Bake for 15 minutes until golden and
slightly crisp. Leave to cool on the
baking sheet for 5 minutes, then
transfer to a wire rack to cool.

Energy 262kcal/1098kJ; Protein 3.7g; Carbohydrate 33.2g, of which sugars 14.4g; Fat 13.6g, of which saturates 6.8g; Cholesterol 27mg; Calcium 71mg; Fibre 2.1g; Sodium 130mg

LUXURY MUESLI COOKIES

IT IS BEST TO USE A "LUXURY" MUESLI FOR THIS RECIPE, PREFERABLY ONE WITH FIFTY PER CENT
MIXED CEREAL AND FIFTY PER CENT FRUIT, NUTS AND SEEDS.

MAKES ABOUT TWENTY

INGREDIENTS
   115g/4oz/½ cup unsalted (sweet)
      butter
   45ml/3 tbsp golden (light corn) syrup
   115g/4oz/generous ½ cup demerara
      (raw) sugar
   175g/6oz/1½ cups "luxury" muesli
      (granola)
   90g/3½ oz/¾ cup self-raising
      (self-rising) flour
   5ml/1 tsp ground cinnamon

1 Preheat the oven to 160°C/325°F/
Gas 3. Line two or three baking sheets
with baking parchment.

2 Put the butter, syrup and sugar in a
large pan and heat gently. Stir
constantly until the butter has
completely melted. Remove the pan
from the heat, then stir in the muesli,
flour and cinnamon until mixed well. Set
aside to cool slightly.

3 Place spoonfuls of the mixture,
slightly apart, on the baking sheets.
Bake for 15 minutes until the cookies
are just beginning to brown around the
edges. Leave to cool for a few minutes
on the baking sheets, then carefully
transfer the cookies to a wire rack to
cool completely.

Energy 120kcal/502kJ; Protein 1.4g; Carbohydrate 17.6g, of which sugars 9.8g; Fat 5.3g, of which saturates 3g; Cholesterol 12mg; Calcium 26mg; Fibre 0.1g; Sodium 68mg.

FRUIT AND MILLET TREACLE COOKIES

THESE LITTLE COOKIES ARE QUICK TO MAKE, AND WILL NO DOUBT BE POPULAR WITH THE WHOLE FAMILY. MILLET FLAKES MAKE AN UNUSUAL ADDITION.

MAKES ABOUT TWENTY FIVE TO THIRTY

INGREDIENTS
90g/3½oz/7 tbsp vegetable margarine
150g/5oz/⅔ cup light muscovado (brown) sugar
30ml/2 tbsp black treacle (molasses)
1 egg
150g/5oz1¼ cups self-raising (self-rising) flour
50g/2oz/½ cup millet flakes
50g/2oz/½ cup almonds, chopped
200g/7oz/generous 1 cup luxury mixed dried fruit

COOK'S TIP
The millet flakes can be replaced with rolled oats, wheat flakes or barley flakes. Golden (light corn) syrup gives a lighter flavour than treacle.

1 Preheat the oven to 190°C/375°F/ Gas 5. Line two large baking sheets with baking parchment.

2 Put the margarine, muscovado sugar, treacle and egg in a large bowl and beat together until well combined. (The mixture should be soft and fluffy.)

3 Stir in the flour, millet flakes, almonds and dried fruit. Put tablespoonfuls of the mixture well apart on to the prepared baking sheets.

4 Bake for about 15 minutes until brown. Leave on the baking sheets for a few minutes, then transfer to a wire rack to cool completely.

Energy 99kcal/416kJ; Protein 1.4g; Carbohydrate 15.7g, of which sugars 10.6g; Fat 3.8g, of which saturates 1.2g; Cholesterol 7mg; Calcium 26mg; Fibre 0.5g; Sodium 33mg.

DATE AND MUESLI SLICE

LEMON-FLAVOURED ICING TOPS THESE SCRUMPTIOUS, LOW-FAT MUESLI BARS. THEY MAKE THE PERFECT MID-MORNING PICK-ME-UP WITH A CUP OF COFFEE.

MAKES TWELVE TO SIXTEEN

INGREDIENTS
175g/6oz/¾ cup light muscovado (brown) sugar
175g/6oz/1 cup ready-to-eat dried dates, chopped
115g/4oz/1 cup self-raising (self-rising) flour
50g/2oz/½ cup muesli (granola)
30ml/2 tbsp sunflower seeds
15ml/1 tbsp poppy seeds
30ml/2 tbsp sultanas (golden raisins)
150ml/¼ pint/⅔ cup natural (plain) low-fat yogurt
1 egg, beaten
200g/7oz/1¾ cups icing (confectioners') sugar, sifted
lemon juice
15–30ml/1–2 tbsp pumpkin seeds

1 Preheat the oven to 180°C/350°F/ Gas 4. Line a 28 x 18cm/11 x 7in shallow baking tin (pan) with baking parchment. Mix together all the ingredients except the icing sugar, lemon juice and pumpkin seeds.

2 Spread the mixture evenly in the tin and bake for about 25 minutes, until golden brown. Allow to cool.

3 To make the topping, put the icing sugar in a bowl and stir in just enough lemon juice to give a thick, spreading consistency.

4 Spread the lemon topping over the baked mixture and sprinkle generously with pumpkin seeds. Leave to set before cutting into squares or bars.

Energy 176kcal/749kJ; Protein 3g; Carbohydrate 38.7g, of which sugars 31.3g; Fat 2.1g, of which saturates 0.3g; Cholesterol 12mg; Calcium 72mg; Fibre 1.1g; Sodium 45mg.

GARBANZO CAKE

THIS CLOSE-TEXTURED, MOIST CAKE IS SUBSTANTIAL RATHER THAN LIGHT. IT IS MADE, SURPRISINGLY, WITH CHICKPEAS AND FLAVOURED WITH ORANGE AND CINNAMON.

SERVES SIX

INGREDIENTS

2 x 275g/10oz cans chickpeas, drained
4 eggs, beaten
225g/8oz/1 cup caster (superfine) sugar
5ml/1 tsp baking powder
10ml/2 tsp ground cinnamon
grated rind and juice of 1 orange
cinnamon sugar (see Cook's Tip), for sprinkling

COOK'S TIP
To make cinnamon sugar, mix 50g/2oz/ ¼ cup caster sugar with 5ml/1 tsp ground cinnamon.

1 Preheat the oven to 180°C/350°F/ Gas 4. Tip the chickpeas into a colander, drain them thoroughly, then rub them between the palms of your hands to loosen and remove the skins. Put the skinned chickpeas in a food processor and process until smooth.

2 Spoon the purée into a bowl and stir in the eggs, sugar, baking powder, cinnamon, orange rind and juice. Grease and line a 450g/1lb loaf tin (pan).

3 Pour the cake mixture into the loaf tin, level the surface and bake for about 1½ hours or until a skewer inserted into the centre comes out clean.

4 Remove the cake from the oven and leave to stand, in the tin, for about 10 minutes. Remove from the tin, place on a wire rack and sprinkle with the cinnamon sugar. Leave to cool completely. Cut the cake into thick slices to serve.

Energy 288kcal/1218kJ; Protein 10.7g; Carbohydrate 52.8g, of which sugars 39.9g; Fat 5.3g, of which saturates 1.2g; Cholesterol 127mg; Calcium 73mg; Fibre 3.2g; Sodium 53mg.

TRADITIONAL HALVAS

HALVAS TAKES VERY LITTLE TIME TO MAKE AND IT USES STAPLE STORECUPBOARD INGREDIENTS, SUCH AS SEMOLINA AND NUTS. IT MAKES A PERFECT ACCOMPANIMENT TO COFFEE.

SERVES SIX TO EIGHT

INGREDIENTS
    500g/1¼lb/2½ cups caster
      (superfine) sugar
    1 litre/1¾ pints/4 cups water
    1 cinnamon stick
    250ml/8fl oz/1 cup olive oil
    350g/12oz/2 cups coarse semolina
    50g/2oz/½ cup blanched almonds
    30ml/2 tbsp pine nuts
    5ml/1 tsp ground cinnamon

1 Put the sugar in a heavy pan, pour in the water and add the cinnamon stick. Bring to the boil, stirring until the sugar dissolves, then boil without stirring for about 4 minutes to make a syrup.

2 Meanwhile, heat the oil in a separate, heavy pan. When it is almost smoking, add the semolina gradually and stir constantly until it turns light brown.

3 Lower the heat, add the almonds and pine nuts and brown together for 2–3 minutes, stirring constantly. Take the semolina mixture off the heat and set aside. Remove the cinnamon stick from the hot sugar syrup using a slotted spoon and discard it.

COOK'S TIP
In Greece, this recipe would be made with extra virgin olive oil, but you may prefer the less pronounced flavour of a light olive oil.

4 Protecting your hand with an oven glove or dish towel, carefully add the hot syrup to the semolina mixture, stirring all the time. The mixture will hiss and spit at this point, so stand well away from it.

5 Return the pan to a gentle heat and stir until all the syrup has been absorbed and the mixture looks smooth. Remove the pan from the heat, cover it with a clean dish towel and let it stand for 10 minutes so that any remaining moisture is absorbed.

6 Scrape the mixture into a 20–23cm/8–9in round cake tin (pan), preferably fluted, and set it aside. When it is cold, unmould it on to a platter and dust it all over with the ground cinnamon.

COOK'S TIP
Coarse semolina is ground from fine durum wheat. It is most usually associated with Indian dishes.

Energy 632kcal/2660kJ; Protein 6.8g; Carbohydrate 99.8g, of which sugars 65.7g; Fat 25.6g, of which saturates 3.1g; Cholesterol 0mg; Calcium 56mg; Fibre 1.5g; Sodium 10mg.

STRAWBERRY OAT CRUNCH

THIS SIMPLE DESSERT LOOKS GOOD AND TASTES DELICIOUS. THE STRAWBERRIES FORM A TASTY FILLING BETWEEN THE LAYERS OF OAT CRUMBLE.

SERVES FOUR

INGREDIENTS
   150g/5oz/1¼ cups rolled oats
   50g/2oz/½ cup wholemeal (whole-
      wheat) flour
   75g/3oz/6 tbsp butter
   30ml/2 tbsp pear and apple
      concentrate
   500g/1¼lb strawberries, hulled
   10ml/2 tsp arrowroot
   natural (plain) yogurt, custard or
      cream, to serve

VARIATIONS
• Use dried apricots (chop half and cook
the rest to a purée with a little apple
juice) instead of the strawberries.
• Add a few chopped almonds or walnuts
to the crumble mixture.
• Pear and apple concentrate is a highly
concentrated, naturally sweet juice
available from health food shops. Golden
(light corn) syrup or honey can be used.

1 Preheat the oven to 180°C/350°F/
Gas 4. Mix the oats and flour in a bowl.
Melt the butter with the apple and pear
concentrate in a pan; stir into the oats.

2 Purée half the strawberries in
a food processor; chop the rest. Mix the
arrowroot with a little of the strawberry
purée in a small pan, then add the
rest of the purée. Heat gently until
boiling and thickened, then stir in the
chopped strawberries.

3 Spread half the crumble mixture over
the base of a shallow 18cm/7in round
ovenproof dish to form a layer at least
1cm/½in thick. Top the crumble with
the chopped and puréed strawberry
mixture, then add the remaining
crumble mixture, patting it down gently
to form an even layer. Bake the oat
crunch for about 30 minutes, until
golden brown. Serve warm or cold, with
yogurt, custard or cream.

Energy 391kcal/1638kJ; Protein 7.4g; Carbohydrate 50.4g, of which sugars 13.1g; Fat 19.1g, of which saturates 9.8g; Cholesterol 40mg; Calcium 50mg; Fibre 5.1g; Sodium 136mg.

BROWN BREAD ICE CREAM

THE SECRET OF A GOOD BROWN BREAD ICE CREAM IS NOT TO HAVE TOO MANY BREADCRUMBS (WHICH MAKES THE ICE CREAM HEAVY) AND, FOR THE BEST TEXTURE AND DEEP, NUTTY FLAVOUR, TO TOAST THEM UNTIL REALLY CRISP AND WELL BROWNED. SERVE WITH A CHOCOLATE OR FRUIT SAUCE.

SERVES SIX TO EIGHT

INGREDIENTS
  115g/4oz/2 cups wholemeal (whole-
    wheat) breadcrumbs
  115g/4oz/½ cup soft brown sugar
  2 large (US extra large) eggs,
    separated
  30–45ml/2–3 tbsp Irish Cream
    liqueur
  450ml/¾ pint/scant 2 cups double
    (heavy) cream

1 Preheat the oven to 190°C/375°F/ Gas 5. Spread the breadcrumbs out on a baking sheet and toast them in the oven for about 15 minutes, or until crisp and well browned. Leave to cool.

2 Whisk the sugar and egg yolks together until light and creamy, then beat in the Irish cream liqueur. Whisk the cream until soft peaks form. In a separate bowl, whisk the egg whites until stiff.

3 Sprinkle the breadcrumbs over the beaten egg mixture, add the cream and fold into the mixture with a spoon. Fold in the whisked egg whites. Turn the mixture into a freezerproof container, cover and freeze.

COOK'S TIP
The Irish cream liqueur can be left out of this delicious ice cream, if preferred, but increase the quantity of double cream or add another favourite liqueur instead.

Energy 417kcal/1734kJ; Protein 4.2g; Carbohydrate 28g, of which sugars 17.2g; Fat 32.5g, of which saturates 19.2g; Cholesterol 125mg; Calcium 62mg; Fibre 0.3g; Sodium 143mg.

DATE AND TOFU ICE

ALL YOU SCEPTICS WHO CLAIM TO HATE TOFU, PREPARE TO BE CONVERTED BY THIS CREAMY DATE AND APPLE ICE CREAM. GENEROUSLY SPICED WITH CINNAMON, IT NOT ONLY TASTES GOOD BUT IS PACKED WITH SOYA PROTEIN, CONTAINS NO ADDED SUGAR, IS LOW IN FAT AND FREE FROM DAIRY PRODUCTS.

SERVES FOUR

INGREDIENTS
  250g/9oz/1½ cups stoned (pitted)
    dates
  600ml/1 pint/2½ cups apple juice
  5ml/1 tsp ground cinnamon
  285g/10½oz pack tofu, chilled,
    drained and cubed
  150ml/¼ pint/²⁄₃ cup unsweetened
    soya milk

1 Put the dates in a pan. Pour in 300ml/½ pint/1¼ cups of the apple juice and leave to soak for 2 hours.

2 Bring the dates to the boil, reduce the heat and simmer for 10 minutes, then leave to cool. Using a slotted spoon, lift out one-quarter of the dates, chop roughly and set aside.

3 Purée the remaining dates in a food processor or blender. Add the cinnamon and process with enough of the remaining apple juice to make a smooth paste.

4 Add the cubes of tofu, a few at a time, processing after each addition. Finally, add the remaining apple juice and the soya milk.

5 Pour the mixture into a plastic tub or similar freezerproof container and freeze for 4 hours, beating once with a fork, electric mixer or in a food processor to break up the ice crystals. Beat again until completely smooth.

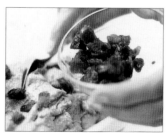

6 Stir in most of the chopped dates and freeze for 2–3 hours until firm.

7 Scoop the ice cream into dessert glasses and decorate with the remaining chopped dates.

COOK'S TIP
Tofu is a non-dairy product that is ideal for making dairy-free desserts that are creamy in texture.

Energy 145kcal/613kJ; Protein 7.6g; Carbohydrate 21.7g, of which sugars 21.3g; Fat 3.7g, of which saturates 0.5g; Cholesterol 0mg; Calcium 384mg; Fibre 1.2g; Sodium 20mg.

FRUITY RICE PUDDING CUSTARD

THERE ARE MANY DELICIOUS VARIATIONS OF RICE PUDDING VARYING FROM COUNTRY TO COUNTRY AND EVEN WITHIN REGIONS OF EACH COUNTRY. LUXURY VERSIONS LIKE THIS ONE INCLUDE CREAM AND FRUIT, BUT ALL ARE DELICIOUSLY FILLING.

SERVES FOUR TO SIX

INGREDIENTS
   60ml/4 tbsp rum or brandy
   75g/3oz/½ cup sultanas (golden
      raisins)
   75g/3oz/scant ½ cup short grain or
      pudding rice
   600ml/1 pint/2½ cups creamy milk
   1 strip pared lemon rind
   ½ cinnamon stick
   115g/4oz/scant ½ cup caster
      (superfine) sugar
   150ml/¼ pint/⅔ cup single (light)
      cream
   2 eggs, plus 1 egg yolk
   almond biscuits, to serve (optional)

1 Warm the rum or brandy in a pan, then pour it over the sultanas. Soak for 3–4 hours or overnight.

2 Cook the rice in boiling water for 10 minutes until slightly softened. Drain.

3 Stir 300ml/½ pint/1¼ cups of milk into the rice in the pan. Add the strip of lemon rind and the cinnamon stick, bring to the boil, then lower the heat and simmer for about 5 minutes.

4 Remove the pan from the heat and stir in half of the sugar. Cover tightly with a damp dish towel held firmly in place with the pan lid. Leave the rice to cool for 1–2 hours.

5 Preheat the oven to 180°C/350°F/ Gas 4. Butter an ovenproof dish (about 1.2 litres/2 pints/5 cups capacity). Sprinkle the sultanas (with any remaining rum or brandy) over the bottom. Stir the rice, which should by now be thick and creamy, most of the liquid having been absorbed, and discard the cinnamon stick and lemon rind. Spoon the rice over the sultanas.

6 Heat the remaining milk with the cream until just boiling. Meanwhile, mix the eggs and egg yolk in a jug. Whisk in the remaining sugar, then the hot milk. Pour the mixture over the rice.

7 Stand the dish in a roasting pan, pour in hot water to come halfway up the sides of the dish and bake for 1–1¼ hours until the top is firm. Serve hot, with almond biscuits, if you like.

COOK'S TIP
This makes a light, creamy rice pudding. If you like your pudding to be denser, cook it for slightly longer.

Energy 326kcal/1366kJ; Protein 8.1g; Carbohydrate 43.7g, of which sugars 33.8g; Fat 11.6g, of which saturates 6.3g; Cholesterol 125mg; Calcium 174mg; Fibre 0.3g; Sodium 79mg.

SWEET FRUITY COUSCOUS

ASIDE FROM ITS SAVOURY ROLE, COUSCOUS IS ALSO EATEN AS A DESSERT OR A NOURISHING BREAKFAST.
THIS SWEET, FILLING AND NUTRITIOUS DISH IS LOVELY SERVED WITH A DRIED FRUIT COMPOTE.
PREPARE THE FRUIT COMPOTE A COUPLE OF DAYS IN ADVANCE.

SERVES SIX

INGREDIENTS
    300ml/½ pint/1¼ cups water
    225g/8oz/1⅓ cups medium couscous
    50g/2oz/scant ⅓ cup raisins
    50g/2oz/¼ cup butter
    50g/2oz/¼ cup sugar
    120ml/4fl oz/½ cup milk
    120ml/4fl oz/½ cup double
        (heavy) cream
For the fruit compote
    225g/8oz/2 cups dried apricots
    225g/8oz/1 cup pitted prunes
    115/4oz/¾ cup sultanas (golden
        raisins)
    115g/4oz/1 cup blanched almonds
    175g/6oz/generous ¾ cup sugar
    30ml/2 tbsp rose water
    1 cinnamon stick

1 To make the compote, put the dried fruit and almonds in a bowl and pour in just enough water to cover. Gently stir in the sugar and rose water, and add the cinnamon stick. Cover and leave the fruit and nuts to soak for 48 hours, during which time the water and sugar will form a lovely golden-coloured syrup.

2 To make the couscous, bring the water to the boil in a pan. Stir in the couscous and raisins, and cook gently for 1–2 minutes, until the water has been absorbed. Remove the pan from the heat, cover tightly and leave the couscous to steam for 10–15 minutes.

3 Meanwhile, poach the compote over a gentle heat until warmed through.

4 Tip the couscous into a bowl and separate the grains with your fingertips. Melt the butter and pour it over the couscous. Sprinkle the sugar over the top, then, using your fingertips, rub the butter and sugar into the couscous. Divide the mixture among six bowls.

5 Heat the milk and cream together in a small, heavy pan until just about to boil, then pour the mixture over the couscous. Serve immediately, with the dried fruit compote.

VARIATIONS
• The couscous can be served on its own, drizzled with clear or melted honey instead of with the dried fruit compote.
• The compote is also delicious served chilled on its own or with yogurt.

Energy 708kcal/2974kJ; Protein 10.6g; Carbohydrate 106.6g, of which sugars 86.8g; Fat 29.5g, of which saturates 12.1g; Cholesterol 46mg; Calcium 165mg; Fibre 6.5g; Sodium 87mg.

INDIAN RICE PUDDING

*THIS CREAMY RICE PUDDING IS FRAGRANT, BEING SCENTED WITH SAFFRON, CARDAMOM AND
FRESHLY GRATED NUTMEG AND HONEY. SHELLED PISTACHIO NUTS GIVE A SUBTLE CONTRAST IN
COLOUR AND ADD A DELICIOUS CRUNCH TO THE DESSERT.*

SERVES FOUR

INGREDIENTS
115g/4oz/¾ cup brown short
   grain or pudding rice
350ml/12fl oz/1½ cups boiling water
600ml/1 pint/2½ cups semi-
   skimmed (low fat) milk
6 green cardamom pods, bruised
2.5ml/½ tsp freshly grated nutmeg
pinch of saffron threads
60ml/4 tbsp maize malt syrup
15ml/1 tbsp clear honey
chopped pistachio nuts, to decorate

1 Wash the rice under cold running
water and place in a pan with the
boiling water. Return to the boil and
boil, uncovered, for 15 minutes.

2 Pour the milk over the rice, then
reduce the heat and simmer, partially
covered, for 15 minutes.

3 Add the cardamom pods, grated
nutmeg, saffron, maize malt syrup
and honey, and cook for a further
15 minutes, or until the rice is tender,
stirring occasionally.

4 Spoon the rice into small serving
bowls and sprinkle with pistachio nuts
before serving hot or cold.

COOK'S TIP
Maize malt syrup is a natural alternative
to refined sugar and can be found in
health food shops.

Energy 228kcal/961kJ; Protein 7.3g; Carbohydrate 44.7g, of which sugars 21.8g; Fat 2.7g, of which saturates 1.6g; Cholesterol 9mg; Calcium 188mg; Fibre 0g; Sodium 106mg.

CARAMELIZED PLUMS WITH COCONUT RICE

RED JUICY PLUMS ARE QUICKLY SEARED IN A WOK WITH SUGAR TO MAKE A RICH CARAMEL SAUCE, THEN SERVED WITH STICKY COCONUT-FLAVOURED RICE FOR A SATISFYING DESSERT. THE GLUTINOUS RICE IS AVAILABLE FROM ASIAN STORES, BUT IT HAS TO BE SOAKED OVERNIGHT BEFORE USE.

SERVES FOUR

INGREDIENTS
6 or 8 firm, ripe plums
90g/3½ oz/½ cup caster (superfine) sugar
For the rice
115g/4oz sticky glutinous rice
150ml/¼ pint/⅔ cup coconut cream
45ml/3 tbsp caster (superfine) sugar
a pinch of salt

1 First prepare the rice. Rinse it in several changes of water, then leave to soak overnight in a bowl of cold water.

2 Line a large bamboo steamer with muslin (cheesecloth). Drain the rice and spread out evenly on the muslin.

3 Cover the rice and steam over simmering water for 25–30 minutes, until the rice is tender. (Check the water level and add more if necessary.)

4 Transfer the steamed rice to a wide bowl and set aside for a moment.

5 Combine the coconut cream with the sugar and salt, and pour into a clean wok. Heat gently and bring to the boil, then remove from the heat and pour over the rice. Stir to mix well.

COOK'S TIP
Sticky glutinous rice does not contain any gluten and is suitable for people with gluten allergies.

6 Using a sharp knife, cut the plums in half and remove their stones (pits). Sprinkle the sugar over the cut sides.

7 Heat a non-stick wok over a medium-high flame. Working in batches, place the plums in the wok, cut side down, and cook for 1–2 minutes, or until the sugar caramelizes. (You might have to wipe out the wok with kitchen paper in between batches.)

8 Mould the rice into rounds and place on warmed plates, then spoon over the caramelized plums. Alternatively, simply spoon the rice into four warmed bowls and top with the plums.

Energy 261kcal/1105kJ; Protein 3g; Carbohydrate 62.6g, of which sugars 41.1g; Fat 0.6g, of which saturates 0.1g; Cholesterol 0mg; Calcium 39mg; Fibre 0.7g; Sodium 45mg.

INDEX

Acknowledgements

Recipes: Catherine Atkinson, Pepi Avis, Valerie Barett, Alex Barker, Ghillie Basan, Angela Boggiano, Georgina Campbell, Carole Clements, Trish Davies, Joanna Farrow, Brian Glover, Nicola Graimes, Rosamund Grant, Rebekah Hassan, Shehzad Husain, Christine Ingram, Manisha Kanani, Soheila Kimberley, Lucy Knox, Jane Milton, Keith Richardson, Marlena Spieler, Biddy White Lennon, Kate Whiteman, Elizabeth Wolf-Cohen, Jeni Wright.
Home economists: Angela Boggiano, Annabel Ford, Silvano Franco, Kate Jay, Jill Jones, Emma Macintosh, Lucy Mckelvie, Jennie Shapter, Linda Tubby, Suni Vijayakar, Jenny White.
Stylists: Shannon Beare, Penny Markham, Marion McLornan, Helen Trent.
Photographers: Frank Adam, David Armstrong, Caroline Barty, Martin Brigdale, Nicki Dowey, Gus Filgate, Amanda Heywood, Ferguson Hill, Janine Hosegood, David Jordan, Sara Lewis, Clare Lewis, William Lingwood, Thomas Odulate, Craig Robertson, Simon Smith.